Space, Time, and Synthesis in Art: Essays on Art, Literature, and Philosophy

Space, Time, and Synthesis in Art: Essays on Art, Literature, and Philosophy

by

Ernst Neizvestny

Edited, with Preface, Introduction, Translations, and Notes

by

Albert Leong

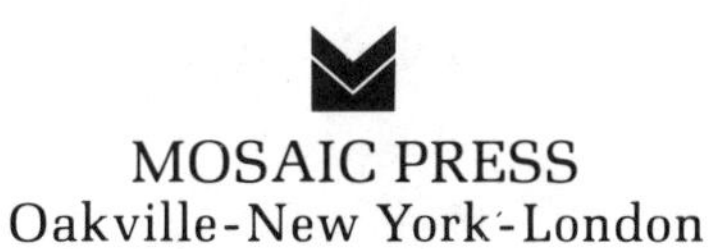

MOSAIC PRESS
Oakville-New York-London

CANADIAN CATALOGUING IN PUBLICATION DATA

Neizvestnyĭ, Ėrnst, 1926-
Space, time, and synthesis in art

Translated from Russian.
Includes bibliographical references.
ISBN 0-88962-436-4 (bound) ISBN 0-88962-437-2 (pbk.)

1. Neizvestnyĭ, Ėrnst, 1926- . 2. Art - Philosophy. 3. Literature - Philosophy. I. Leong, Albert. II. Title.

NB699.N4A35 1990 730'.92 C90-095335-7

Published by MOSAIC PRESS, P.O. Box 1032, Oakville, Ontario, L6J 5E9, Canada. Offices and warehouse at 1252 Speers Road, Units # 1&2, Oakville, Ontario, L6L 5N9, Canada.

Mosaic Press acknowledges the assistance of the Canada Council and the Ontario Arts Council in support of its publishing programme.

Design by Marion Black
Typeset by Aztext Electronic Publishing Ltd.

Printed and bound in Canada.

ISBN 0-88962 436-4 CLOTH
ISBN 0-88962 437-2 PAPER

MOSAIC PRESS:

In Canada:
MOSAIC PRESS, 1252 Speers Road, Units # 1&2, Oakville, Ontario L6L 5N9, Canada. P.O. Box 1032, Oakville, Ontario L6J 5N9

In the United States:
Distributed by National Book Network Inc., 4720-A Boston Way, MD. 20706, USA.

In the U.K.:
John Calder (Publishers) Ltd., 9-15 Neal St., London, WCZH 9TU, England.

Beauty will save the world.
Dostoevsky

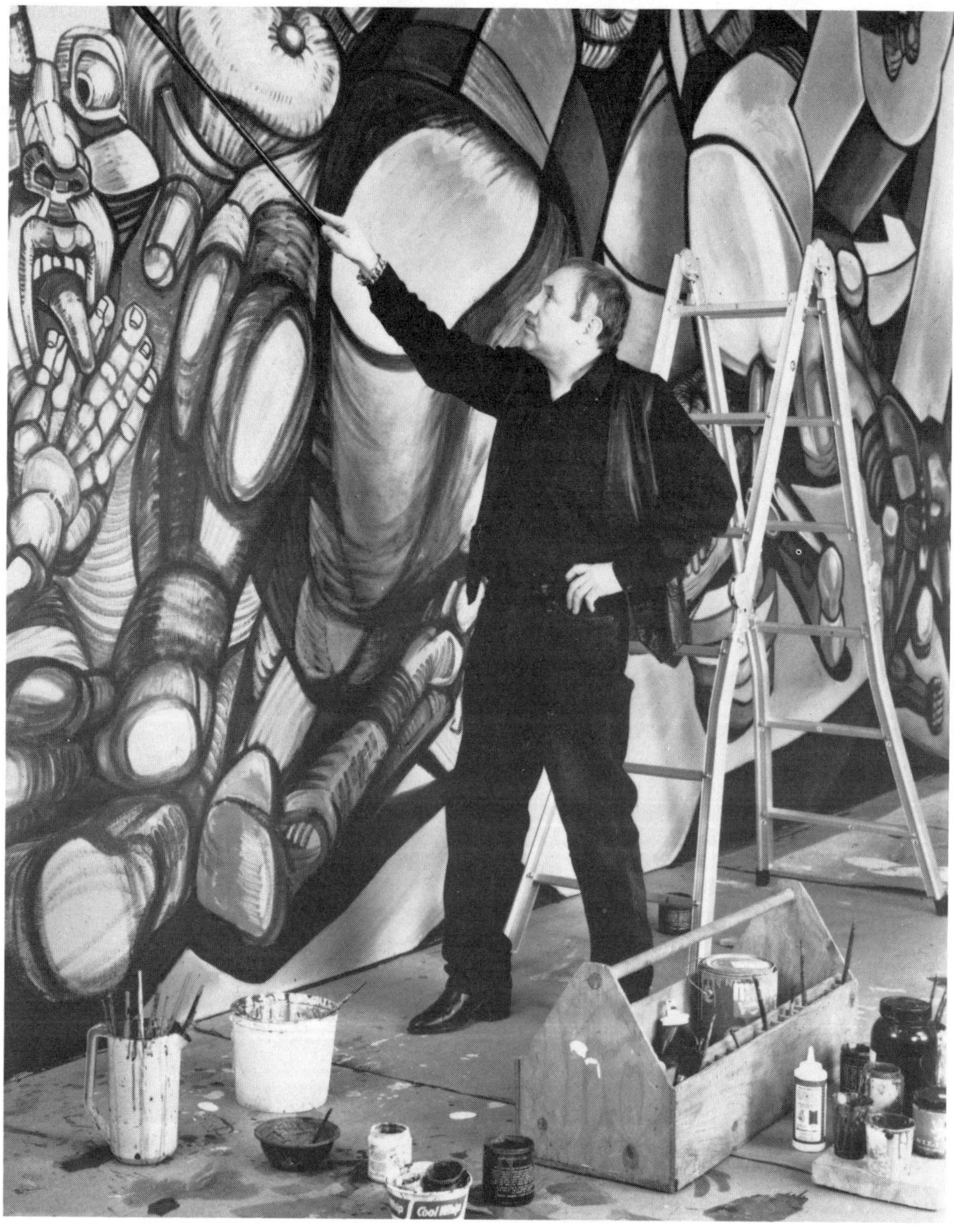
Cool Whip

CONTENTS

ILLUSTRATIONS

FIGURES

PLATES

(Following Page 64)

Krik (The Outcry)
Kentavr i krest (Centaur and Cross)
Raspiatie vniz golovoi (Upside Down Crucifixion)
Kentavr (Centaur)
Raspiatyi v tekhnike (Man Crucified in Machinery)
Polurobot ((Semi-Robot)
Kosti i plot' (Bones and Flesh)
Rozhdenie iz smerti (Birth from Death)
Terrorist (Terrorist)
Krysa v zheleznykh rukakh (Rat in Iron Hands)
Sarkafag liubvi (Sarcophagus of Love)
Padaiushchie totemy: Gitler, Stalin, Mussolini, Mao i t.d.)
(Falling Totems: Hitler, Stalin, Mussolini, Mao, etc.)
Byk revoliutsii (Bull of Revolution)
Kentavr i rab (Centaur and Slave)
Begstvo iz zheleznogo uzla (Escape from Iron Knot)
Zheleznyi uzel (Iron Knot)

(Following Page 96)

Ptitsa iz tsikla "Sud'ba" (Bird from Cycle, "Fate")
Chelovek - Maska (Man - Mask)
S. Beket (Samuel Beckett)
Kentavry (Centaurs)
Sviatoi Sebastian (Saint Sebastian)
Minotavr (Minotaur)
S. Beket: Khromoi (Samuel Beckett: The Cripple)
Shag cherez liubov' (Stepping Over Love)

S. Beket: Ten' (Samuel Beckett: Shadow)
S. Beket: Dialog s ten'iu (Samuel Beckett: Dialogue with a Shadow)
Stol Beketa (Beckett's Table)
S. Beket: Dialog s ten'iu (Samuel Beckett: Dialogue with a Shadow)
Tanets s kukloi (Dance with a Puppet)
S. Beket: Labirint (Samuel Beckett: Labyrinth)
Stol Beketa (Beckett's Table)
S. Beket: Maska (Samuel Beckett: Mask)

(Following Page 128)

Drevo zhizni (Tree of Life)
Detail, *Ruka i ia* (The Hand and I), from *Prometei* (Prometheus)
Chelovek i nauka (Man and Science)
Detail, *Chelovek i nauka* (Man and Science)
Rel'ef (Relief)
Prorok (The Prophet)
Novaia statuia svobody (New Statue of Liberty)
Dvulikii (Man with Double Face)
Pamiatnik v chest' mertvykh (Monument in Honor of the Dead)
Zheleznyi prorok (Iron Prophet)
Atomnyi vzryv (Atomic Explosion)
Kentavr bez ruk (Centaur without Hands)
Totem (Totem)
Serdtse Khristosa (Heart of Christ)
Tors kentavra (Centaur's Torso)
Raspiatyi gigant (Crucified Giant)

FOREWORD

Long before *glasnost'* and *perestroika* were implemented in the Soviet Union by Mikhail Gorbachev, I wrote in *Neizvestny Speaks* that change in the USSR was inevitable, but that altering the Soviet system was impossible. All my life I have found myself in the odd, dualistic, and incomprehensibly contradictory position of thesis and antithesis. Having lived many years in the Soviet Union, I sensed that this situation could not persist much longer. As a sculptor and artist, I looked upon Soviet society from two perspectives – the diachronic and horizontal, as well as the synchronic and vertical – and drew the conclusion that to maintain the status quo was out of the question.

I do not believe in historical determinism. The changes in the socialist system that I foresaw as inevitable have come about not from objective, economic conditions, but from a psychological outburst, an almost mystical ferment and change in mass consciousness. As a result, these changes are at once inevitable and irreversible.

At the birth of Solidarity in Poland, I wrote that I saw the hand of fate guiding the workers' movement. Workers' movements normally develop in reaction against religion and communist institutions, and move in the direction of materialism and revolution. But the Solidarity movement in Poland developed along different lines: from materialism to mystical, spiritual values. Stalin was fond of asking, "How many divisions does the Pope have?" Yet in Poland we saw huge throngs of workers rallying to the banner of the Black Madonna. For me this process was symbolic, and I anticipated the same transformation in Europe and Russia.

People have often asked how I was able to predict the sweeping changes taking place in East Europe and the Soviet Union. I am no prophet, nor did I actually foresee those changes. But an artist is a seismograph who can sense the slightest shifts and movement in an epoch, whether in politics or in philosophy. The artist is a person from whose hand the skin has been stripped, and the nerves thus exposed feel the breath of change much more acutely than does healthy skin. The artist, therefore, is a barometer of popular sentiment. In that sense I had a premonition of inevitable change in Europe and Russia.

In the final analysis I cannot believe in historical determinism. The 1917 Russian Revolution was anticipated by a number of Russian poets, but not by Lenin himself. No one has been able to give a rational, objective explanation for such phenomena. Revolutions resemble strange, spiritual earthquakes caused by unexpected shifts in various strata of the population.

What is happening in East Europe and the Soviet Union today, in principle, is a situation where society has reached the limits of despair, and change is imperative. I first heard the thesis of *perestroika* thirty years ago from friends, philosophers, and dissidents – a number of whom presently serve as advisors to Gorbachev. And *perestroika* is based on dissatisfaction alone. But the historical process is something else. Think of the Soviet Union as a great tree which, beneath the lush foliage, is hollow and rotten to the core. It does not take a very strong wind to topple that tree.

We are witnessing the beginning of the demise of communism. Communism has reached not only an impasse, but total bankruptcy. Communism, not as an idealistic utopia nor as a poetic idea, in reality is bankrupt in all respects. There was an ascetic period of Soviet culture in the 1920s when there was no bread, but the people were given spiritual food. There was a period when bread was plentiful. There was a time when the Soviet people were deprived of both bread and freedom, and instead were given the illusion of dynamic change. And there was a period under Stalin when everything was taken away: illusions, spiritual nourishment, bread, freedom, and even honor itself.

ERNST NEIZVESTNY

PREFACE

A synopsis of the life of Russian-American sculptor and philosopher Ernst Neizvestny (pronounced ne-iz-VEST-ny) has the contours of myth, legend, and film scenario: a Russian child prodigy in art becomes a decorated war hero who survives clinical death on the battlefield and transcends the pre-Gorbachev Soviet totalitarian state as a visionary artist of genius.

Complex and controversial, Neizvestny's life and work have given rise to a number of conflicting interpretations. *Art and Revolution: Ernst Neizvestny and the Role of the Artist in the USSR* by British art critic John Berger conceives of Neizvestny as a Marxist artist whose sculpture is "an interim monument to the endurance necessary at the beginning of the world struggle against imperialism."[1] *Ernst Neizvestny: Art and Reality* by Russian emigré sociologist Nikolai Novikov, more accurately depicts the artist as a monumentalist who toiled in isolation in the Soviet Union.[2] An Italian compedium of documents and essays, *Ernst Neizvestny,* by Mario De Micheli portrays Neizvestny as a religious artist close to Roman Catholicism.[3] The documentary film version of Aleksandr Solzhenitsyn's *Nobel Lecture* on literature, *One Word of Truth,* features Neizvestny as a humble artist joyfully working as "a common apprentice under God's heaven."[4] *Ernst Neizvestny: Life and Work* by Norwegian art critic Erik Egeland describes Neizvestny as a "spiritualistic Dionysian figure."[5] Both Boris Ogibenin's *Ernst Neizvestny: Créateur d'une archaïque nouvelle*[6] and Franco Miele's *Dinamismo Plastico in Ernst Neizvestny*[7] analyze the semiotic and compositional elements of Neizvestny's sculpture without addressing the Russian cultural context that energizes his art.

If one were to juxtapose these divergent images of Neizvestny, one would come up with a creature more grotesque than the centaurs and fanciful combinations of men and machines that characterize the artist's sculptures, paintings, and drawings. When a historian of Russian culture encounters an artistic talent as expansive, prodigal, and prodigious as Neizvestny's, what critical framework can be devised that would adequately encompass his gifts and properly place him in the context of Russian and world culture? What critical approach and method can resolve the dilemma of the blind men attempting to describe an elephant as a whole and arrive at a comprehensive, scholarly assessment of a man who resembles a "baggy monster," a phrase that Henry James once applied to another monumental and multifaceted Russian, Lev Tolstoy?

My approach to Neizvestny's life, art, and thought differs from those scholars and critics cited above in three important respects. First, as a historian of Russian literature and culture who has systematically researched Neizvestny's theoretical writings on art, literature, and philosophy, I have come to regard Neizvestny as an original artist, critic, and thinker in the tradition of Russian social, political, and philosophical thought. Now translated into English in a single collection, these essays clearly delineate Neizvestny's aesthetics and poetics for the first time and make his ideas accessible to scholars and general readers with little or no background in Russian language and culture.

Secondly, I look upon Neizvestny's art as a unique fusion of East and West. He is not a Russian nationalist like the Slavophiles, nor is he a Westernizer who indiscriminately embraces the institutions and technologies of the West.[8] Nurtured at the crossroads of East and West in the Ural Mountains of Siberia, Neizvestny's art attempts to synthesize some of the formal and substantive elements of Eastern and Western culture. In his latest monumental projects – the *Tree of Life*, the *New Statue of Liberty*, and the memorials to the victims of Stalinism and the Holocaust – Neizvestny encompasses the great cultural achievements of East and West: the *Tree of Life* as a monument to human creativity in art, science, and technology; the *New Statue of Liberty* as a fusion of traditional Chinese culture based on the teachings of Confucius with the modern technology of the West that has developed from it; and the memorials to the victims of Stalinism and the Holocaust as a celebration of the resistance and resilience of the peoples of East and West.

And, thirdly, I regard Neizvestny as a model of human resistance to the modern totalitarian state and a living example of how art, artist, and human beings can develop even under the constraints of a closed society, such as censorship, surveillance, and the imposition of a State aesthetics of "socialist realism."

This collection of Neizvestny's essays on art, literature, and philosophy – the first in any language – begins to fill the large gap in scholarship on Neizvestny by defining his place in Russian and, thereby, world culture. These brilliant, provocative essays – individually and collectively – dispel the notion that Neizvestny is merely a "dissident" artist. His widely-publicized confrontation with Nikita Khrushchev at the Manège exhibition in 1962 on the subject of modern art has long obscured and colored critical judgment as to the intrinsic merit of his art and ideas. My critical biography in progress, *The Art of Freedom: Ernst Neizvestny and Russian Culture,* by discussing the man and his art in the context of Russian intellectual and cultural history, also supports the view of Neizvestny as a major figure in Russian and world culture.

A number of people have assisted me in the preparation of this book, and I wish to acknowledge their contributions with gratitude. Portions of Chapters Seven and Twelve are based on the taped interviews with Neizvestny which Tanya Gorokhovskaya and Marina Lukanova transcribed. Susan Mende and Christine Sperber provided me with documentary material for the bibliography, and Martha Sherwood-Pike integrated illustrations with text in Chapter Two. An equipment grant from Apple Computer facilitated the preparation of the manuscript, and Roy Singer performed the data transfer from the Macintosh to the IBM format. Suggestions by George Beltran, Dean McKenzie, Howard Robertson, and Ann Muller have been incorporated into the book.

My wife Ann made a number of valuable suggestions, proofed sections of the book, and was a source of inspiration during the entire project. Ernst Neizvestny selected the illustrations, proofed my translations, gave me access to his personal library and archives, and offered me gracious hospitality at his studio in New York City as we brought the project to a conclusion. Grant funding in 1983 from the Oregon Committee for the Humanities for a Summer research project on Neizvestny and for a public humanities symposium featuring Neizvestny, "Freedom and Culture in the Soviet Union," enabled me to complete preliminary research on the artist. I also wish to thank the University of Oregon and Donald Van Houten, Dean of the College of Arts and Sciences, for release time to complete this book. And, finally, Howard Aster of Mosaic Press has provided timely assistance, suggestions, and enthusiastic support throughout the preparation of this manuscript for publication.

ALBERT LEONG

[1] John Berger, *Art and Revolution: Ernst Neizvestny and the Role of the Artist in the USSR* (New York: Pantheon Books, 1969), 153. See my review in *Slavic and East European Journal,* Vol. XV, No. 2 (Summer 1971): 253-54. Neizvestny rejects this Marxist interpretation of his work.

[2] Nikolai Novikov, *Ernst Neizvestnyi: iskusstvo i real'nost'* (Ernst Neizvestny: art and reality) [New York: Chalidze Publications, 1981].

[3] Mario De Micheli, *Ernst Neizvestny* (Milan: Giangiacomo Feltrinelli Editore, 1978).

[4] *One Word of Truth* (Produced by Ailsa Hamilton, Harry Howlett, and Finn Harald Wetterfors) [Cambridge: Anglo-Nordic Productions Trust, 1981). Neizvestny is shown working on a centaur sculpture in Sweden.

[5] Erik Egeland, *Ernst Neizvestny: Life and Work* (New York: Mosaic Press, 1984), 195.

[6] Boris Ogibenin, *Ernst Neizvestny: Créateur d'une archaïque nouvelle* (Ernst Neizvestny: creator of a new archaism) [Lisse: Peter De Ridder Press, 1975].

[7] Franco Miele, *Dinamismo Plastico in Ernst Neizvestny* (Plastic dynamism in Ernst Neizvestny) [Rome: Prospettive, no date].

[8] The Slavophiles *(slavianofili)* placed faith in indigenous social institutions such as the Russian peasant commune *(mir)* as the basis for the future development of Russia. Their ideological opponents, the Westernizers *(zapadniki),* favored the adoption of foreign technology and social reform on the European model.

CHRONOLOGY

1926-42 Born April 9, 1926, in the Ural Mountain city of Sverdlovsk. Wins national competition and attends special school for artistically gifted children from 1939-42, first in Leningrad, then in Samarkand during the war years.

1942-45 Volunteers for service in the Red Army and attends military school in Kushka. Commissioned as airborne commando officer and sees action on Second Ukrainian front. Gravely wounded in Austria on April 22, 1945, declared dead, and "posthumously" awarded the Order of the Red Star for heroism.

1945-46 Teaches drawing at Suvorov Institute in Sverdlovsk.

1946-47 Studies at the Academy of Fine Arts in Riga, Latvia.

1947-54 Studies art at Surikov Institute of Art and philosophy at Moscow State University.

1955-76 Member of Sculpture Section of Union of Soviet Artists, Moscow Branch.

1954-62 Participates in youth, republic, and all-union exhibitions in Moscow.

1956 Begins work on *Tree of Life* project.

1957 Awarded two prizes at the Fourth International Festival of Youth and Students in Moscow.

1958 Begins work on *Gigantomachia* series. *Heart of Humanity* evolves into *Tree of Life* architectural monument to human creativity in art, science, and technology.

1959 Wins national competition for *Victory* war monument commemorating Soviet victory over Nazi Germany.

1962 Takes part in Manège exhibition in Moscow and discusses art with Soviet premier Nikita Khrushchev.

1963 Begins work on series of etchings and drawings to the works of Fedor Dostoevsky.

1965 Exhibition at Museum of Contemporary Art in Belgrade. Takes part in symposium, "Sculpture in Free Space," and erects two sculptures – *Centaur* and *Stone Tears* – in Yugoslavia. Joint exhibition with Marc Chagall at Grosvenor Gallery, London.

1966 Executes 150-meter decorative relief, *Prometheus,* for Artek Pioneer Camp in the Crimea. Begins work on series of etchings and drawings to the works of Dante. Exhibition at Museum of Contemporary Art in Vienna and at Lambert Gallery in Paris.

1968 Illustrates Dante's *Short Works* (Moscow: Nauka, 1968). Wins international competition with design for *Lotus Blossom* monument, the largest sculpture in the world, for the Aswan Dam in Egypt.

1969 Exhibition of illustrations to Dante's *Inferno* at Astley Gallery in Köping, Sweden.

1970 Exhibitions at Museum of Modern Art in Paris, and Museum of Fine Arts in Locarno, Italy. Takes part in exhibition by Veterans of World War II and exhibition commemorating the Centennial of Lenin's Birth in Moscow. Publication of Fedor Dostoevsky's *Prestuplenie i nakazanie* (Crime and punishment), with illustrations by Neizvestny.

1972 Executes sculpture for main pavilion of *Electro-72* exhibition in Moscow. Exhibition at Museum of Contemporary Art in Tel-Aviv, Israel.

1973 *Crucifix* sculpture exhibited in collection of Pope John Paul I.

1974 Executes tombstone for Nikita Khrushchev at Novodevichy Monastery in Moscow, 970-meter decorative relief for Institute of Electronics and Technology in Moscow, and sculptural monument *Wings* for Institute of Light Alloys in Moscow. Takes part in "Progressive Currents" exhibition at Bochum Museum in West Germany. Sculpture, *Large Crucifix,* acquired by Vatican Museum.

1975 Designs monumental architectural facade for headquarters of Central Committee in Ashkhabad, Turkmenia. Exhibitions in Vienna, Berlin, and at Lincoln Center, New York.

1976 Emigrates to the West and settles in Zurich, Switzerland. Completes bronze head of Dmitri Shostakovich for Kennedy Center for the Performing Arts in Washington, DC.Aleksandr Zinoviev's *Ziiaiushchie vysoty* (The yawning heights) published, with Neizvestny as its hero.

1977 Moves to New York City. Begins to lecture on art and philosophy at universities in the United States.

1981 Featured in film version of Aleksandr Solzhenitsyn's *Nobel Lecture* on literature, *One Word of Truth.* Guest speaker at national meeting of American Association for the Advancement of Slavic Studies at Asilomar, California.

1982 *On Synthesis in Art* published.

1983 Appointed Humanist-in-Residence at the University of Oregon, USA, and conducts course on "Synthesis in Russian Culture." Lecture tour on "Art and Freedom" to twelve Oregon cities. Holds exhibition at Museum of Art, University of Oregon, and takes part in symposium on "Freedom and Culture in the Soviet Union." Appointed distinguished visiting lecturer in art and philosophy at Columbia University.

1984 First collection of essays in Russian, *Govorit Neizvestnyi* (Neizvestny speaks) published. Lectures on "Art and Society" at Harvard University.

1985 Essay on "Art and Freedom" published.

1986 Elected to the Swedish Royal Academy of Sciences and the New York Academy of Arts and Sciences. Visiting lecturer in summer Russian seminar sponsored by U. S. Department of Education at the University of Oregon.

1987 "Tree of Life" Museum dedicated to Neizvestny's works opens in Uttersberg, Sweden. "Body: Man as Visual Sign" and "Art and Society" published.

1988 Designs *New Statue of Liberty* honoring the Republic of China and the Third World. Tours major cities of Taiwan with traveling exhibition of his works.

1989 Completes illustrations to jubilee edition of Samuel Beckett's works. Lectures on culture at Moscow State University. Commissioned to design Holocaust monument in Riga, Latvia, and memorial to victims of Stalinism in Vorkuta, USSR. Soviet documentary film, *V otvete l' zrachii za sleptsa* (Will the visonary answer for the blind?) released in USSR. "O sinteze iskusstv" (On synthesis of the arts) published in *Voprosy filosofii* (Problems of philosophy) after twenty-year delay. Elected to full membership in European Academy of Arts, Sciences, and Humanities.

1990 First collection of essays in English, *Space, Time, and Synthesis in Art: Essays on Art, Literature, and Philosophy*, published. Commissioned to design memorials to the victims of Stalinism in Magadan and Sverdlovsk, USSR.

Neizvestny Museum established in Sverdlovsk.

Centaur: The Life, Art, and Thought of Ernst Neizvestny

Albert Leong

1. A Centaur's Life

In his essay "On Synthesis in Art," Neizvestny defines synthesis as "the combination of the many, the diverse, into one."[1] The equivalent concept in Russian philosophical thought is *sovokupnost'*, a totality characterized by wholeness. Neizvestny's polyphonic art is based on this concept of synthesis. In the modern age, high technology in the form of computers, robots, and spacecraft has become a "second nature" that interacts with, and complements, Mother Nature herself. In Neizvestny's eyes, contemporary culture, East and West, is a fusion or synthesis of people and machines.

Neizvestny's paintings, sculptures, and drawings depict the enormous variety of these hybrids in the modern world. The central image of his art is the centaur, a mythical creature that conjoins man and horse to create a new expressive synthesis. For Neizvestny, the peoples of East and West now live in a "civilization of centaurs." Within this concept of synthesis, Neizvestny brilliantly exploits the Formalist and Cubist device of deformation to reduce heterogeneous elements into a single living whole.[2] His polyphonic style of composing sculptures, paintings, and drawings allows Neizvestny to juxtapose the most diverse combinations of nature, the second nature of technology, and styles of art in expressing the spirit of the modern age. The personification of the centaur as the expressive synthesis of heterogeneous elements is Neizvestny himself.

Ernst Iosifovich Neizvestny was born April 9, 1926, in Sverdlovsk, formerly Ekaterinburg, a city situated in the Ural Mountains, the dividing line between Europe and Asia in the Soviet Union. Neizvestny describes Sverdlovsk as "a city of exiled intelligentsia, aristocracy, and criminals . . . a city that embodies, as no other, the antinomy of the European and Asiatic traits of the Russian soul."[3] A bastion of diversity and freedom, Sverdlovsk was a close-knit community where the cultures of East and West met, where Russians, Tatars, and a large number of Chinese lived and worked. Even the uncommon family name, Neizvestny ("the unknown one"), may have been adopted by freed exiles reluctant to disclose their true identities.

The Neizvestnys are descended from an old Siberian military family. Neizvestny's grandfather was a prosperous entrepreneur who owned a printing establishment in Orenburg and other business interests in the Urals. Of his parents Neizvestny writes: "My father, a former White officer from a wealthy merchant family, was a pediatric surgeon. Due to this background, he encountered difficulties throughout his life. My mother was a biochemist, as well as a poet and writer of children's books. Because she was Jewish, my mother was accused of Zionism and cosmopolitanism. Our home and meetings with people in my parent's circle were my first universities."[4] Their background and wealth made the Neizvestny family *lishentsi*, or Soviet citizens deprived of civil rights. But his father's eminence as a surgeon enabled the family to survive the Stalin years.

Ernst and his younger sister grew up in a comfortable, three-story home with a garden. He had his own nursery and a nanny who was to play an extraordinary role in his fate.[5] His father Iosif had taken part in the Civil War of 1918-21 as a White officer. Neizvestny remembers him as an athlete, a figure skater, a champion dancer, and an expert billiards player. If his Russian Orthodox father was conservative and aristocratic, Ernst's Jewish mother, Bella De Jour, was liberal and democratic. Of mystical bent, she investigated Rudolf Steiner's anthroposophy,[6] Tibetan mysticism, and the theosophical teachings of Madame Blavatsky[7] and Annie Besant.[8]

Although the Mendelian school of genetics was banned as bourgeois and reactionary during the Stalin era, his mother, a biochemist who was trained at Leningrad State University, continued to conduct experiments with guinea pigs, rabbits, and birds in an animal laboratory disguised as a household menagerie. Young Neizvestny assisted her in these experiments, and he recalls those scientific investigations as his first contact with underground or "catacomb" culture.

After his mother began to write poetry, she was introduced to literary circles, where she met the poet Nikolai Zabolotsky,[9] to whom she later became engaged. Although Zabolotsky was arrested in 1938 and vanished into the GULag for a number of years,[10] he managed to have his poems smuggled out to Bella, who entrusted them to the memory of her son.[11] Bella De Jour recently was awarded a prize by West Germany for her lyric poetry. In addition to poetry, she has written children's books on nature, animals, and ecology, as well as monographs on glass and dolls.

The man who was to become one of Russia's greatest artists and philosophers of art was brought up to value family, education, religion, self-discipline, art, science, cultural traditions, and moral responsibility before society and the world. The boy was named Eric by his mother after a king in a Norse saga. Since the name sounds childish in Russian,[12] Neizvestny changed it to Ernst when he became older. To this day Neizvestny speaks of "Erik" and "Ernst" as two sides or stages of his personality: the child versus the adult.

Young Neizvestny started to talk at a rather late age; but, once he did, he learned to speak and read rapidly at about the same time. His parents introduced their precocious son early to the mysteries of art and science, and young Neizvestny quickly absorbed the family's large library of pre-Revolutionary books. The Neizvestny family were members of the Siberian cultural and scientific intelligentsia who maintained a tradition of independent political thought tracing back to the Decembrists, members of the Russian nobility who were exiled to Siberia for participation in the December 1825 revolt in St. Petersburg against tsarist autocracy.

As a boy, Ernst was a natural leader who liked to box and play soccer. His father wanted him to become a geologist and arranged for Ernst to study at a local institute. Neizvestny found these lectures tedious and preferred to go the Palace of Young Pioneers where he could draw and paint. Even then Ernst liked to draw skeletons, skulls, masks, hands, and dying people: "I was never particularly interested in the natural world around me and how a tree looked, but, rather, what a tree was. I was interested in what went on inside, in how things lived."[13] When it was raining or snowing, young Neizvestny would gaze at the surface of a window and conjure up images of himself as Alexander the Great,[14] Spartacus,[15] Paracelsus,[16] Pasteur,[17] or the explorer Amundsen.[18] The boy longed to perform great deeds and knew, even as a child, that he would someday be famous.[19]

A child prodigy who was drawing, painting, and modeling clay as long as he could remember, young Neizvestny, now fourteen, passed a national art competition and was admitted into a new elite school established by Lazar Kaganovich[20] in Leningrad for artistically gifted children. There, the five students in Neizvestny's class were given instruction in classical academic subjects by sixteen renowned scholars. When World War II broke out, this elite school was moved to Samarkand in the Central Asian republic of Uzbekistan. There, the sixteen year old boy enunciates his artistic credo in a letter to his parents: "There is only one way for art – the path of absolute truth. Anything that is not true is not art. There is no excuse for untruth, not even that of being young. Untruth becomes a habit. One must learn to be truthful right from the start, . . . and never just out of cleverness. One must stick to the truth. Only this will bring me to my goal."[21] In Samarkand Ernst contracted typhoid fever and suffered from a temporary loss of hair, strength, and memory.

Though he was exempt from military service due to his exceptional artistic talent, Neizvestny decided to volunteer for service with the Red Army to fight fascism after a close friend was killed in action. Altering his age at the recruiting office,[22] Ernst was accepted for training in desert warfare as an airborne commando officer at Kushka, a rigorous military academy in a Turkmen town near the border of Afghanistan. Trained in assault and landing operations, the seventeen year old Neizvestny was assigned to the 45th Assault Regiment attached to the 86th Guards Division on the Second Ukrainian Front. Neizvestny's unit, through parachute drops, armored assaults, and landings by sea, fought its way from the Ukraine into southern and eastern Europe. From 1943, Lieutenant Neizvestny, only eighteen years old, led his unit of 120 men into battle in Romania, Hungary, and Austria, and was wounded on several occasions. The last time, on April 22, 1945, near Heisendorf, Austria, an exploding bullet entered his chest, shattered his spine and ribs, damaged his internal organs, and made a crater in his back.[23]

The extraordinary events that occurred afterwards have permanently shaped Neizvestny's life, art, and outlook. According to Neizvestny, his mangled body was taken to a field hospital, where the woman who washed his wounds recognized him by certain distinctive birth marks. This nurse, by sheerest coincidence, had also served as his childhood nanny in Sverdlovsk. She identified him and took special care of him. Neizvestny, suffering excruciating pain, was encased in plaster. Despite doctors' orders to the contrary, his nurse obtained pain-killing drugs for him. Neizvestny recalls:

> One morning I woke up completely free from pain. I was at peace and content. But I could not open my eyes, could not say a word, not move a limb. I could, however, hear what was going on around me. I heard that there were doctors standing by my bed. They were saying that I was dead and gave the Latin name for my condition. I had grown up in a doctor's house, so I knew the terminology. I wanted to let them know that I was alive, but could do nothing. I was completely unafraid, calm, and happy. . . I knew only peace and was free from pain.
>
> The stretcher bearers came to take my body to the mortuary in the cellars, down a great many stairs. I was particularly heavy because of all the plaster. They could not be bothered to carry me, so they heaved me over the banisters and went on their way. The plaster cracked open as I hit the ground at the bottom of the stairs, and this presumably

> touched off something in my mutilated back. I began to scream with pain, I know not for how long.
>
> In the meantime my old nursemaid had come into the ward and found my bed empty. She found out that I had died and had been taken to the mortuary. So she went down there to take her last farewell of me. And on her way down she found me lying screaming. I was carried up again, back to life and pain. But the bureaucrats had already managed to send the news of my death to my family.[24]

Neizvestny's remarkable recovery from clinical death and physical mutilation has left an indelible mark on the central images of his paintings, drawings, and sculptures, in which the human body undergoes dramatic transfiguration and synthesis. For Neizvestny, death and unbearable pain became the measure of all things, and human endurance developed into a major motif of his postwar art. Inverting the meaning of the title of Pasternak's lyric cycle, *My Sister – Life,* Neizvestny proclaims that his own "sister" is death.

Neizvestny returned from the war a hero and an invalid. He was admitted to the Academy of Art in Riga, Latvia, but the hostility that he, as a Russian, felt from the Latvian students obliged him to transfer in 1947 to the Surikov Institute of Art in Moscow.[25] While a student at the institute, Neizvestny also undertook to study philosophy at Moscow State University. He worked as a caretaker to two sculptors to pay for his lodgings and had to stoke stoves with coal in the early hours of the morning before attending classes that started at eight o'clock. However, his physical disabilities, in addition to malnutrition and extreme overexertion, led to complete exhaustion and even a suicide attempt. Now aware of Neizvestny's plight, senior sculptors at the institute began to hire him as an assistant, and his lot gradually improved.

Neizvestny's development as as an artist can be divided into three stages: the student period (1947-54); the period of intermittent Soviet recognition and repression (1955-75); and the "Western" period (1976 to the present). From 1947 through 1954 Neizvestny studied at the Surikov Institute of Art and, with a small group of friends, formed a "catacomb culture" study group that passed itself off as a student drinking club with the motto: "Love and Hunger Rule the World." The group studied banned books, writers, artists, and philosophers in what spare time they had. Ernst would copy classical statues by day and model modernist sculptures at night. One of his neo-classical works, *Female Torso* (1949), was acquired by the Tretiakov Gallery in Moscow. In his last year at the institute, Neizvestny was invited to join the Moscow branch of the Union of Soviet Artists, an extraordinary honor for a fledgling artist.

Russian museums, Western art books, and visiting exhibitions supplemented Neizvestny's education in the history of art. In them Neizvestny discovered Pre-Columbian art, primitive art, Aztec sculpture, Mexican art, Picasso,[26] Leger,[27] and works by the banned masters of the Russian avant-garde, such as Kandinsky,[28] Malevich,[29] and Tatlin,[30] the master of Constructivism who was his mentor in Moscow. Finding true affinity with the theories and creations of the Russian avant-garde, Neizvestny openly repudiated the state aesthetics of socialist realism and began to model and exhibit constructivist sculptures after Stalin's death in 1953. His teachers at the Surikov Institute, who had expected the gifted young artist to follow in their footsteps as a "socialist realist" executing monuments on sanctioned Soviet themes, were appalled. Thus began Neizvestny's long struggle against the cultural establishment in the Soviet Union.

After Stalin's death, an open art competition was announced for a monument to commemorate the union of the Ukraine with Russia. These and other open competitions for which designs could be submitted anonymously and evaluated by peers instead of bureaucrats, enabled Neizvestny's star to rise rapidly by the sheer force of his talent and personality. At the 1957 Sixth International Youth Festival at Sokolniki Park in Moscow, Neizvestny was awarded the three top prizes in a competition consisting of 4,500 works by young artists from fifty countries: the gold medal for his granite sculpture *Nature;* the silver medal for a granite figure *Mulatto;* and the bronze medal for another granite figure *Female Torso.* Because one person garnishing three medals was somewhat awkward, the Soviet Minister of Culture, Aleksandr Mikhailov, ordered Neizvestny to relinquish the gold medal.[31]

The major events of 1956 in East Europe – Khrushchev's secret speech denouncing Stalin and Stalinism at the Twentieth

Congress of the Communist Party of the Soviet Union, the revolution in Hungary, and unrest in Poland – affected Neizvestny directly. Accused of "revisionism" and sympathy for the Hungarian cause, Neizvestny found all doors closed to him and was obliged to return to Sverdlovsk to work in a foundry, where at night after work he would fashion sculptures out of scraps of metal. He began to suffer from intense depression and to drink heavily. It was there that Neizvestny saw his vision of the *Tree of Life*.

Motivated by this artistic vision, Neizvestny returned to Moscow in 1960. He won a national competition to design a vast monument outside Moscow to commemorate the Soviet victory over Nazi Germany. His war memorial project brought Neizvestny the attention of talented young Soviet architects, who began to collaborate with him on monumental works. Their first joint effort was a successful design for an immense bas-relief honoring the children of the world at the Artek Pioneer Camp in the Crimea. During the Khrushchev "Thaw" of the early 1960s,[32] exhibitions of unofficial art could be held outside the purview of the Union of Soviet Artists, and artists would hold showings in scientific institutes, workers' clubs, and universities. In 1960 Neizvestny exhibited his works at the *Druzhba* (Friendship) Workers' Club in Moscow; in 1962 he held an exhibition at Moscow State University. Later that year Neizvestny took part in the December 1962 exhibition of modernist Soviet art at the Manège[33] exhibition hall in Moscow to celebrate the thirtieth anniversary of the Union of Soviet Artists. This event was to mark another turning point in Neizvestny's fortunes.

In the West one cannot easily imagine artist and autocrat locked in debate over the issue of what is art, but it is a recurring theme within the Russian tradition going back at least to Aleksandr Pushkin's confrontation as a Decembrist sympathizer with Tsar Nikolai I in the early nineteenth century.[34] The Soviet premier with his official entourage came to the opening of the exhibit, was outraged by what he saw, and held Neizvestny responsible for works that Khrushchev considered excrement, filth, and a disgrace. Neizvestny now believes that the whole affair was a provocation to embarrass Khrushchev.[35] Despite threats and intimidation Neizvestny defended the art and artists exhibited and won Khrushchev's respect: "You are the kind of man I like. But there's an angel and a devil in you. If the angel wins, we can get along together. If it's the devil who wins, we shall destroy you."[36]

What ensued was a crackdown on nonconformist artists and writers, including Neizvestny. Khrushchev was intent on driving the "devil" out of Neizvestny, and intense pressure was brought to bear on the artist. Neizvestny was expelled from the Union of Soviet Artists and persecuted in numerous ways.[37] The Soviet Academy of Art intervened to kill his War Memorial project.[38] He was subjected to a psychiatric examination. When Khrushchev asked how he could withstand the pressure of the State for so long, Neizvestny replied: "There are certain bacteria – very small, soft ones – which can live in a super-saline solution that could dissolve the hoof of a rhinoceros."[39] He was found sane by the psychiatrists. In October of 1964 Khrushchev was ousted by Brezhnev[40] and Kosygin in a coup, but the story has an unexpected denouement: after Khrushchev's death in 1971, Neizvestny agreed to execute Khrushchev's headstone at Novodevichy Monastery at the request of the late Premier's family.

The years of disfavor from 1962 to 1970 were difficult for Neizvestny. He relocated temporarily to Riga, worked on the Artek project, and completed his illustrations to Dante and Dostoevsky. His sculptures *Orpheus* and *The Prophet* were crafted in 1962, and his sculptural ensemble *Gigantomachia* was begun. The albums for the *Tree of Life* originated in 1965, and a model of the monument was constructed in 1968. In 1965 the Soviet magazine *Iunost'* (Youth) published an account of Neizvestny's wartime exploits together with a poem by Andrei Voznesensky which dramatized the fact that war hero and nonconformist artist were one and the same person.[41] Neizvestny survived by selling his works to foreign visitors and working anonymously for established architects. In 1969 he learned of an international competition for a monument at the Aswan Dam in Egypt. With two architects Neizvestny designed in secret a *Lotus Blossom* monument and smuggled the plans for the project out of the country. Neizvestny's design won the competition and obliged the Soviet cultural establishment to acknowledge his achievement as a symbol of Soviet-Egyptian cooperation. His membership in the

Union of Soviet Artists was restored, and he was to enjoy full rehabilitation and artistic success for the next five years.

Neizvestny had caught the eye of Soviet technocrats, scientists, architects, intellectuals, and even Communist Party officials such as Kosygin – the same group of people who advocated a break from the dogmas of the Stalinist past. The Kosygin circle – which included the ministers for electronics, electrification, and hydroelectric development – was able to award Neizvestny commissions for new sculptural-architectural works against the wishes of the Academy of Art, the Union of Soviet Artists, and the Ministry of Culture. Thus, in 1974, Neizvestny's massive relief for the Moscow Institute of Technology and Electronics was completed. Also, in 1974-75, was accomplished his monumental relief for the headquarters of the Central Committee of the Communist Party in Ashkhabad, the capital of Turkmenia. With the assistance of Sergei Korolev, designer of the first Soviet space satellite, and the Nobel laureates in physics, Petr Kapitsa and Lev Landau, Neizvestny was able to hold a one-man show at the Kurchatov Atomic Research Institute.

In 1973 Neizvestny was invited to Poland as a guest of prominent Polish communists. Upon his return, the Soviet authorities barred him from further foreign travel, despite repeated invitations from France, Italy, and England. To dramatize his plight, Neizvestny held a press conference with Western journalists in March of 1974 and announced that he had made more than fifty applications for travel abroad in the past ten years without success. In September of 1974 nonconformist artists from Moscow and Leningrad held an outdoor joint exhibition near Moscow, but the authorities ordered the exhibition bulldozed into the ground.

Neizvestny was subjected to artistic and ideological pressure and kept under continuous surveillance by the KGB. Under these conditions Neizvestny decided to apply for emigration on the grounds that he was unable to work as an artist in this atmosphere of censorship, harassment, and repression. The authorities responded with a threat to take away his studio; and, in the summer of 1975, Neizvestny was physically assaulted outside Moscow. Thanks to the intervention of Prime Minister Bruno Kreisky of Austria and international publicity, Neizvestny finally received his exit visa in March 1976 and arrived in Geneva,

Switzerland, in May of that year. Neizvestny, the centaur, was now free to pursue his artistic visions in the West.

Like other Russians who have emigrated to the West for purely artistic reasons, Neizvestny and his art have blossomed in the atmosphere of tolerance and cultural pluralism characteristic of Western Europe and the United States. Attracted by the dynamism, diversity, and freedom of America, Neizvestny moved to the SoHo district of New York City in 1977 and eventually relinquished his Swiss citizenship, There, in a cavernous studio on Grand Street, Neizvestny, acclaimed as an artist in Europe but virtually unknown in the United States, laid the foundations for the future development of his art.

The sculptures of Neizvestny's Western period were executed with greater technical refinement, and the artist began to paint large canvases in brilliant hues as a new form of self-expression. Under the sponsorship of Freedom House, Neizvestny gave slide lectures in Russian on topics such as "Dante and Dostoevsky" and "Synthesis in Art" at American colleges and universities. But his lack of knowledge of English and his habit of working long hours in seclusion or with a few Russian emigré assistants effectively isolated Neizvestny from the mainstream of Western cultural life.

The rise of Neizvestny's reputation in the United States and in Asia, too, dates perhaps from the Spring of 1983, when he accepted my invitation to come to the University of Oregon as Humanist-in-Residence to teach a course in Russian on *Synthesis in Russian Culture*, to lecture on "Art and Freedom" in twelve Oregon cities, to hold a major exhibition of his paintings and sculptures at the university's Museum of Art, and to take part in a symposium on "Freedom and Culture in the Soviet Union" sponsored by the Oregon Committee for the Humanities. As a result of that sojourn in Oregon, Neizvestny acquired a working knowledge of English that made him more accessible to Western intellectuals, the mass media, and the general public. That stay in Oregon also led to the first appearance of an essay of his in English translation.[42]

Since it was his first teaching position at a university, Neizvestny prepared for it with characteristic energy and thoroughness. The year before he had exhibited a collection of his prints and drawings and had lectured on "Dante and Dostoevsky" and "Synthesis in Art" before large audiences at the University of Oregon. These and other lectures that Neizvestny composed for the course – "Man as Visual Sign," "The Tree of Life," "Space and Time in Tolstoy and Dostoevsky," "Time and Space in Russian Icons and Egyptian Reliefs," "Artists of Flow and Artists of Masterpieces," "Messianic Tendencies in Russian Culture," and "Art and Freedom" – form the basis of this collection of essays.

Neizvestny chose to take his meals in the student dining hall and to live in an austere dormitory room on campus, "like a soldier" as he put it. Continuous contact and discussions for three months with American college students, often late into the night, enabled him to begin to communicate in English. He was a dynamic, learned, charismatic, and creative teacher who held 150 students spellbound for 90 minutes twice a week while lecturing in eloquent and expressive Russian. I had the challenging task of translating his lectures simultaneously into English and serving as his interpreter during his statewide lecture tour. In the course of traveling hundreds of miles together by Volkswagen camper from Eugene to Corvallis, Albany, Salem, Portland, Roseburg, Coos Bay, Ashland, Klamath Falls, Bend, Pendleton, and Astoria, Neizvestny and I became friends and decided to collaborate on several book projects: a biography and a collection of his essays on art, literature, and philosophy.

I particularly remember the way Neizvestny conducted the final oral examinations for the course. In the Russian tradition, the students would come into his room one at a time; within fifteen intense minutes, Neizvestny the master teacher was able to assess their term papers and projects, ascertain their grasp of the ideas he had expounded in his lectures, and gently lead them to new discoveries. Neizvestny was to return to the University of Oregon for the third time to take part in a Russian Seminar for advanced teachers of Russian in the Summer of 1986,[43] the same year that he was elected to the Swedish Royal Academy of Sciences and to the New York Academy of Arts and Sciences.

Since his return to New York, Neizvestny has designed a *New Statue of Liberty* to honor the Republic of China as a symbol of the Third World, a memorial to his friend Andrei Tarkovsky,[44] and a monument to the humanitarian, Raoul Wallenberg.[45] His mother and sister were permitted at last to emigrate and now live near

Neizvestny. His daughter came to visit him in New York for six months. In July of 1989 Neizvestny returned to the Soviet Union as part of an American delegation attending a conference at Moscow State University on the future of culture, and delivered a lecture on "Art and Culture." His triumphant return to his homeland was marked by extensive coverage in the Soviet press.[46] Moscow Film Studios filmed Neizvestny at his summer studio in Sweden as part of a full-length documentary film about the artist that was released in 1989.[47] He has been commissioned to design a memorial to the victims of fascism in Riga, Latvia, and monuments to the victims of Stalinism in Magadan, Vorkuta, and Sverdlovsk. Neizvestny, now an American citizen and a major figure in world art, has been restored at last to a rightful place of honor in his native land.

2. Neizvestny's Art and Thought

Neizvestny as an artist and thinker was inspired, first of all, by the theories and achievements of the Russian avant-garde in the first decades of the twentieth century. In an interview he said: "I consider myself a pupil of the Russian avant-garde – Malevich Kandinsky, and partly the Cubo-Futurists. But unlike my mentors, who moved from man to machine, I am going in the opposite direction – from machine to man. . . . I strive for synthesis, which was a constant aim of the Russian avant-garde. Kandinsky's book concludes with the words: 'The future is in monumental synthesis.'"[48]

In his essay, "Content and Form, 1910" Kandinsky predicted the appearance of a monumental, spiritualized art that would unite all the arts in a single work.[49] Kandinsky's vision of spiritualized art is embodied in Neizvestny's immense architectural-sculptural monument to human creativity, the *Tree of Life*: "The *Tree of Life* is the apotheosis of the human soul and human knowledge. . . . By spiritually uniting art with contemporary science and technology, the *Tree of Life* represents the symbiosis of Faith and Knowledge. In unity they enrich one another and thus impart purposefulness to the spiritualized universe."[50]

Moreover, Neizvestny's physical description of the *Tree of Life* bears a striking resemblance to the grandiose *Monument to the Third International* of Vladimir Tatlin, which was described as an "organic synthesis of architectural, sculptural, and painterly principles."[51] While Tatlin's monument was conceived as a secular temple, Neizvestny's *Tree of Life* is meant to be a holistic contemporary cathedral.

The third avant-garde master who shaped Neizvestny's concept of art was Kazimir Malevich. In his manifesto, "From Cubism and Futurism to Suprematism: The New Painterly Realism, 1915," Malevich wrote: "To create means to live, forever creating newer and newer things.... The artist can be a creator only when the forms in his picture have nothing in common with nature. For art is the ability to create a construction that derives not from the interrelation of form and color and not on the basis of aesthetic taste in a construction's compositional beauty, *but on the basis of weight, speed, and direction of movement*."[52]

Thus, deformation of nature and the Cubo-Futurists' compositional principle of dynamism distinguish Neizvestny's paintings, drawings, and sculptures. In "On Synthesis in Art," Neizvestny describes a world in which nature, including humankind, interacts dynamically with a "second nature" created by human beings as an extension of their hands, brains, eyes, and hearts.[53] Defining sculpture as a dialogue between flesh and spirit, Neizvestny sees unique possibilities in the art of sculpture for the monumental synthesis of heterogeneous elements. Because modern life is an endless dialogue between living nature and the "second nature" of machines, robots, and computers, monumental polyphonic sculptures – such as the *Tree of Life*, the *New Statue of Liberty*, and the memorial to the victims of Stalinism at Vorkuta – epitomize contemporary civilization. Neizvestny's fundamental technique of deformation or reduction (*svedenie*) of nature enables him to juxtapose and synthesize the most diverse elements – from extreme abstraction to the most naturalistic representations – in a single work.

The key to Neizvestny's art and aesthetics is contained in the famous poem, "The Prophet" (*Prorok*), composed in 1826 by Russia's national poet, Aleksandr Pushkin:

> Dukhovnoi zhazhdoiu tomim,
> V pustyne mrachnoi ia vlachilsia,
> I shestikrylyi serafim

Na pereput'e mne iavilsia.
Perstami legkimi kak son
Moikh zenits kosnulsia on.
Otverslis' veshchie zenitsy,
Kak u ispugannoi orlitsy.
Moikh ushei kosnulsia on, –
I ikh napolnil shum i zvon:
I vnial ia neba sodrogan'e,
I gornyi angelov polet,
I gad morskikh podvodnyi khod,
I dol'nei lozy proziaban'e.
I on k ustam moim prinik,
I vyrval greshnyi moi iazyk,
I prazdnoslovnyi i lukavyi,
I zhalo mudryia zmei
V usta zamershie moi
Vlozhil desnitseiu krovavoi.
I on mne grud' rassek mechom,
I serdtse trepetnoe vynul,
I ugl', pylaiushchii ognem,
V grud' otverstuiu vodvinul.
Kak trup v pustyne ia lezhal,
I boga glas ko mne vozzval:
'Vosstan', prorok, i vizhd', i vnemli,
Ispolnis' voleiu moei
I, obkhodia moria i zemli,
Glagolom zhgi serdtsa liudei'.[54]

(By spiritual thirst exhausted,
In desert's gloom I dragged, –
And a six-winged seraphim
On the crossroad to me appeared.
With fingers light as dream
My orbs he touched.
And my prophetic orbs opened
As a frightened she-eagle's.
My ears he touched, –
And noise and ringing filled them:
And heard I the heaven's shudder,

And angels' steep flight,
And sea monsters' underwater walk,
And vale's vines growing,
And he affixed himself to my lips,
And tore out my sinful tongue
So idle and cunning,
And a wise serpent's sting
Into my frozen lips
With bloody hand he placed.
And cleft he my chest with sword
And fluttering heart withdrew,
And a coal aglow with fire
Into my open chest inserted.
Like a corpse in the wilderness I lay,
And God's voice to me called out:
'Arise, prophet, see and heed,
Carry out my will
And, seas and lands traversing,
With my Word sear humankind's hearts.')[55]

Pushkin's description of a pilgrim's spiritual rebirth in many respects parallels documented experiences of clinical death and recovery.[56] In World War II, Neizvestny, gravely wounded, was declared dead by field medics, but later miraculously revived.[57] John Berger has noted Neizvestny's preoccupation with mutilation motifs in his early postwar sculptures: Neizvestny appears to deform or reduce human figures in his art as his own body had been deformed by man-made instruments of war.[58] Similarly, his illustrations to Dante's *Inferno* depict the human body transfigured by the torments of Hell. Neizvestny's more recent drawings, such as his illustrations to the works of Samuel Beckett,[59] dramatize Beckett's characters, like those of Dante[60] and Dostoevsky,[61] as masks of bodies conducting an endless dialogue with death and with space. In Pushkin's poem, the prophet created by the sculptor-seraphim exemplifies Neizvestny's reduction of heterogeneous elements (eyes, ears, tongue, heart) into a single, indivisible, living essence (the prophet). And it is Neizvestny's sculpture of Pushkin's prophet that stands at the center of his monument to the *Tree of Life*.

In recorded clinical death experiences, a common image or vision is that of a passageway leading to the world beyond death, and quite often there is a guide or angel who conducts the human soul through this passage. In Neizvestny's *Tree of Life*, the Moebius strips spiralling upwards appears to represent the passage from life to afterlife, since the Moebius symbolizes infinity.[62] Similarly, Pushkin's seraphim, the pilgrim's guide in the poem, is the agent of the artist's spiritual transfiguration. According to Neizvestny, the *Tree of Life* – complete to the last detail – appeared to him in a dream-like vision at the nadir of his fortunes in the Soviet Union.[63] Moreover, the Tree of Life is a multiple symbol of life (the tree, the heart), as well as death and resurrection (Christ, the Cross).[64]

Neizvestny's conception of art as a holistic, spiritual phenomenon and his image of the artist as a creator of myths and archetypes to unite the human community stem from the Russian philosophical tradition of holistic synthesis established by Vladimir Soloviev,[65] Nikolai Fedorov,[66] Fedor Dostoevsky, and Pavel Florensky.[67] Like the medieval Russian icon painter, Andrei Rublev,[68] Neizvestny "philosophizes in colors" (*umozrenie v kraskakh*); and, like Dostoevsky in *The Brothers Karamazov*, he longs for *sobornost'*, a harmonious spiritual community of free men and women that embodies the Slavophile ideal.[69] Neizvestny's philosophical ideas are inseparable from his life and art. While American art historians and critics may be familiar with the formal and constructivist aspects of the Russian revolutionary avant-garde, Neizvestny observes that, because they are unaware of the foundations on which this movement was built in the period before and after the October Revolution, they cannot entirely understand what he, the successor to the Russian avant-garde, is trying to do.[70]

In Neizvestny's view the concept of synthesis was central to the Russian avant-garde, and to Russian philosophy as well. Kandinsky, Malevich, Filonov,[71] and Tatlin were all holistic artists whose work pointed to a future synthesis. Kandinsky's *Concerning the Spiritual in Art* (1912) regarded abstraction as a form of purifying art in preparation for the monumental synthesis of the future. Filonov conceived of perfected works of art, like trees, undergoing universal flowering. Tatlin saw Constructivism as a rational structure and his *Monument to the Third International* as a secular temple. Influenced by Fabian socialist philosophy, in which technical progress leads to utopia,[72] Tatlin espoused a metaphysical approach to technical progress similar to that of Nikolai Fedorov, who equated technical and moral progress with the idea of God. In Neizvestny's view, Fedorov "was a Christian believer whose conception of the world was one of universal atonement. He considered technical progress to be deeply meaningful. The advent of the new technological civilization meant the realization of God's purpose, which was that humanity, as His instrument, should dominate the earth. Technology was part of God's plan for creation."[73] At the present time Neizvestny describes his own views as a fusion of "post-religious Russian philosophy and the ideas of the Russian avant-garde."[74] He cites the work of Father Pavel Florensky, whose pioneer work on sign systems suggests a synthesis of mathematics, aesthetics, and topology, of sounds and words with space.

In Neizvestny's view, the second concept shared by Russian philosophy and the Russian revolutionary avant-garde is *maximalism*. Maximalism is part of the eschatological temperament of Russian philosophy and art that is closely related to the eschatological, maximalist, and revolutionary nature of the Russian avant-garde.[75] Therefore, the Russian Revolution drew upon the political slogans and expectations of the Russian avant-garde.[76] Neizvestny believes that philosophy as a formal discipline developed rather late in Russia and that the first Russian philosopher in the Western sense of the word was Grigory Skovoroda.[77] As a result, the Russian school of philosophical thought owes much to poetic and artistic creativity. According to Neizvestny, the first philosophers in Russia were artists. Andrei Rublev was an artist who "philosophized in colors," and Vladimir Soloviev was a "philosophizing poet." And Nikolai Fedorov's philosophy is essentially a form of Christian utopianism. Thus, there is a most intimate relationship between Russian philosophy and the Russian avant-garde. Fedorov believed in a particular form of reincarnation and profoundly influenced avant-garde artists such as Tatlin and Vladimir Mayakovsky.[78]

The nexus between Russian philosophy and art provides the cultural and intellectual context by which Neizvestny and his art can be understood. Neizvestny not only continues the traditions of the Russian revolutionary avant-garde of the 1920s, but also has created a new visual language and a new kind of synthesis in his monumental art. This synthesis is based on a powerful fusion of natural forms, such as the human body, with the tools and technology that extend the senses in what Neizvestny calls humankind's "second nature." The most notable of these hybrids is Neizvestny's extraordinary tribe of contemporary centaurs, those creatures – half human, half machine – who roam freely in his paintings and drawings and who command space in his powerful sculptures.

Melding past, present, and future, Neizvestny's centaur is an arresting metaphor and symbol of modern civilization. The centaur evokes antiquity and the realm of myth and archetype.[79] To apply Yury Tynianov's distinction, Neizvestny is both an archaist and an innovator.[80] He draws inspiration from the ancient metaphysical cultures of Egypt, India, China, Greece, and Mexico in which art and artist were part of a transcendental worldview. At the same time, he makes use of high technology as themes and tools in the construction of his art. The primacy of "deformation," "device," and "reduction" in Neizvestny's aesthetics and poetics also connects him directly to the Russian Formalis; movement of the 1920s.[81] For example, Mikhail Bakhtin's concept of monologic and dialogic discourse is applied by Neizvestny to the art of sculpture as a quintessential dialogue between spirit and matter. In his synthesis of art, life, and thought, Ernst Neizvestny personifies the centaur he celebrates in his prolific, polyphonic art.

As his life work, the *Tree of Life* embodies Neizvestny's concept of universal synthesis and reconciles the dualistic contradictions of man and nature, of man and machine. The *Tree of Life* is also the fruition of Neizvestny's central theme of polyphonic synthesis, a motif developed in his illustrations to Dante, Dostoevsky, and Beckett. From his mentor Tatlin, he developed the idea of creating a monumental construction combining purely artistic forms with utilitarian applications. From Malevich, Neizvestny was inspired to create an abstract sculpture at once eternal and futuristic on the basis of weight, speed, and motion. And from Filonov, Neizvestny assimilated the idea of crafted perfection in art that will undergo universal flowering. From Russian philosophy and the Russian revolutionary avant-garde, Neizvestny conjoined the concepts of holistic synthesis and eschatological maximalism in the process of philosophizing through art. A monumental synthesis of art and idea in the great tradition of Russian culture from Rublev to Fedorov, Soloviev, and the Russian avant-garde, the *Tree of Life* symbolizes the spiritual union of art, science, and technology, the harmonious symbiosis of Faith and Knowledge, and the possibility of peace and reconciliation in the nuclear age.

[1] See Chapter One, "On Synthesis in Art".
[2] Cubism in art and Russian Formalism in literature both "deformed" the work to heighten its effect.
[3] From Neizvestny's unpublished autobiographical sketches, *Lik, Litso, Lichina* (Visage, Face, Mask).
[4] *Ibid.*
[5] According to Neizvestny, it was the same nanny who rescued him from the cellar where he was left for dead on the Second Ukrainian Front in World War II. See Egeland, *Ernst Neizvestny*, 50-52.
[6] Rudolf Steiner (1861-1925), Austrian social philosopher and founder of anthroposophy, which held that self-discipline can lead to cognitive spiritual experiences.
[7] Elena Petrovna Blavatsky, founder of Theosophical Society advocating eclectic world religion based on Buddhism and Brahmanism.
[8] Annie Besant (1847-1933), English theosophist.
[9] Nikolai Alekseevich Zabolotsky (1903-58), Russian modernist poet, children's writer, and translator. His art combined a pantheistic outlook with a primitivist style.
[10] GULag (*Glavnoe upravlenie lagerei*), Central Administration of Labor Camps that destroyed approximately 40 million people between 1918 and 1956, according to Soviet statistics recently released.
[11] When Zabolotsky was freed from exile and came across Neizvestny again, he was astonished to hear the sculptor, now in his thirties, recite those poems flawlessly. Zabolotsky subsequently revised and published those poems. See Egeland, *Ernst Neizvestny*, 40.

[12] The suffix -ik, when attached to proper names in Russian, signifies a diminutive or affectionate form of address.
[13] Quoted in Egeland, *Ernst Neizvestny*, 42.
[14] Alexander the Great (356-323 BC), King of Macedonia (336-323 BC) and conqueror of Persian empire.
[15] Spartacus, Thracian gladiator, slave, and insurrectionist who died in 71 BC.
[16] Phillipus Aureolus Paracelsus (1493?-1541), Swiss alchemist and physician.
[17] Louis Pasteur (1822-95), French chemist and bacteriologist
[18] Roald Amundsen (1872-1928), Norwegian explorer who discovered the South Pole in 1911.
[19] Egeland, *Ernst Neizvestny*, 43.
[20] Lazar Moiseevich Kaganovich [Kogan] (1893-), Bolshevik revolutionary, politician, and close associate of Stalin.
[21] Quoted in Egeland, *Ernst Neizvestny*, 45.
[22] Both 1925 and 1926 are given as his year of birth.
[23] See Egeland, *Ernst Neizvestny*, 50.
[24] Quoted in Egeland, *Ernst Neizvestny*, 50-52.
[25] Because Latvia was incorporated by force into the Soviet Union as a result of the Hitler-Stalin pact, Latvians bear considerable resentment towards Russians.
[26] Pablo Picasso (1881-1973), great Spanish painter, sculptor, ceramicist, and graphic artist who created Cubism together with Braque.
[27] Fernand Léger (1881-1955), French Cubist painter
[28] Vasily Kandinsky (1866-1944), Russian painter and a founder of abstract art.
[29] Kazimir Malevich (1878-1935), Russian pioneer of abstract art and founder of Suprematism.
[30] Vladimir Tatlin (1885-1955), Russian artist and founder of Constructivism, an art movement of the 1920s that combined modern technology, practical function, and aesthetics into its works.
[31] Subsequently, Prime Minister Aleksei Kosygin presented the sculpture *Nature* to Urho Kekkonen, then President of Finland.
[32] "Thaw," from the 1954 novel *Ottepel'* by Ilya Grigor'evich Erenburg (1891-1967) refers to Nikita Khrushchev's brief period of cultural liberalization connected with his policy of de-Stalinization.

[33] Manège, former riding school now used to house exhibitions.
[34] Aleksandr Sergeevich Pushkin (1799-1837), Russia's national poet who was killed in a duel in what is believed to be a provocation planned by the tsarist government.
[35] A transcript of the Khrushchev-Neizvestny debate is given in Berger, *Art and Revolution*, 82-86.
[36] Also quoted in Egeland, *Ernst Neizvestny*, 86.
[37] Expulsion from the union deprived Neizvestny of access to art supplies, official commissions, and exhibition space.
[38] Elements of this project, such as pools of water symbolizing a sea of tears, are preserved in his proposed memorial to the victims of Stalinism at Vorkuta.
[39] Quoted in Berger, *Art and Revolution*, 85-86.
[40] Leonid Ilyich Brezhnev (1906-82), Soviet political leader and head of state (1964-82).
[41] Andrei Voznesensky, "*Neizvestnyi – rekviem v dvukh shagakh, s epilogom*" (Neizvestny – a requiem in two steps with an epilogue), *Iunost'* (June 1965).
[42] Ernst Neizvestny, "Art and Freedom," translated by Albert Leong, *Studies in Comparative Communism*, Vol. XVII, Nos. 3 & 4 (Fall/Winter 1984-85): 235-39.
[43] Two of his lectures, "Body: Man as Visual Sign" and "Art and Society" were published in the *Proceedings of the Summer 1986 Intensive Workshop in Chinese and Russian*, ed. Albert Leong (Eugene: University of Oregon Press, 1988) and made his ideas better known in the academic community.
[44] Andrei Tarkovsky (1932-86), major Soviet filmmaker, director of *Andrei Rublev.*
[45] Raoul Wallenberg (1912-47?), Swedish diplomat who saved the lives of 5,000 Hungarian Jews from the Nazis and was arrested by Soviet authorities as a spy. His fate is unknown.
[46] Essays on or by Neizvestny have appeared in *Moskovskie novosti* (Moscow news), *Sovetskii ekran* (Soviet screen), *Iskustvo kino* (Film art), *Izvestiia* (News), *Voprosy filosofii* (Problems of philosophy), *Novoe vremia* (New times), *Komsomol'skaia pravda* (Komsomol truth), and other periodicals.
[47] *V otvete l' zrachii za slepogo* (Will the visionary answer for the blind?)

[48] See Bella Ezerskaia, *Mastera* (Masters) [Ann Arbor: Hermitage, 1982], 90.
[49] Vasily Kandinsky, "Content and Form, 1910," *Russian Art of the Avant-Garde: Theory and Criticism*, ed. John E. Bowlt (New York: The Viking Press, 1976), 21-22.
[50] See Chapter Two, 63.
[51] N. Punin, *Pamiatnik Tret'emu Internatsionalu: Proekt V. Tatlina* (Monument to the Third International: A project by V. Tatlin). Peterburg, 1920), 1.
[52] Kazimir Malevich, "From Cubism and Futurism to Suprematism: The New Painterly Realism, 1915," in *Russian Art of the Avant-Garde*, ed. Bowlt, 21-22.
[53] See Chapter One, 6.
[54] A. S. Pushkin, *Izbrannye proizvedeniia* (Selected works), III (Moscow: Khudozhestvennaia literatura, 1965), 108-09.
[55] Translation mine.
[56] See case histories in Kenneth Ring, *Life at Death: A Scientific Investigation of the Near-Death Experience* (New York: Coward, McCann & Groghegan, 1980).
[57] Neizvestny's family received official notification of his death in battle.
[58] Berger, *Art and Revolution*, 97-101. Neizvestny notes, however, that the theme of death appeared frequently even in the drawings and paintings of his childhood (see Egeland, *Ernst Neizvestny*, 52-53).
[59] Samuel Barclay Beckett (1906-89), Irish dramatist, novelist, and Nobel Laureate in Literature (1969).
[60] Dante Alighieri (1265-1321), Italy's greatest poet, author of *The Divine Comedy*.
[61] Fedor Mikhailovich Dostoevsky (1821-81), major Russian novelist, author of *Notes from the Underground, Crime and Punishment,* and *The Brothers Karamazov*.
[62] The Moebius is a topological space having only one side and formed by joining two strips of material after turning one of the ends through an angle of 180 degrees. Because the Moebius is circular and covers the same surface over and over, Professor Howard Robertson suggests that it may also symbolize reincarnation.

[63] Interview with Neizvestny (9 April 1983). I am indebted to Professor Henryk Baran for noting the striking convergence of Neizvestny's biography with essential elements of Siberian shamanism: Neizvestny's full recovery from physical mutilation and clinical death; his rebirth as a visionary artist; and his shamanic vision of the Cosmic Tree with its roots in the underworld, its trunk in the world, and its branches in the Cosmos.
[64] Egeland, *Ernst Neizvestny*, 31. See also Mircea Eliade, *A History of Religious Ideas*, Vol. 2 (Chicago: University of Chicago Press, 1982), 401-03, for a discussion of religious symbolism embodied in the Cross and the Tree of Life: "The notion of salvation merely takes up and completes the notions of perpetual renewal and cosmic regeneration, of universal fecundity and sacrality, of absolute reality, and, in the last analysis, of immortality – all notions that coexist in the symbolism of the World Tree." (p. 402).
[65] Vladimir Sergeevich Soloviev (1853-1900), influential Russian philosopher and poet.
[66] Nikolai Fedorovich Fedorov (1828-1903), Russian Christian philosopher, author of *Philosophy of the Common Task*.
[67] Pavel Aleksandrovich Florensky (1882-1943), Russian theologian, scholar, folklorist, poet, and religious philosopher; author of *The Pillar and Foundation of Truth* (1914).
[68] Andrei Rublev (c1370-c1430), greatest Russian religious artist.
[69] *Sobornost'*, which comes from the word *sobor*, meaning "cathedral" or "congregation," is discussed in Chapter Three. See also Preface, note 8.
[70] Interview with Neizvestny (April 9, 1983).
[71] Pavel Filonov (1883-1941), Russian exponent of Analytical Art, the central concepts of which are "madeness" (*sdelannost'*), the crafted perfection of a work of art, and "universal flowering" (*mirovyi rassvet*), the organic evolution of a work of art. See John Bowlt, "Pavel Filonov and Russian Modernism" in *Pavel Filonov: A Hero and His Fate: Collected Writings on Art and Revolution* (Austin: Silvergirl Inc., 1984).
[72] Cf. Lenin's dictum that "Communism is Soviet Power plus electrification."
[73] Egeland, *Ernst Neizvestny*, 31.
[74] Lecture, "On Synthesis in Art," by Neizvestny at University of Oregon (23 April 1982).

[75] The Russian avant-garde looked upon the Russian Revolution as Apocalypse.
[76] Conversation with Neizvestny (20 September 1985). See also Chapter Three.
[77] See Grigorii Skovoroda, *Sochineniia v dvukh tomakh* (Works in two volumes) [Moscow: AN SSSR, 1973]. See discussion of Skovoroda in Chapter Three.
[78] Vladimir Vladimirovich Mayakovsky (1893-1930), Soviet Futurist poet, playwright, and artist.
[79] Neizvestny admires the writings of Carl Jung and Joseph Campbell on archetype and myth.
[80] Yury Nikolaevich Tynianov (1894-1943), Russian writer, critic, and translator affiliated with Russian Formalist movement.
[81] Russian Formalism, a school of literary criticism of the 1920s that expounded purely intrinsic analysis of the "devices" (*priemy*) used in the composition of verbal art. Other leading Russian Formalists include Viktor Borisovich Shklovsky (1893-1984), Boris Mikhailovich Eikhenbaum (1886-1959), and Mikhail Mikhailovich Bakhtin (1895-1975).

CHAPTER ONE

On Synthesis in Art

1.

Everything in this article concerns my inner experiences as an artist. The words were born afterwards. I do not attribute any value to what is uttered in words. Words are instruments of thought that assist me in my work.

We artists speak more and more often about a so-called "synthesis of the arts." I too had to dwell on this matter, all the more so because everything on which I work – whether it is an album of drawings, a series of etchings, or separate sculptures and groupings – is part of a holistic monumental schema which is in principle polyphonic, but at the same time unified. After rejecting a number of causes that have no direct bearing on art, one can say, in the first place, that this notion of synthesis of the arts interferes with the prevailing notion of a distinct delimitation of their possibilities and laws. But painting is painting; sculpture is sculpture, architecture is architecture, and music is music, and so forth people will say. This thought came to us in precisely such terms; it was formulated as the antithesis to the post-Rodin,[1] post-impressionist collapse of the formal signs of art. Sculptors striving for external verisimilitude began to abuse their art by using the devices of painting. Light and shadow on a sculpture's surface began to destroy the tectonics of volume and space. In expressionism[2] the representation of a psychological state became the main aim, and traditional qualities of plasticity as well as the structure of the material were ignored. Some sculptors tried to compete directly with literature, and their works became arbitrary salon and genre sculptures.

It was precisely these and similar tendencies that produced, as an antithesis, a whole series of theoreticians and practitioners of art who tried to prevent the collapse of representational art by establishing the boundaries and criteria of separate forms of art. And, to give them their due, this basically simplistic idea of course was a professional one in the narrow sense of the word. This idea indeed was and is based on a bookish understanding of the discipline of a profession, of what I would call the body of a profession. Of course, striving for harmony, honesty, and professionalism is better than the raging and unprincipled international salon of dilettantes. Therefore, by being principled, this idea bore fruit. But as human knowledge, like any thought attempting to sunder a single whole into its parts, it bore with it the imprint of barrenness. It seems to me impoverished and fundamentally ignoble. This tendency is particularly provincial in the context of that spiral on which we now find ourselves.

At the present time human awareness, despite the endless abundance and diversity of information and, perhaps because of it, is striving for unity, for knowledge of origins, and a focus for all that exists. And artists envision themselves as not only craftsmen producing more or less professional objects, but inevitably aspire to create works that are innately essential events. Therefore, the greatest masters of schools which strive for doctrinal strictness in preserving the boundaries of the arts often destroyed their own theories in practice.

It is paradoxical for theoretical discussions about pure plasticity to be conducted by people who are working in an essentially literary form. These are not plastic artists who reverently address proportions, correlations of weight, precise distribution of spatial elements of a sculpture, who profess a vitalistic love of nature and its stateliness purified of fleeting picturesque vicissitudes. These are not Constructivists,[3] who consider that only the construction itself and its rhythm comprise the soul of spatial art. Nor are they pantheists,[4] who view the imitation of the plant and mineral world as the highest form of plastic vision. No, guarded discussions of the separation of the arts are conducted not by authentic artists who may have set limits to their tasks, but by artists of literary anecdotes who have realized their trivial visual tasks in eternal materials. Indeed, their talk of pure plastic form, endless "scientific" constructions when speaking of matters elementary, commonly known, and obligatory for everyone having at least an average education in art is simply a fig leaf covering the lack of an artistic world view. Their struggle against the established functions of art is an attempt not to merely kill time in the guild, or to play the game of "good" or "bad" artist, but to do something reflecting the spiritual interests of people, to combat the metaphysical and philosophical content of art. Hence arises their collective prejudice that only the visual is appropriate for representational art, and that a world view, since it cannot be seen in nature, cannot be depicted, for it is no longer representational art, but abstract reasoning.

Life itself demands a certain scale of design, wholeness, synthesis. Unfortunately, synthesis is often perceived in the following nonwhimsical manner: "How can we place a very good sculpture in such a way, so that it would not interfere with a very, very good picturesque painting nearby or inside an architectural design?" But the striving for synthesis is not a narrowly professional attempt to drive diverse forms of art towards some kind of external harmony, but a holistic idea.

Synthesis is not eclecticism, where everything is brought together whimsically. Synthesis in art is an organism in which each part performs its proper function, and the parts comprise an aesthetic unity as a whole. The more complex the inner life of a work, the larger the circle of phenomena which it incorporates, and the more symphonic the experiences, the greater are the number of parts, the greater the diversity. But this diversity is not unified by the initial energy of the design. Therefore, a good book, a good piece of music, or a good sculptural-architectural ensemble is a microcosmos.

In a single fragment of Egyptian sculpture inhere the laws of Egyptian architecture; in its tiniest part pounds the pulse of the entire structure. For ancient peoples had a holistic relationship to the world. Artists were not simply craftsmen, but always found themselves at the focal point of spiritual life. And the interconnection and interdependence of phenomena, whether as scientific truth or poetic premonition of it ("instant knowledge"), were always obvious to the ancient artist, as past ages of great art attest.

At the present time objective systematic laws in the structure of matter have been revealed, and these laws find support in psychological research on cognition. There is comparative study of sign systems, from signals to natural languages and the formalized languages of science. The unity of words, sounds, color, light, and forms is confirmed by research. Identity has been found among verse forms and the organization of crystal structures. We have evidence of links between aesthetic phenomena and the form of the "golden section"[5] even in film art. One can cite endless examples of typological and semantic interconnections. And it is clear that if one seriously does a structural analysis of the plastic arts, a juxtaposition of various systems of representational symbols will lead us to the concept of linking kinds of representational art not only with myth and ritual (which is obvious), but also with music, cosmogony,[6] and mathematics. Moreover, the same systematic regularities going beyond the bounds of human activities and found in nature itself are possible. Therefore, the fundamental division of conditional signs of architecture, sculpture, painting, and so forth is viewed not only as fruitless, but also as inaccurate.

When speaking of synthesis, one prefers to think not about the more or less successful combination of disparate elements in art, for their formation yields no result, just as in mathematics an infinite series of zeroes will, all the same, produce no number. Our age has given rise to a large number of local discoveries, and the technical possibilities of representational art have been broadened. Ages of culture and art show that a holistic perception of the world reconciles opposing signs in a single, variegated whole, that is, in a synthesis. And the antagonism of artists connected with these partial, narrow definitions is senseless, because we have yet to create an art comparable to a temple where each professes its own in the context of the whole. We cannot intellectually decide how to produce this synthesis, this unity in creating a new holistic plastic language, but we can strive for this goal. Precisely for this reason tolerance with respect to individual approaches and discoveries of someone working in this area is not simply the ethical norm, but also a sign of professional and human maturity.

Archaeology has given us incomparable opportunities to see perfected works of ancient art, to see that the form of each of them is not accidental, not capricious, but a world view. The absence of perspective in Egyptian art, the reverse perspective of Russian icons, the zero sign in Eastern painting, and various architectural monuments from India to Mexico are neither caprice, nor the exercises of an individual artist, but the sensuously materialized representations and knowledge of ancient peoples about the structure of the world. With more attentive study within the stylized art of these stone chronicles can be discerned the passion of individual efforts of architect and artist. The sensitivity and temperament common to art in general even spontaneously affect the unsophisticated person, one who has not studied the hermetic symbols and myth making of ancient peoples. But we artists sense and know that architectural forms, their structure and proportions, as well as their system of space and means of representation, are signs, without knowledge of which it would be impossible to comprehend fully the entire depth and sublimity of the designs of ancient peoples.

We create our orthography, syntax, and new books in exactly the same way. Whether we wish it or not, this is how the eternally old, yet ever new world is born. This is how things are, and cannot be otherwise. At the present time the human world consists not only of nature, people, earth, and the heavens, not only of animals and plants that are either friends or foes, totems, or simply objects of representation. Human beings are already realized in their deeds: they have generated a second nature, objects which are extensions of their hands, brain, eyes, nerves, and heart. The human world is not only a pantheistic cosmogony, but so to speak also a technical cosmography,[7] and the natural search for symbols and metaphors consonant with our times (or, rather, to find other terms, for symbols and metaphors ultimately cannot express the content of the complex questions that are raised).

In this connection I would like to say a few words about sculpture, which we shall provisionally describe as dialogical. Or, more precisely, we shall speak about the possibility of developing the synthesis inherent in sculpture. In speaking of dialogical sculpture, it is difficult to think about the beautiful while proceeding only from the classical monological notion of the human body. Rather, what is beautiful about it is the state of soul of a person, that is, what is indifferent and under tension as manifested in the form of a sculpture. But it is not merely what is under tension as physical form, but form and space in their interaction as expressing psychology and, more than psychology, the spiritual life of a person. In this instance, sculpture is not simply a quantity of surrounding physical material, organized according to the external form of a person, animal, or other natural or geometrical forms and situated in space: the sculpture contains within itself a dialogue between spirit and flesh. The sculpture is one, but it is not homogeneous.

Look at how creatures combining dissimilar elements – animal and human (person-fish-water nymph, lion-person-sphinx, horse-person-centaur, and so forth) – coexist with ancient peoples. The creation of such images in general is characteristic of popular grotesque fantasies. But this is not just the creation of forms. These personages have definite moral meaning. True, these combinations, these reductions *(svedeniia)* are pantheistic fusions of the living with the living. All elements appear in nature, and nature is living, not dramatic. And that is why Rodin's sculpture, *Female Centaur,* with a woman's body desperately breaking out from a horse, in spite of its fine sculpting and quite accessible literary design, does not produce a stronger impression than those sculptures of his restricted to a single human body. Because tragic dialectics, antinomy of the human soul, and dualism for us are connected with the contemporary world.

A second nature[8] is entering the human world, and the human bond with it is genuinely dramatic, because this second nature is inanimate. No matter how it imitates and replaces man, technology is more lifeless than minerals, and infinitely more lifeless than a tree. And yet this second nature of technology is "indivisible." Although dead and formless, it assumes the functions of life. It both elevates and annihilates man: it is both good and evil. And our contemporary life is an endless dialogue, not only with living nature, with the earth, the sea, and the sky with their inhabitants, but also with the technology we have created with our own hands.

Naturally, this cannot help but influence the forms of representational art. A sculpture has appeared in which heterogeneous elements, realistically existing parts comprise the whole in the conflict, engulfment, and collaboration of many principles, where everything is fraught with contradiction, a sculpture caught up in Heraclitean flux, a form emerging into space or engulfing it, one part restraining the other or repelling it. The metallic and the softly organic appear in combat and interlocked: the soft flows into the hard, the hard compresses and transforms the soft. A sculpture, its volume as if compressed from all sides by an external force, but resisting this force or expanding from the center, as though someone were tugging it apart from without, but the central nucleus keeps it from the final rupture.

In this manner the dramatic quality of the sculpture is conditioned by the presence within it of heterogeneous principles and impulses, and its movement becomes not only a pose or a form in space, but mainly motion inside the form itself. This kind of sculpture can contain within itself the Apollonian principle of perfected form (man) and the Dionysian principle of movement (destruction of man). In its movement it implants the man in man, the child in an old man, and a person into stone. Machinery containing both male and female principles and a tree contain in themselves people, just as people contain in themselves the whole evolution of earthly creatures and the most complex products of their hands. In this manner a sculptural composition is created in which all things exist everywhere and the least part is just as great and intense as a a large one.

And only the sculptor's will, the flow of the composition's rhythm magnifies or diminishes the scale of what is depicted. But each part of the representation is a titan finished in its form and breaking out of its small dimensions, a giant attempting to part, broaden, and fill everything. Such a sculpture, obviously, cannot be contained within the bounds of Euclidean or Kantian space and does not look upon space in general as homogeneous. In this way the parts of a sculpture make up a whole in struggle, engulfment, and repulsion. Such a sculpture is not a static object, but an object of a contradictory process of being, where each thing, fraught with its very opposite, has not one but several meanings.

We say "atom" and simultaneously visualize the smallest particle, the greatest source of energy, and a world catastrophe. This no longer confuses us, for after all among the ancient Greeks the goddess Athena[9] was at once a woman, the sea, a snake, an owl, and a horse. Sculpture in principle can be polyphonic in its form, since its aim is to integrate externally heteregeneous elements: human flesh and urban construction, a concrete subject and a kinetic object, form and color and lighting. But the main condition is organicity, the content of these reductions, so that they would not be simply aesthetic combinations, but full of content and spiritual reality.

The reduction of externally heterogeneous elements yields infinite possibilities for an artist's individual development. The principle itself excludes the canonical, the static, ossification. Therefore, all is possible – from extreme forms of abstraction to the most precise and deceptive representations. But for me personally the main principle of organization in my compositions is always living nature at the core of all: anthropomorphism, the beginning and end of what exists. Therefore, fantastic machinery is only part of the rhythm that develops according to the laws of anatomy, such as blood circulation, organ function, growth. No matter how perfect a technical construction is, even if it should surpass human capabilities a thousand fold, it will always be less sensitive and fantastic than a human being. Moreover, even the latest piece of equipment designed, the most unexpected and expressive construction sooner or later begins to age in our consciousness. But the form of a human being, like that of a tree or a flower, does not age.

It seems to me, therefore, that compositions developing along the lines of organic matter have greater possibilities. I do not rule out and am even convinced that there is a way whereby the systematic laws of construction and mathematics can be the foundation of sculpture. But the Pyramids,[10] like other mathematical and geometric forms, as well as the decorative patterns of the ancients, were the result of occult, magical notions at the heart of which always stood human beings, their link with life and death, the reincarnation of the soul, its wanderings, and its final union with Logos.[11]

Important for mature Classical and Neo-Classical art were closed constructions of body, setting, and measure that placed the eyes and nose on the face and head in relation to the torso according to proportion and canon. Let us take, for instance, classical Greek sculpture of the Golden Age, the highest example of monologic art.[12] Man is usually depicted at the peak of his powers. His figure radiates life, not destruction or death. His volumes are proportional, structured, and enclosed. There are no sharp protrusions of form, deep hollows, or holes within the volume. This is an orderly mass that occupies a defined space, and its life takes place in this space. Such a sculpture does not depict human beings as we understand them, but only their corporeal, physical existence as creatures. It is an abstraction, because a whole person is not only highly organized flesh, but also embodies complex problems of the soul. A monologic sculpture of a person is exquisitely mute. I have boundless admiration for the creators of such sculptures, but I love another kind of sculpture. Monologic sculptures cannot respond to my problems. And in order to sculpt in such a way, one must experience man as a finished three-dimensional object.

For polyphonic art man and space are not concepts to be studied and depicted from without. They are reality itself. Ecstasy and tension do not contradict what is human. They underscore the antinomy of human life and the soul. They strip away habitual external form. But they do not annihilate man, but merely make possible the visual representation of the infinite human "I."

2.

My principal work is an enormous monument that I provisionally call *The Tree of Life*. It incorporates the problems of man's dualistic contradictions, of man and nature, of man and second nature. By definition this theme is polyphonic. That's why Fedor Dostoevsky's works attract me.[13] True, before I took on Dostoevsky, I had illustrated some of the works of Dante,[14] Plato, and Empedocles.[15] All these drawings were a kind of preparation for my monument and find their embodiment in *The Tree of Life*.

But Dostoevsky is close to me by virtue of the polyphonic quality of his art, his use of multiple voices, and the clash of contradictions in his works. Like Dante, he is for me an inspiring example, because I see what they have in common. Dante's and Dostoevsky's art is not monologic like that of Ivan Turgenev[16] or Henry Moore,[17] but dialogic. That is, their works are not enclosed, but open and projected into an idea. Dostoevsky's world view is coordinated, but his forms of expression are subordinate to his world view. Artists who are attracted by ideas are dearer to me.

I do not have a favorite work by Dostoevsky. I experience his works as a whole. I do not understand people like Vissarion Belinsky,[18] who divided his works into good and bad ones. For instance, Dostoevsky's *The Double (Dvoinik)* is considered inferior, but from my viewpoint it is a brilliant work and the key to understanding Dostoevsky's corpus. Dostoevsky is not an artist of a single masterpiece *(khudozhnik shedevra),* but an artist of flux *(khudozhnik potoka).*[19] His works resemble the construction of a temple, which develops freely but in a single organic burst of inspiration.

My illustrations of Dostoevsky's works are connected with his inner themes, for instance, "Doubles" *(Dvoiniki),* "The Whole Child" *(Vse ditia),* and so forth. That is, I note separate themes which I have come upon in various novels. Besides, if one immerses oneself in the reading of Dostoevsky, one can see that his heroes are not characters, but ideas that course through all his novels, articles, diaries, and notebooks. Therefore, one can compare Dostoevsky's works to those of Dante, whose *Divine Comedy* is a complex of philosophical and religious ideas enclosed within the structure of a single work. We know that Dostoevsky had a similar style of contruction, though not in any one novel, but in his world view as a whole.

In general it is impossible to love Dostoevsky and his heroes. For instance, how can a person love a doctor! People who say they love Dostoevsky are lying. One can admire, fear, share his experiences, or suffer for him, but I cannot find a single hero of his whom I could love, even among his most beautiful heroes.

Nowhere does Dostoevsky formulate the main thought and idea of his works. He presents it in the form of thesis and antithesis. Each person chooses one or the other. Of all of Dostoevsky's thoughts, the dearest to me is his idea that, before one can become a person, one must develop one's humanity: man must struggle to become himself. Dostoevsky expressed this idea by means of the semantics of religion. Unlike many literary critics who try to apply Dostoevsky to the needs of the moment, I consider him both enormously realistic and a religious thinker, not merely an elemental dialectician. Dostoevsky's main idea is man's struggle with himself for self-perfection.

Unlike the ancient Greek idea of man as a closed, self-contained phenomenon, man in Dostoevsky has a cosmic dimension within his soul. Man is as infinite as the cosmos. Dostoevsky's anthropomorphic awareness that man is the beginning and end of all approximates my own views.

Visual illustrations of Dostoevsky are inadequate. Dostoevsky is an artist of ideas and themes, not of plots and stories. For Dostoevsky ideas comprise the milieu in which he works. We have excellent illustrations of Dostoevsky by Shmarinov, Dobuzhinsky,[20] and others. Their portraits are respected and serious. However, these artists illustrated Dostoevsky's situations and visual spirit. But I wished to illustrate Dostoevsky's inner spirit and themes. Rather, I do not illustrate Dostoevsky but note certain ideas with graphic means. Why is this now possible? Because at the present time our semantics in representational art makes it possible to depict Dostoevsky's internal themes. This was impossible until our semantics could be perceived in a purely visual manner.

I like Perov's[21] portrait of Dostoevsky. I have also made a portrait of Dostoevsky. I tried to render it without concrete psychological states, to fashion it as a new mask, as a mystery. But this attempt is also inadequate. The fact is, it is quite difficult to depict Dostoevsky's inner world, which is quite multifaceted, through his facial appearance. Lev Tolstoy,[22] for instance, resembles himself, but Dostoevsky externally bears little resemblance to his inner self. I can imagine a whole series of portraits of Dostoevsky: for example, Dostoevsky as "an old woman" *(babka)* smirking. One can imagine Dostoevsky cruelly grinning or weeping or pensive. These would all be local portraits. If we were to speak of plumbing the depths of Dostoevsky's inner world by means of his portrait, then that seems to me to be quite complicated.

At one time I was engaged in analyzing Dostoevsky's use of space and color. And I undertook to affirm, especially in *Crime and*

Punishment (Prestuplenie i nakazanie) that Dostoevsky's space was metaphysical. His space is neither the landscape of St. Petersburg,[23] nor three-dimensional. Everything he has written bears a definite fantastic character. The transition from space to space has a deeply ideological, non-visual character. It is no accident that nature in *Crime and Punishment* bursts in powerfully only once, at Raskol'nikov's moment of illumination in Siberian exile, when he falls on his knees before Sonia.[24] There you will find a landscape, space, and air. Up till then there was no air. There were only two or three walls, some kind of strange stairs, weird alleys. This is all metaphysical space, sick space, even St. Petersburg itself.

The same thing with dialogue. Dostoevsky's dialogues cannot be transferred simply to the stage without transforming them radically, because as recitation Dostoevsky's breathless phrases contain extraordinary tension, which is lost when heard in an auditorium. Dostoevsky's non-theatrical art lies in the fact that, while reading his works, we at once enter the heart of intrigue without understanding what is happening, for we do not know the beginning or the end. Herein lies his intellectual secret.

Let's take the stage version of *The Gambler (Igrok)* for example. The General awaits retribution, the death of his wife. But suddenly she drives up. This is the culmination point. And when several personages stand on stage while the general's wife unmasks her husband, we do not experience the tension of Dostoevsky's phrases in the novel. Dostoevsky has a climactic, nightmarish moment of utter shame that occurs in a dream when a person finds himself in a terrifyingly vile position. A resolution of this situation on stage is possible by recourse to non-realistic devices. Perhaps emptying the whole theater, or have people crawling out from all the cracks in the walls, or to have some of the audience standing and shaming the general. I do not know, for I am not a stage director.

The same thing with color. Dostoevsky is quite modest in his use of color. What color is *Crime and Punishment?* Yellow, a burnt-out, ashen yellow like the color of the sun, the same color throughout the work. Nor does *The Brothers Karamazov (Brat'ia Karamazovy)* have all those colors presented in the Russian film version. Those range of hues are more appropriate for the plays of Ostrovsky.[25] Such vast landscapes, the tolling of church bells, the cries of flying jackdaws, and so forth are not characteristic of Dostoevsky's works.

Dostoevsky's power lies in his mercilessness. His scenes resemble a dream within a dream. For instance, you dream of a thief or murderer climbing through your window. You wake up in horror and touch the floor with your feet, but the intruder keeps crawling through the window. You again wake up in horror, but the burglar keeps coming closer. That's Dostoevsky's method of inducing horror in us. We read on and think we can't bear it any more, that we might even perish with his heroes. But then new characters appear, and the shame goes on and on and on. In the theater it is impossible to introduce all the characters indicated by Dostoevsky. Therefore, his verbal texture cannot be transferred to a texture of sounds and sights on stage. The semantic linkages here are profound and typological, but never superficial nor purely external.

3.

Pushkin's "The Prophet" *(Prorok)* [26] remains my most favorite work, and the finest sculptor I know is the six-winged seraphim in that poem.

> And cleft he my chest with sword,
> And fluttering heart withdrew,
> And a coal aglow with fire,
> Into my open chest inserted.

Thus the Prophet is created. In this poem is expressed the idea of reducing heterogeneous elements in nature into one invisible, living, and essential whole. Representational art is not merely the reflection of visual interest in the world. The plastic arts mirror essential problems in man's spiritual life. Any attempt to reduce representational art to merely visual tasks turns out to be a struggle against its age-old functions, that is, to express a metaphysics and a world view.

In principle, I stand for the creation of a new polyphonic language. The linguistic diversity that exists in the world is a phenomenon that deeply contradicts human nature. If impenetrable barriers trouble scholars, when mathematicians cease to understand one another, then localized discoveries by artists, at the very nature of which lies knowledge of the truth as a holistic book of existence, seem to me to be spiritually wrong. An artist ought to strive for all-encompassing unity, that is, we ought to create a new kind of orthography. Books are written in letters, and letters make up phrases. We have fragmented books not only into letters of the alphabet, but even masters of the comma have made their appearance. Obviously, a new synthesis is needed. How this synthesis will come about, we do not know. But this synthesis will be a living organism. Synthesis, obviously, is a combination of a number of individual spiritual principles that gradually will create a new organic, living unity, as in the construction of a temple.

Creative work is a contradictory process of being. That which the artist has already created no longer exists. In a certain way creative work is an objective form of meditation. And the greater and broader the flow of creativity, the less the artist is attached to the fruits of his labor. That is, as soon as creativity assumes the form of an object, it is no longer a part of me, but outside of me.

Two forms of artistic modesty exist. One is dissatisfaction with the result of one's labor because it did not attain the lofty heights of some existing classical standard. This is what I call immodest modesty, or rather the striving to be great. Another kind of modesty exists, when an artist is internally alienated from vainglory and end results. This artist is merely a transformer and conductor of certain feelings and ideas that took form within him. He appears to be their rectifier or amplifier. And in no way does he consider himself the sole, unique producer of these feelings and ideas.

An artist is fated to be alone. But this does not mean that he will be. For if he authentically gives concrete form to a state of mind, then this fact must hold true for someone else, too. And this solitude is essentially illusory. On the other hand, democracy no doubt is an excellent thing as a form of social structure, but not in the form of collective assessment of the fruits of creativity. One must unquestionably consider the opinion of professionals. But, unfortunately, were it left to collective consensus, we would have no Michelangelo,[27] Dante, or Dostoevsky. These artists made collective experience concrete, but only through individual means.

The very act of artistic creation as a spiritual act directed at resolving non-pragmatic problems is an active act of faith. Creative work without faith is impossible. I am not speaking of the meaning and symbols of faith. An artist must have faith that man is not merely an animal, but a complex being consisting of two dualistic principles: the cosmic and the carnal. What makes an artist an artist is precisely this innate knowledge.

Faith is a feeling, but it is difficult to define this feeling in words. To give an approximation, faith is a striving, attempt, and means of overcoming man's cosmic solitude and a premonition of the ultimate answer that is found simultaneously inside and outside oneself. Christianity is one of the loftiest forms of religious self awareness, because in it exist the heroic principle, individual free will of human personality, and the understanding of history as an eschatological Mystery. In this sense Judaism-Christianity as a world view is closer to me than impersonal Buddhism or other religions lacking an anthropological sense of being.

The role of representational art in the modern world is to strive to create certain universal symbols and metaphors. Perhaps one should use other terms here, because "symbol" and "metaphor" semantically no longer encompass those problems that face the modern world, such as the task of revealing the value and infinitude of the human "I" overwhelmed by a surfeit of information. This is the meaning of art. I think that the quest for synthetic, holistic man will unify all human acts.

This problem, however, is so complex, that quite often one will encounter distortions and incomprehension. For instance, it's wrong when people treat icons as art objects or as exotic archeological curiosities. An icon in principle is a holistic world view linked with a religious cult. Father Pavel Florensky[28] revealed and explained this quite well in his work, *The Iconostasis*.

On the other hand, eccessive reliance on tradition often turns out to be a pretext for something else. But, all the same, there are certain elements of tradition in what I do. As a boy, I came across wooden sculptures from the Perm' region that made a rather great impression on me. It was not a direct analogy, I would say, but there were certain associative links. The sculpture of Perm' to a certain degree is a unique phenomenon in Russian religious art. In Perm' sculptures there is a specific system of deformation[29] somewhat uncommon for Orthodox crosses to be worn on the chest. To a certain extent this kind of deformation resembled the kind of sculpture I wished to create. That is, not only mercy, but also an element of the dramatic, are present in the Perm' style of deformation that attracted me to these works. Besides, among the works of Perm' are remarkable sculptures of the seated Christ and of the grieving Mother of God. And these figures to a degree recall their counterparts in Catholic cathedrals. In the Russian tradition this is a very strange, but powerful phenomenon.

I once had the dream of executing a crucifixion in the form of a memorial. That is, I imagined a field on which were erected crosses of this kind, where, say, a dying crucified man is perishing not alone, as if the whole human race were expiring. Therefore, my crucifixions often have many heads, from those of old women to those of children. A human being is dying, and in him die the past, present, and future. It resembles a forest of crucifixions of different sizes standing on the spot of a mass grave of war victims. In this instance I envision such a sculpture as secular, and not strictly religious. Such a feat would encompass its own metaphysics.

In one way or another, all these works are intended to be constitutent parts of my principal design project, the cycle of sculptures, drawings, and engravings that I call *The Tree of Life*. This monumental structure in the form of a Moebius[30] spiral contains diverse elements of the human "I." Besides a pantheistic cosmogony, the element of technical cosmography produced by humanity also enters into *The Tree of Life*. My representation of dismembered, maimed, and mutilated people is not an effort to take human beings apart, but merely to exhibit man's infinitude. That's why I am interested in sculpture not as a volume cast into space and interacting with it, but as a process of being in interconnection, repulsion, and interpenetration.[31]

[1] Auguste Rodin (1840-1917), major French sculptor whose works include *The Thinker, The Kiss,* and *The Burghers of Calais.*
[2] Expressionism, early twentieth century movement that held that art and literature should express subjective feelings.
[3] Constructivism, Russian art movement based on contemporary technology and founded by Vladimir Tatlin (1885-1956).
[4] Pantheism, philosophical and religious view that equates God and the universe.
[5] Golden section, division of line segment into two segments in which ratio of original segment to larger division equals ratio of larger to smaller division; proportions of Golden Section considered aesthetically ideal in art and architecture.
[6] Cosmogony, the science of the origins of the universe.
[7] Cosmography, a description of the universe.
[8] Second nature of technology: Neizvestny's concept of modern man's dual nature as a centaur conjoining nature and technology.
[9] Athena, Greek goddess of war and wisdom, known as Minerva in Roman pantheon of gods.
[10] Pyramids, polyhedrons erected in ancient Egypt as tombs for the Pharoahs.
[11] Logos, unifying principle of the world in Greek and Hebrew metaphysics.
[12] Neizvestny's opposition of dialogic to monologic art is derived from the concept of polyphony developed by Mikhail Bakhtin (1895-1975).
[13] Dostoevsky (See Introduction, note 60).
[14] Dante Alighieri (1265-1321), Italy's greatest poet, author of *The Divine Comedy.*
[15] Empedocles (c.490-430 BC), Sicilian Pythagorean philosopher who conceived of four fundamental elements in nature – air, earth, water, and fire.
[16] Ivan Sergeevich Turgenev (1818-83), pro-Western Russian writer, author of *Fathers and Children* (1862).
[17] Henry Moore (1898-1986), major English sculptor and artist noted for his perforated natural forms.
[18] Vissarion Grigorevich Belinsky (1811-48), influential radical Russian literary critic.
[19] Neizvestny divides all artists into these two categories.

[20] Mstislav Valer'anovich Dobuzhinsky (1875-1957), Russian painter and stage designer associated with the journals *Mir Iskusstva* (World of Art), *Zolotoe Runo* (Golden Fleece), and *Apollon* (Apollo).

[21] Vasily Grigorievich Perov (1833-82), major Russian realistic portrait, historical, and genre painter.

[22] Lev Nikolaevich Tolstoy (1828-1910), major Russian writer, educator, publicist, and thinker; author of *War and Peace* and *Anna Karenina*.

[23] St. Petersburg, now Leningrad, was founded by Peter the Great in 1703 as his new imperial capital and window onto the West.

[24] Sonia, the embodiment of Christian compassion and "holy wisdom" in the novel.

[25] Aleksandr Nikolaevich Ostrovsky (1823-86), Russian dramatist, author of *The Storm* (1860).

[26] Metapoem composed in 1826 by Aleksandr Sergeevich Pushkin (1799-1837), Russia's national poet.

[27] Michelangelo (1475-1564), renowned Italian sculptor, painter, poet, and architect.

[28] Florensky (See Introduction, note 67).

[29] Deformation, Russian formalist concept in which artistic form is distorted to heighten its expressiveness. See *Permskaia derevian-naia skul'ptura* (Wooden sculptures of Perm'), edited by D. M. Vlasova (Perm': Permskoe knizhnoe izdatel'stro, 1985).

[30] Moebius (See Introduction, note 61).

[31] This essay was published in Russian in Ernst Neizvestny, *O sinteze v iskusstve (On synthesis in art)* [Ann Arbor: Hermitage, 1982], 9-26. Twenty years after it was commissioned by the journal, it appeared under the title, "O sinteze iskusstv" (On synthesis of the arts), in *Voprosy filosofii*, No. 7 (1989): 73-82.

CHAPTER TWO

Body: Man as Visual Sign

In my childhood I agonizingly tried to imagine infinity. Somewhere out there, far-far away was the end of the universe. But what was beyond that? My small brain ached with curiosity and horror. The concept of emptiness terrified me especially. The end. And beyond it was emptiness. There was nothing, absolutely nothing. It was absolutely empty. What, then, was this? Confusion gripped me. And, to save myself, I tried to imagine the universe in the form of an infinite series of bodies, one encompassing the other, like a nest of Russian wooden dolls. In the most immense, huge, unimaginably gigantic body of infinity nested small bodies, housing still smaller bodies containing even tinier bodies holding teeny-weeny bodies encompassing micro-bodies. The universal body attained unimaginably gigantic dimensions by filling up the emptiness outside, or it would compress itself and become infinitely smaller and smaller. All these bodies – from the supergrandiose to the super small – were similar. They were like my own body. And in the center was I. And, depending on me, everything kept getting larger or smaller. But since the gigantic body was also me, and the rest of the bodies – including mine – were situated within this gigantic body, the center of the universe for this gigantic body was its own self, just as in me lived millions of worlds and beings that were also me. The center of the universe for each of these worlds is its own self, and all these selves think and think (what is this – the infinitely large or the infinitely small?). These thoughts were the energy of infinitely large and small bodies. These thoughts link everything, everything from the most gigantic of giants to the smallest of the small, and the vacuum of distance is filled by the energy of thought that binds bodies together.

I temporarily, alas, only temporarily freed myself from terror and intently examined my little finger, the tip of which housed billions and billions of galaxies and billions and billions of beings like me, all thinking about the endlessly large and the unimaginably small. Emptiness ceased to frighten me. I felt myself part of the most enormous **I.** And even when I wet myself, this act became significant in many ways: it was not merely pee-pee, but a universal flood. I looked at my little penis with respect, for in it rested whole worlds and civilizations.

A child's thinking, like the fantasies of folk cultures, strives to sunder the scale of everyday life. The uncommon is customary, and only the grandiose and tiny, giants and dwarfs, become heroes of life's mysteries.

THE ARTIST IS ALWAYS A GULLIVER.[1]

IDEALIZATION OF MATTER AND MATERIALIZATION OF IDEAS

Abstract content is symbolized. A symbol, striving to become concrete, is transformed into a sign. The self sufficiency of a sign is "the being of another." A symbol is concrete, but its content is abstract. Without symbolism a man would be imprisoned in Plato's Cave of Shadows[2] and transformed into a biological being interested only in procreation and satisfying other material needs, "A Free Practical Worker"[3] liberated from an "ideal world" that strives to discover religion, art, philosophy, science. Myth is the basis of symbolism. But a symbol is not only expressed, but also perfected in the fine arts.

A myth is filled with symbols. A symbol contains the sign in itself. A myth, like a symbol, is inexhaustible. A sign is finite. A myth is submerged in mystery. Symbols are constituent parts of a myth. In a symbol pounds the pulse of a myth: its multiple facets, its multiple meanings, its inexhaustibility. In order to be understood, an image acquires the form of a sign. But on the surface of a sign lies the imprint of a higher inner quality, that is, the rhythm of a mysterious whole from which emerged Myth, Symbol, and Sign.

THE HUMAN BODY

In cosmological myths the universe is often engendered by disparate parts. Bodies are perceived as symbols and signs of the cosmos. Symbolic anatomy becomes cosmological anatomy. Interest towards the depiction of man cannot be extinguished. The expressive possibilities of the body are inexhaustible. Different civilizations and individual artists demonstrate to us this endless diversity. Engaged in the study of the structure of the human body and the use of this structure in various civilizations, we see that the techniques used in depicting man in various cultures, and by artists whom we consider great, are not accidental, but connected with their world view. We shall see that plastic art is a language with its own regular features, just as we find rhymes, rhythms, alliteration, and so forth in poetry. In music harmony, rhythm, tone, and other features distinguish it from everyday sounds. Many people do not sense this, because – while we are taught to speak, read, write, and be good – we are not taught how to see, to experience space and form as an aesthetic category. For many reasons in modern civilization the ability to hear is more quickly refined. Anyone can say "What an ugly sound!" but rarely will anyone say "What an ugly space!" The underdevelopment of vision produces the error of considering everything depicted as plastic art.

While the languages of different peoples are distinguished from one another, at the basis of each are definite laws based on universal laws of human thought. It is the same with representational art. The Greek idea of the body differs greatly from the idea of a grotesque body. But both Greek and grotesque art have their own distinctive regular features. Rhythms organize the links between the parts of the body – different rhythms, but rhythms nonetheless: the rhythms of deep tranquil breathing or the rhythms of ecstasy; the rhythms of elegy, laughter, lamentation. Rhythm is the link. In plastic art the connection of various forms occurs in space. This linkage creates tension. Expressiveness is art. Life itself is under tension. An apple is in a state of tension, as is a fish. We exist in a state of tension, and art expresses various kinds of tension in form – perhaps the tension of movement, the tension of a body in transition from one state to another. Dynamism: a running athlete. Michelangelo.[4] The Baroque.[5] Rodin.[6] Perhaps a static state of tension: Egyptian sculpture. Brancusi.[7] The tension of a glance. The tension of hollows, holes, and protuberances of the body. The Grotesque.[8] In Greek philosophy there was the term *tonus* (tension), by which philosophers such as Heraclitus[9] or the Stoics[10] characterized all beings as a whole. True, for them it was not things in space that were under tension, but space itself which was perceived as strings under different kinds of tension.

Representational art does not imitate life. It creates life, the intense life of plastic form. To become expressive, the body is generalized, deformed,[11] or transformed. A body in art begins to live its own life, different from the life of a living body, and in a space unlike real space. And at its highest point of tension, purification, and generalization the depiction of a person and the parts of the body becomes a sign.

But not every representation of the human body, nor just any part of the body can be recognized as a sign for "man."

We see that this is a man:

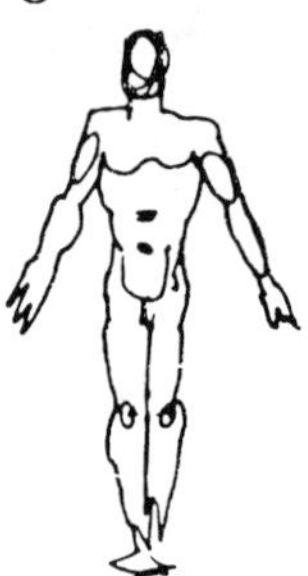

And this is also a man:

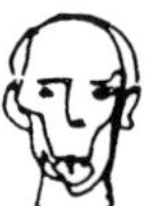

A head without a body does not confuse us.

A hand is also a man: 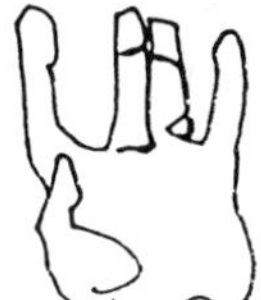

Can one reduce the body further without losing the link with the whole concept: "This is a man"?

A head separated from the body is still a man: 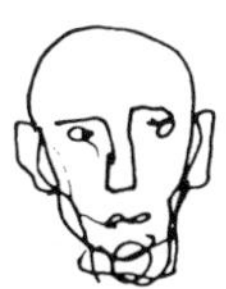

And an eye separated from the head is perceived as human:

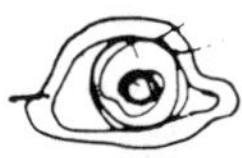

But, for some reason, an eye depicted in profile and separated from the head is not recognizably human:

In any case, this eye cannot serve as the sign: "This is a man." And all civilizations using the eye as a symbol for man or as a universal orb resembling man depict the eye only from the front. The sign (eyes=man) is applicable only from a front view. This was dictated by anatomy itself: **an eye looks**. Therefore, an Egyptian head in profile always has an eye facing us.

A head in profile:

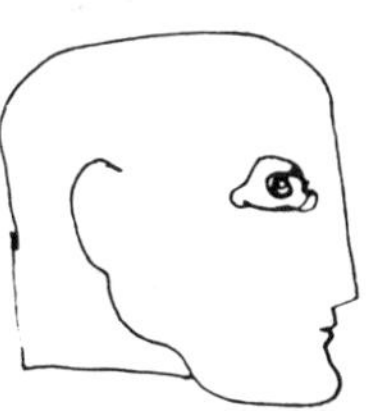

An eye facing front:

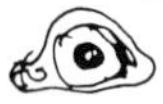

A hand separated from the body is a man: 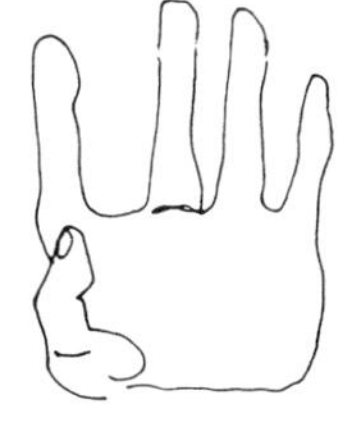

Even a finger separated from a hand is recognized as a person:

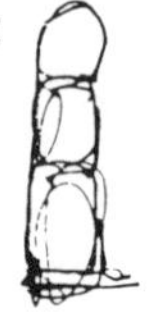

In many cultures a phallus is represented and secretly substituted, for it too is a man:

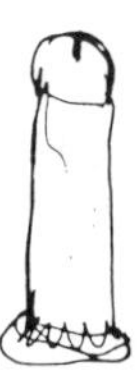

A fingerprint of a "man":

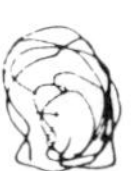

For the police a fingerprint is greater than the sign of man. It is the person himself. In Babylon and Syria footprints were taken. While a footprint is a "man," the representation of a foot did not become a sign. Let us proceed further. For some reason the bone of the finger from which a print was taken is not perceived by us as a sign of man. Similarly, a finger foreshortened cannot serve as a sign.

Can a human fingernail be a sign? Among many peoples an animal claw is a sign of the animal itself. No, it cannot be. Why? Possibly because we clip it and destroy its natural form. At any rate ancient Chinese aristocrats let their nails grow, but they did not become a sign, although fingernails in Chinese and Indian art were expressive elements. Hair is an ornament in all artistic cultures, but an individual hair was not transformed into a sign. The scalp for the American Indians was a sign of a man. One could give other examples. The parts of the body are separate from the body and can live their own independent lives by incorporating in themselves the concept of the whole body. But only those parts are separated that contain a representational sign in their structure. Even in literature bodily parts that live independent lives – such as heads, eyes, noses, phalluses, and so forth – are elements of the body that can be depicted graphically and become a sign. Flesh is a thing becoming significant. In representational art the **idealization of matter and the materialization of ideas** are particularly clear. **The sign and what is signified can change places.**

Ancient Greece

Greek aesthetics is basically mythology, from Homer's myths[12] to the myths of the Neoplatonists.[13] The essence of the beautiful for Greek aesthetics is neither personality, society, history, nor even nature, but the healthy human body. The body is equidistant from birth and death. Man is always depicted at the peak of his powers. For that reason birth, as well as death, is only a transition from one quality into another. Although there is much physical motion, the Greeks were interested in stasis – not in the sense of motion – but in a person who is static, that is, enclosed in his corporeal envelope. This body is three dimensional and closed. Thus, for Lucretius,[14] the atom was an indivisible, closed, three-dimensional object. In the Greek body there were no holes nor sharp, protruding exits. The body comprised a self-sufficient world moving in space. Classical art did not know of any spiritual experiences in our sense of the word. In Anaxagoras' view,[15] the body contains in itself the germ of all things in general. It was the symbol of the cosmos as a whole. According to Anaxagoras, internal thinking life and the life of the body were one and the same. Schiller[16] once said that psychologism and the stirrings of the soul were unknown to the Greeks.

The beautiful in Greek aesthetics appears when the physical elements are harmonized in a living and perfect human body. Abstract beauty. Beauty in its universality, the beauty of all that exists between heaven and earth, from a stone to a tree. The beauty of all beings and phenomena. Beauty in its quintessence is concentrated in the human body.

The Greek gods were human bodies universalizing the semantic principle of existence. They were already symbols and, if you wish, signs. Thus, Zeus[17] was an ideal body, an image of Heaven. Poseidon[18] was an image of water and the sea; Hephaestus,[19] of fire; Aphrodite,[20] of love; and so forth. Democritus[21] affirmed the identity of the universal and the particular. Aesthetics was transformed into cosmogony, that is, into teaching about number, measure, rhythm, and the harmony of elements making up the cosmic whole.

It was thought that all these elements were concealed in the structure of rhythms and proportions of the human body. Therefore, the universal principle of the beautiful was beauty that merged the body with itself. Symmetry of the bodily parts lies in its rhythmic distribution.

Let us take a look at several linkages of bodily parts that one might relatively call anatomical. They are relative because there is no superman who can flex his muscles like a Greek sculpture. Although the Greeks underscored anatomical elements, they would select in anatomy precisely the essence of a sign. The Greeks used anatomical linkages, but made them more expressive, eliminating the inessential and intensifying the essential, thereby creating tension, tension of form with the co-rhythms of these parts with others in the space of an enclosed body.

Let us consider these combinations:

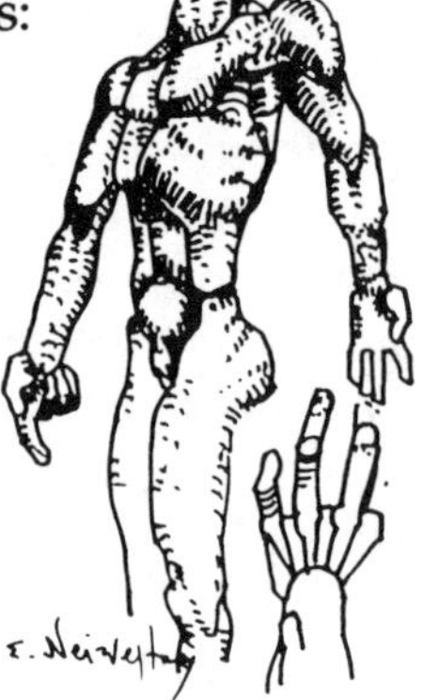

In this schema it turns out that, after taking the precise network of proportions of the body of classical Greek works and drawing a line where large and the most significant groups of muscles are attached with cartilage to the skeletal bones of an athletically developed human body, we have a schematic depiction in signs of the Greek body. In Greek vases that graphic principle of combining parts attained the level of a sign. Laconic representation acquires the character of a hieroglyph. **This device can be called anatomical deformation.**[22]

Egypt

Egyptian representational art as a whole is symbolical and exhibits a striving to view the human body as a sign. Hieroglyphic depiction of everything can be seen in Egyptian reliefs. Therefore,

I shall say a few words about the representation of space and perspective in Egyptian art.

Geometrical perspective, according to legend, was invented by Anaxagoras, but perspective was applied in the theater of Pompeii to create the illusion of three-dimensional space. That perspective was first used in the theater has its logic, since perspective does not exist in nature. No object becomes smaller when it approaches the horizon. This is an optical illusion that arises when one is sitting motionless while looking at a single point – which is what happens in a theater. An ideal illusion of perspective arises if one looks with one eye. The German artist Dürer[23] invented a device for reproducing an illusion of perspective that was based precisely on this principle. And since there is no perspective in nature, various civilizations perceive space in the light of their own world view. In China and Japan, for example, a scattered perspective was applied.

Reverse, Byzantine perspective (that is, objects moving toward us become smaller) was used in the Russian icon. But the Egyptians employed no perspective, and not because they did not know its laws. They understood perspective. They understood geometrical proportions and knew how to apply reduced and augmented scales. The Egyptians measured direct perspective with mathematical formulae, for they were geometricians and astronomers. Artistically the Pyramids are mathematical phenomena: the Egyptians knew that the axis of the Pyramid of Cheops coincided with that of the Polar Star. It is hard to imagine that the Egyptians did not employ perspective due to naiveté. They did not use perspective because they did not need it to depict the human body. In great artistic civilizations the common principle of the concept of perspective, proportions, and volume comprises a single system, which is not only a part of their aesthetics, but also a part of their general world view. Consequently, a part always contains elements of the whole. From a single fragment of Greek or Egyptian sculpture one can assess the whole work. In this particle beats the whole scale of values of a civilization.

The principle of tectonic[24] understanding of space in Egyptian art and its hieroglyphic essence is quite apparent in the structure of the Egyptian relief. How is the human figure constructed in an Egyptian relief? Imagine a narrow box made of glass. The space between the front and back walls of this box must be filled with human figures. Or, imagine a thin book in which a human figure must be placed between the front and back covers. Morever, this figure must be placed in such a way so that all the parts of the body can be recognized at once as signs (for the first condition of a sign is its intelligibility). Naturally, it will not occur to you to place this figure with feet first and head back, that is, from a front view with the face turning its nose towards you, so that the nose would protrude from the surface or be pressed up against the front glass wall, while the back of the head is resting against the back glass wall. The most sensible solution would be to turn the head in profile. But an eye in profile does not resemble an eye, or serve as a sign for an eye. Therefore, the eye is turned to the front.

From shoulder to shoulder the torso would occupy much space and, if one shoulder presses against the back wall, then the other inevitably would jut out beyond the front wall to shatter the given space for the figure (that is, breaking the glass of the front wall). Therefore, the torso is turned towards the front:

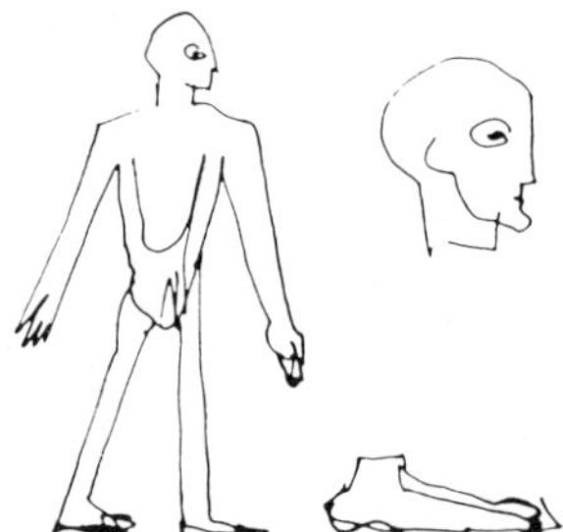

The legs are in profile so that, if the heel rests against the back wall, then the toes would protrude beyond the boundaries of the front wall. Similarly, the hands face front for the same reasons:

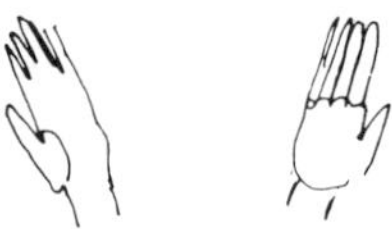

But why did the Egyptian artists complicate their lives by choosing a stone space as flat as a book? Would it not have been simpler, like the Greeks, to use thick chunks of stone for their reliefs, where one could freely place the figure of a man in any pose and in any combination of positions? That is, to simply create a real space for a real figure, or to change perspective?

But unity of space in art is not necessarily the space of Euclid[25] or Kant.[26] And all of Egyptian civilization – beginning from the earliest excavations to tombs located by the archaeologist Petrie,[27] through all the classical epochs and distinctions until the Ptolemaic period[28] – bears witness to an astonishingly holistic understanding of relative space. The whole history of Egyptian art is a striving for symbols and signs. Figures have a hieroglyphic essence and, therefore, organically become hieroglyphs. The combination of figures and their poses are signs. Gesture is also a sign.

What is artistically phenomenal is that extraordinarily vital representations appeared within a closed aesthetic system (not in spite of, but evidently thanks to it), as if the given schema compressed powerful, living flesh regardless of those restrictions. And this schema creates tension. The constraint of Egyptian sculpture is not tranquillity, but restricted motion within a form. What do I have in mind? If day by day one shoots a film about the ripening of an apple and then projects it in fast-motion, we shall see how the apple's flesh swells up, how a vital force ruptures the apple from within. Looking at an apple, we always sense its energy. Precisely such a sense of energy within tense flesh is present in Greek sculpture and, with still greater force, in Egyptian sculpture. Depending on lighting, the character and depth of a relief of a figure and hieroglyph are changed while preserving the contours of signs within the representation. It is like a single musical theme which contains many diverse variations within it.

Thus, there is an external contradiction: constraint and canonic form versus vivid, vital spiritual content. These qualities in general are characteristic of folk art, which is produced by protracted repetitions and refinement at a time of defined devices of representation.

The means of depicting the body in Egyptian art can be called **deformation of sign and symbol.**[29]

IMAGES OF MIXED BODIES

The Egyptian system of metaphors and fantastic juxtapositions reached a point wherein a single plastic image often linked what was externally impossible: elements of a man and an animal (jackal, lion, snake, hippopotamus); a man and a plant; parts of a body (eye, hand, phallus) transformed into a symbol or semantic sign. These metaphors were meaningful, but were not deprived of the sensual principle characteristic of art in general. Metaphor in Egyptian art was transformed into a symbol.

Centaurs, sphinxes, and other mixed beings were born in the period between matriarchy and patriarchy, as were hermaphrodites. These dual beings could not be called grotesque, since the grotesque employed another system of deformation that we shall examine later.

In Empedocles[30] we find the idea of combining unlike elements of the body together in an unexpected way. All the parts of the body were born separately, striving to unite themselves in a harmonious whole. Initially, they sprouted in an absurd manner, without any harmony, sundering the body's anatomy. Everything was mixed up – arms, legs, eyes, and ears. Over a long period of time, combining and separating by trial and error, the human body was put together according to the laws of anatomical expediency.

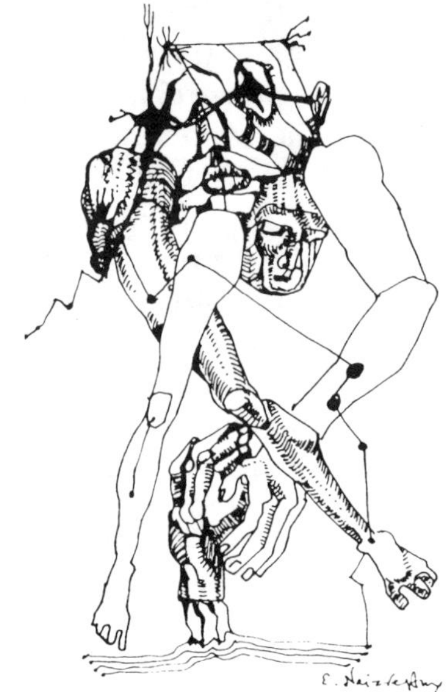

After illustrating Empedocles, I continued this theme in my series entitled *Strange Births*, where all was born from everything: Adam from the earth; Eve from Adam's rib; Athena[31] from the head of Zeus; Aphrodite from sea foam; Pantagruel[32] from an ear; and so forth. Prototypes of strange births can be found in all the metamorphoses of the cosmological Myth of all the world's peoples.

For the fusion to be organic in these metamorphoses and animal-human figures of Greece and Egypt, the connections and rhythms had to correspond to a definite system of deformation. Moreover, they could be perceived as a sign in even the simplest schema. Let us take a look at the construction of a centaur.[33] Here the human torso is attached to a human pelvis, but in reality these are the front leg bones of a horse. The fusion is so organic that we are fully convinced that such a being can really exist. The stasis and dynamics of a centaur are anatomically perfect, as are those of a faun,[34] *rusalka*,[35] or sphinx.[36]

In Egypt, Syria, and Greece these dual beings became canonical in their construction and were transformed into signs. Their expressiveness was achieved by the very same principles, which I call anatomical and symbolical deformation.

ON SYMMETRY

In the rhythm of a body there is always symmetry. But, deforming the body, the ancients departed from absolute symmetry, from the conditions of a "closed" system. Minor (but not total) asymmetry creates a sensation of an open system, of a readiness for change.

This asymmetry contains in itself the magical effect of the swastika.[37] It is not perfect symmetry that arouses action, but repetition that is not a mere mirror reflection.

ON FUNCTIONS IN DEPICTING THE BODY

Before speaking about deformation in the grotesque, let us see how a child draws a figure of a person. Dot, dot, comma, minus sign, a crooked little mug; stick, stick, little cucumber, little legs – and you have a little man:[38]

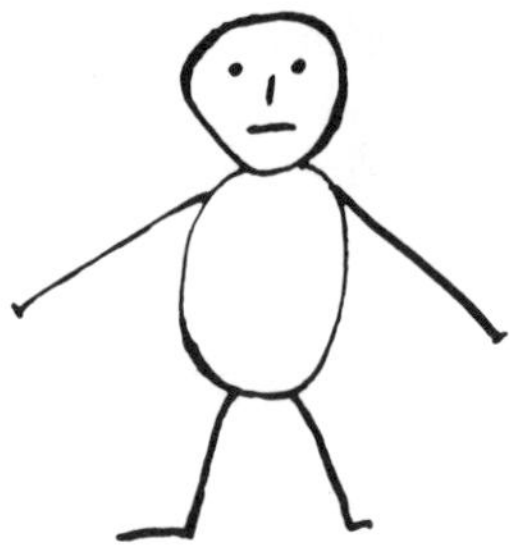

For a child a person is only what physically functions: eyes that see; a nose and mouth as openings that breathe; legs and arms as sticks that move. For a child, the sign of a person is not the anatomical construction of a body, but only the functions of its most significant parts from a child's viewpoint, that is, **functional deformation.** We can observe functional deformation not only in children's drawings, but also in the very mysterious, ancient, and expressive Mexican art. Look at Mexican figures, and you will see that they differ from Greek figures, in which the body's construction – but not its functions – is obvious. Look at Egyptian art and you will see that it manifests symbolism and a hieroglyphic system. And then look at Mexican art. You will immediately see the difference, because the element of functions present in the grotesque can now, of course, be found in the puppet theater and in contemporary television monsters.[39]

ON THE GROTESQUE

A grotesque type of imagery already arose in pre-Classical antiquity: hydra,[40] harpy, [41]cyclops,[42] and other images of archaic grotesquery.

The grotesque is boundless; it is horrible and comic. A carnival perception of the world lies at the basis of the grotesque.[43] From the most ancient mysteries ritual, mask, gesture, and pose were inseparable and, infusing one another, made up the whole. The grotesque was the product of freedom by sundering conditions and stasis. The grotesque often appears terrifying, but it is actually a triumph over terror. The intellectual fear of death is overcome by a belly laugh. Life and death are perceived not as antinomies, but as a single dialectical process of dying and rebirth.

In his brilliant study of Rabelais, Mikhail Bakhtin[44] spoke about the union of two principles in grotesque culture: the higher and the lower. One can apply this definition in general to the loftiest phenomena of world culture. The temples of various religions and their rituals and mysteries unite in their sweep both the lofty intellect of hermetic culture (the higher level) and folk culture, the culture of the crowd, the "culture of town squares" (the lower level), thereby creating a mighty fusion that can only be called culture in the literal sense of the word. A similar synthesis appeared among all the great artists of Egypt, India, Mexico, Greece. In the modern period we sense this sweep of fusion in Dante, Michelangelo, Rabelais, Picasso,[45] Charlie Chaplin,[46] Walt Disney,[47] and several others. The ability to unite the "high" and the "low" is the strength of artists of this type. They could walk a tightrope over two abysses and not fall either into the arrogant snobbery of the "lofty" or the vulgar coarseness of the "lowly."

MOTION – PUPPET – MASK

In 1810 the German scholar Kleist,[48] after laying the foundations of scientific bionics[49] in the theater, wrote a work about the motion of marionettes. He explained why the movements of puppets were psychologically more vivid than those of a person.

A human actor stands on legs and is subject to the laws of his own weight. His movements, while demonstrating psychology, are not freed from physiology. But a marionette is suspended in air. A puppet master directs it by tugging at strings attached to the body parts of the puppet. Each of its gestures becomes a sign of emotions imparted to the marionette's body by the puppet master and actor. Therefore, grief, gladness, tranquillity, confusion, and so forth are presented in their purest form. Developing this idea, one can observe that symbolism of gesture and puppet-like movements are generally characteristic of the theater of masks, part of the traditions of which have come down to us. The Japanese theater (beginning of seventh century), quite close to the art of Greek mimes, can be cited as an example, along with the Noh theater.[50] The same tradition was continued by the Kabuki theater (seventeenth century), performances of which can still be seen today.[51] Although there are no masks as such in the Kabuki theater, masks are mimicked by the makeup worn on the actors' faces. The transformation of a face into a mask is an ancient tradition. Modern mimes and clowns decorate their faces to create masks of laughter and sorrow. The mask occupied an important place in the consciousness of the ancients. It is impossible to study the tradition of the mask separate from religion, mystical mysteries, and the scientific notions of ancient peoples. Even the precise description of the face of a mortally-ill person by the physician Hippocrates[52] approximates a mask-symbol and was called the "Hippocratic mask of death." Independent of Hippocrates, folk masks of death and makeup – whether African, Mexican, or Chinese – repeat this schema. Tattooing also often converts a face into a mask. Charles Darwin,[53] while researching concepts among various peoples, tells about young African women who wore tattoos on their faces to mimick old age and death. This ancient tradition is alive even today. Look at various television monsters depicting phantoms. Their faces repeat the mask of death described by Hippocrates. While the mask is only one detail in the art of the theater, it is nevertheless a detail by which we can assess the character of the entire art. Masks, makeup, and gestures are intended to make it clear to the spectator whom it is he or she is seeing on stage. On the whole, this kind of art aspires towards the symbolism of image and gesture by becoming a sign. In this way, theater merges with representational art. We find this interpenetration in the cultural traditions of Mexico, Bali, and Indonesia. Marcel Marceau[54] and Charlie Chaplin are vivid examples of the vitality of these ancient traditions in today's world. Chaplin refined his gestures until they became symbols by transforming himself into a sign. Look at the little figure of Chaplin moving away from us, and you will see two bowlegs parallel to the back. This grotesque representation of walking is so convincing psychologically that it has been converted into a television sign and advertisement. A similar device of positioning parts of the body in space can be seen in the dances of India, Indonesia, and China. Legs and arms are turned parallel to the torso on a flat surface, so that the spatial devices of Egyptian or Assyrian reliefs are repeated – namely, hieroglyphic **symbolic deformation**.

The symbolic motion of marionettes can often be seen in medieval sculptures, which appear to be free from the body's gravity.

In the late works of Francisco Goya,[55] after he had become deaf, his depiction of figures was no longer subject to the law of gravitation and assumed the sharply psychological and tragic character of men-marionettes propelled by fate. It was the romantic motif of the "tragic puppet."

A puppet is often more expressive than a person. One often remembers a mask better than a real face. For us the face of a puppet is more alive than the face of the puppeteer. This becomes quite obvious if one recalls television programs in which people and puppets appear at the same time. The program ends, and we remember the puppet-mask, but not the puppeteer's face. And we remember it only when the puppet is a grotesque representation of the man himself.

THE GROTESQUE BODY

A grotesque body is universal. But it is not closed and harmonious, as it was with the classical Greeks, but the open and eternally transformed **flesh of being.** The body at birth. The cosmic body. It is open to entries within. Occasionally it is even turned inside out. The element of functions. The element of **functional** deformation.[56]

Eyes in the grotesque do not simply see: they literally **protrude from their sockets.** They try so hard to see that they flee from the face in order to function solely as eyeballs. Eyes in the grotesque are not the "mirror of the soul" as in the realism of Lev Tolstoy,[57] but "peering little balls." The mouth is a maw, a swallowing hollow, an ever-gaping grotto, enormous gates into another world. Everything that protrudes from the body reaches out to us. Everything that sinks into the body invites us to enter. The contemporary personage of American television, Cookie-Monster, is the embodiment of the grotesque. Its eyes protrude beyond the boundaries of the head and dance about on threads. Its face is only a gaping maw, a corporeal abyss. The grotesque body consists of exits and entrances, of death or birth in overcoming the boundaries between the world and the body. The grotesque body is never static; it is always in motion. Parts of the body attempt to separate and live their own independent lives. Fingers, phalluses, and noses grow to the size of the entire body or even bigger and finally replace it. The fingers of the giant Gargantua[58] become mountains in France. Parts of the body acquire the symbolism of "man." Thus, the finger is a symbol of man. The finger is a synonym for the phallus. Therefore, the phallus is also a man. The nose is a synonym for the phallus. The nose is also a man, or even an entire person as in Nikolai Gogol's short story, *The Nose.*[59] Noses walk about gravely in the paintings of Bosch,[60] or cavort about in Hans Sachs' *The Dance of the Noses*.[61] Parts of the human body easily replace one another in the symbolic apology of the grotesque. These concepts even penetrate into the realm of science. Joubert[62] in the eighteenth century with complete seriousness asserted that the size of a man's nose corresponds to the size of his phallus.

Representational anatomical symbols enter into colloquial speech and survive to this day. When one says "to be duped" *(ostavit' s nosom:* "to be left with a nose") or "to taunt" *(pokazat' nos:* "to show one's nose"), it is quite clear to everyone today what the speaker wants to express.

In the grotesque, as a body and its symbols, only that appears which can function immediately and openly: to eat is to defecate and so forth.

The grotesque is a manifestation of functional deformation.

ON TELEVISION

The festive madness of the grotesque is an essential element of animated films and television puppet programs. The images of folk culture are always bold and accustom everyone to their boldness, to the sweep of a gesture unrestrained by conventions imposed by an effete culture of snobs. Television monsters and masks mock the dead sea of abstract concepts. While they were spawned only recently, they are not the product of salons: they were produced by life itself. Archetypes evolving for thousands of years can be found in these monsters and masks. Similar and dissimilar, they have existed on a number of continents, in a number of folk cultures. Without knowing one another, they were yet related. Thus, disdaining sterile analysis of distinctions, these masks and monsters affirm their kinship, and the American culture of cartoons and puppet theater – the product of a refined mastery of deformation and selection of expressive means – brought them together into one family. It were as if they knew Freud's words about laconic expression: "The brief and laconic is not yet witty. The brevity of wit is precisely a special kind of witty brevity."[63]

The manners of television characters remind one of the manners of medieval schoolboys in the "Festival of Fools."[64] They are bored with the vacuum of minimalism.[65] They are turbulent, like sexually active youths who find profound, impotent men ridiculous. Cleverly, laconically they stick out their taunting tongues and say: "So what if you are minimalists; we shall be maximalists."[66]

It is impossible to link any kind of pure art with those cultural phenomena that were formed historically and are characterized by the fusion of many different principles and devices, such as the modern television puppet theater. And this phenomenon is not accidental, but structural. It is not simply the union of many aspects, but the creation of a **new aspect** altogether, an attempt at synthesis.

The mask and the character-sign are the foundation of television spectacles. The mask is the most complex and polysemantic motif in folk culture. The mask is not an object, but an image of the most ancient and ritually spectacular forms. To describe the multiple faces and complexities of the mask is impossible.

Parody, caricature, grimace, clowning, making faces, and striking poses are a continuation of the mask. The mask is the essence of the grotesque: images of mixed bodies on television, people-animals, people-trees, people-stones, personified cars, machine-like animals, robot-people, all kinds of transformations, a body dismembered into its parts, the lives of separate parts of the body. All this wins the approval of the viewer and is transformed into a character constantly in action. Television is a spectacle only when these combinations are converted into a mask-sign according to the internal laws of synthesis. Rich fantasy and the free play of the body are similar to the anatomical combinations of ancient grotesquery. Human beings never seen before appear, such as sirens,[67] giants, dwarfs, and humanoid creatures with hooved feet, with a single leg, with faces on their chests, or simply headless. Or people with one eye on their forehead (like the Greek cyclops), or with eyes on their shoulders and backs. Creatures with six arms or many arms. Other beings ride with the help of their noses and speak with their stomachs. These unbridled, grotesque, anatomical medieval images were spawned by new technical possibilities. Television seems to illustrate Rabelais' prophecy, in which he, a symbol of human technical culture, and Pantagruel make human unity – that is, the union of different cultures – possible.

Of course, the images of mixed bodies in film animation are not constructed on the same principles of combination as in images of mixed bodies in Egypt, Assyria, or Greece, that is, according to the structural and anatomical laws of physical conjunction. Furthermore, intuition tells us that combinations are constructed according to certain laws of perception innate in us. Precisely for that reason, character masks die out quickly after making their appearance. Others, however, remain, settle into our consciousness, become symbolic and – as symbols and signs – spread throughout the world to become a part of the design of magazines, catalogs, and costume jewelry. In the form of masks and signs they travel on trucks, trains, airplanes, and quite soon possibly will fly to other worlds on decorated rockets. It is an enviable fate to be part of real life, a lot attained by their elder brethren – the masks of the great civilizations of the past.

Television teaches garrulous conceptualism[68] that TV has become an essential element of life, not to speak of those who live by it. And real life quite often encompasses vulgarity, arrogance, and disproportionate elements. Let us forgive the shortcomings of television, my high-brow colleagues, and look at ourselves. Contemplating ourselves, we shall see that we are as symmetrical as Greek anatomy, as polysemantic as an Egyptian symbol, and as provocative as the grotesque.[69]

[1] Reference to *Gulliver's Travels* by Anglo-Irish satirical writer Jonathan Swift (1667-1745), a work that contrasts extreme scales of size and proportion.
[2] From Plato's *The Republic*.
[3] Soviet political slogan.
[4] Michelangelo Buonarroti (1475-1564), Italian sculptor, painter, poet, and architect of genius.
[5] Baroque, a movement in European art (c1600-1750) that rejected Renaissance Classicism in favor of a dynamic and expressive style.
[6] Rodin (see Chapter One, note 1).
[7] Constantin Brancusi (1876-1957), Romanian sculptor known for simple, polished forms such as *Bird in Space* (1919).
[8] Grotesque, a decorative style characterized by incongruous combinations of forms that developed in sixteenth-century Italy.
[9] Heraclitus (c540-c480), Greek philosopher who believed in universal impermanence and the interrelation of all things.
[10] Stoicism, Greek school of philosophy founded by Zeno of Citium (c335-263 BC), who held that wise men should desire only virtue and be indifferent to all else.
[11] Neizvestny applies the Russian Formalist concept of deformation to the plastic arts.
[12] Homer (c8th century BC), Greek epic poet to whom *The Iliad* and *The Odyssey* are attributed.
[13] Neoplatonism, school of philosophy developed by Plotinus (205-70 AD) and based on the teachings of Plato.
[14] Lucretius (c95-55 BC), Roman poet and greatest exponent of atomism.
[15] Anaxagoras (c500-c428 BC), Greek philosopher who held that the elements were infinite in number.
[16] Johann Christoph Friedrich von Schiller (1759-1805), leading German playwright, poet, and essayist.
[17] Zeus, supreme god of Greek mythology, god of earth and the sky.
[18] Poseidon, brother of Zeus and Hades and god of horses, earthquakes, and the sea in Greek mythology.
[19] Hephaestus, son of Zeus and Hera and god of fire in Greek myth.
[20] Aphrodite, Greek goddess of love, beauty, and fertility.
[21] Democritus of Abdera (c460-370), Greek materialist philosopher and exponent of atomism.

[22] Neizvestny's theory of anatomical deformation is a central element in his art and aesthetics.

[23] Albrecht Dürer (1471-1528), German artist influenced by the traditions of the Italian Renaissance and the Gothic and known for his detailed drawing, , engravings, and woodcuts.

[24] Tectonics, the art or science of constructing large buildings.

[25] Euclid (c300 BC), Alexandrian mathematician whose *Elements* is the basis of Euclidean geometry.

[26] Immanuel Kant (1724-1804), great German philosopher, author of *Critique of Pure Reason*, *Critique of Practical Reason*, and *Critique of Judgment*.

[27] Sir William Matthew Flinders Petrie (1853-1942), British archaeologist who devised the system of sequence dating of artifacts.

[28] Ptolemaic period (323-30 BC).

[29] Neizvestny's concept.

[30] Empedocles (c490-430 BC), Sicilian Pythagorean philosopher who conceived of four fundamental elements in nature: air, earth, water, and fire.

[31] Athena, Greek goddess of war and wisdom, known as Minerva in the Roman pantheon of gods.

[32] Pantagruel, reference to *Gargantua and Pantagruel* by François Rabelais (1494?-1553), French monk, doctor, and humanist writer

[33] The centaur is one of the central archetypes in Neizvestny's art.

[34] Faunus, giver or oracles and god of shepherds and agriculture in Latin mythology; corresponds to Greek god Pan.

[35] *Rusalka*, mermaid in Russian folklore.

[36] Sphinx, mythical beast of ancient Egypt depicted as recumbent lion with the head of a man; symbol of Pharoah as incarnation of sun god Ra.

[37] Swastika, ancient cosmic or religious symbol of good luck formed by a Greek cross with the ends of the arms bent at right angles.

[38] In Russian: "Tochka, tochka, zapiataia, minus, krivaia rozha;/ Palka, palka, ogurechek, nozhki – i vykhodit chelovechek."

[39] Neizvestny is particularly fond of the grotesque monsters from the American children's program, *Sesame Street*.

[40] Hydra, mythical monster with snakes for hair.

[41] Harpies, winged monsters who carried people off in Greek mythology.

[42] Cyclops, mythical one-eyed monster.

[43] A reference to Mikhail Bakhtin's concept of carnival in his study of Rabelais.

[44] Mikhail Mikhailovich Bakhtin (1895-1975), Russian literary theorist, scholar, and philosopher of language.

[45] Picasso (See Introduction, note 26).

[46] Sir Charles Spencer Chaplin (1889-1977), British actor and director, great comedian of the silent cinema.

[47] Walt Disney (1901-66), American pioneer of animated films and cartoons.

[48] Heinrich von Kleist (1777-1811), German writer and dramatist known for psychological insight.

[49] Bionics, the application of biological principles to the study of engineering systems.

[50] Noh, classical court drama of Japan employing mime, speech, singing, instrumental music, and dance.

[51] Kabuki, traditional Japanese popular theater that blended song, dance, and mime.

[52] Hippocrates (c460-c377 BC), Greek physician called the "Father of Medicine."

[53] Charles Robert Darwin (1809-82), English naturalist who formulated theory of evolution by natural selection.

[54] Marcel Marceau (1923-), great French mime.

[55] Francisco Goya (1746-1828), Spanish painter and graphic artist known for his etchings, *The Disasters of War* (1810-14).

[56] Deformation – whether functional, symbolical, or grotesque – is the key to Neizvestny's aesthetics.

[57] Lev Nikolaevich Tolstoy (1828-1919), great Russian realistic writer, author of *War and Peace* and *Anna Karenina.*

[58] Gargantua, a monster from *Gargantua and Pantagruel* by François Rabelais (1494?-1553).

[59] Nikolai Vasil'evich Gogol' (1809-52), Russian-Ukrainian writer of grotesque works such as *The Overcoat, Dead Souls,* and *The Government Inspector.*

[60] Hieronymous Bosch (c1450-1516), Dutch painter noted for grotesque fantasy.

[61] Hans Sachs (1494-1576), popular German poet and dramatist, one of the *Meistersingers.*

[62] Joseph Joubert (1754-1824), French moralist and author of *Pensées*.
[63] Sigmund Freud (1856-1939), Austrian neurologist and psychiatrist, founder of psychoanalysis.
[64] Festival of Fools, burlesque medieval religious festival occurring during Christmas and New Year's revels.
[65] Minimalism, art movement of 1960s that emphasizes pure color and geometric forms devoid of emotionalism.
[66] Maximalism, a term Neizvestny applies to Russian culture in general and to his own art in particular, comes from *maksimalist*, an extreme faction of the Russian Socialist-Revolutionary Party that was formed in 1906.
[67] Sirens, legendary sea nymphs whose songs enchanted all who heard them.
[68] Conceptualism, a philosophic doctrine that abstract concepts exist only in the mind and have no external reality. It is the basis of Conceptual Art, a movement of the 1960s that affirms that art is the leap of the imagination and, consequently, can dispense with galleries, the public, and even the work of art itself.
[69] An earlier form of this translation was published in the *Proceedings of the Summer 1986 Intensive Workshop in Chinese and Russian*, edited by Albert Leong, 89-106 (Eugene: University of Oregon Press, 1988). Reprinted with permission from *Oregon Studies in Chinese and Russian Culture*, edited by Albert Leong (New York: Peter Lang Publishers, 1990).

CHAPTER THREE

Messianic Tendencies in Russian Culture

In Russia, practically speaking, there is no distinction between art and philosophy. In principle, philosophy is art and art is philosophy. Russians, independent of their intellectual rank and social position, will always have something to tell you and their ideas will always be imbued with a desire to change the world. When a person of insufficient talent strikes this pose, it becomes ridiculous and a caricature. But, at the same time, a caricature is a grotesque representation of something essentially real, as we can see in the characters of Dostoevsky[1] or Tolstoy.[2] A graphomane is a writer without talent. If we took away the energy of genius from Balzac,[3] Dickens,[4] or Dostoevsky, they would simply be graphomanes.

In Russia there have been no philosophers like Kant[5] or Spinoza.[6] All Russian philosophers, in essence, have been poets. As we know, Plato[7] in his *Republic* simply exiled artists and poets from his utopia because he believed they would disrupt the harmony of society and philosophy in general. But, having exiled myth and Homer,[8] Greek society in Plato's scheme began to create its own myths. For Greek philosophy was not anthropomorphic, but cosmic. By driving out the artists, the philosopher could establish his own order.

But Russian philosophy is anthropomorphic through and through. It is a philosophy about human beings in historical context. Russian philosophy appropriated portions of European philosophy, as Byzantium did.[9] The Byzantine Empire after Alexander the Great[10] achieved a strange, harmonious union of two principles that underlie European and Russian civilization today – the Judeo-Christian and the Hellenistic. We sense this dualism not only in Byzantine institutions and laws, but also in ourselves. The Roman attitude towards the body and sexuality was univocal and clear. For other peoples, however, two principles clash – the Roman and the Judeo-Christian one.

For the Greeks space and time were cosmic and all-encompassing, while for the Jews, the medieval mind, and the peoples of Europe time and space were particular. In the Judeo-Christian tradition, time is eschatological,[11] historical, and anthropomorphic – from birth to the Last Judgment. In this tradition, people do not find themselves in an abstract cosmos, but instead are interconnected links in the historical process. The Greek concept of fate ruled out both free will and conscience. Why did Byzantium combine these two principles? And how did Byzantium achieve such an astonishing, organic, dialectical fusion?

After Constantinople was taken by the Turks in 1453, some Byzantine intellectuals fled to the West, and others to the East. The major Byzantine philosophers fled to the West because Latin was a common language. They did not know Russian, and there was nothing for them to do in Russia. Therefore, important Byzantine thinkers did not come to Russia, but missionaries did, as well as icon painters. Since there were no Byzantine philosophers in Russia, Russia received the Judeo-Christian branch of philosophizing, that is, philosophy as prophecy and as the poeticization of objects. For Russians, Solomon[12] was as much a philosopher as Socrates.[13] I am not suggesting that there was no poetical philosophizing in Western thought – there were St. Augustine,[14] St. Thomas Aquinas,[15] Nietzsche,[16] Schopenhauer,[17] Kierkegaard,[18] and Camus[19] – but only that there was a duality in European consciousness.

But, on the whole, there was no basis for poetical philosophizing in the European conception of philosophy, which considers Kant, Descartes,[20] and Spinoza philosophers, but Nietzsche to a lesser degree. In Russia, however, even before the appearance of philosophy as a distinct discipline, you will find the artist and icon-painter Rublev[21] listed under philosophers in philosophical works of the time. Why? Rublev never gave lectures on philosophy. In fact, he did not even speak, for he took a vow of silence as a monk. Why, then, is he a philosopher? Because in Russia there was the concept of "philosophizing in colors" *(umozrenie v kraskakh)*. That is, high art was considered one of the forms not only of cognition, but also of creating structures equal to philosophy.

And this is the key to the tendency of Russian artists and intellectuals, in general, to be not merely narrow specialists. If you consider the simple Russian word *pravda,* you will find that it cannot be translated fully into any European language, because the word conjoins the concepts of "truth" *(istina)* and "justice" *(spravedlivost')*. But in European thought, especially in positivism,[22] "truth" and "justice" are separate concepts. For positivists "justice" is a moral imperative, while "truth" is objective, so that "truth" can exist without "justice." This notion of "truth" = "justice" *(pravda)* is the source of Russian philosophical maximalism, for there are different conceptions of *pravda*. This accounts for Russian extremism: revolution and counterrevolution, dissidence and repression.

For the European and American mind, which is nourished on pluralism and dialogue, extremism is incomprehensible. For instance, the best journalists in the United States are objective and refrain from expressing their personal points of view. They merely reflect reality. But we Russians believe that even science is not objective, because if it were, then the best scientists would be idiots. Why? Because an idiot – lacking imagination, feelings, and emotions – would only consider objective facts with his brain. But even the selection of objective data is subjective, because each of us sees what he or she wants to see: homosexuals see other homosexuals; dog fanciers, dogs; old men, other old men. Even the natural sciences concede that the results of a scientific experiment are linked with the will of the experimentor.

Thus, only in Russia could appear an idea astonishing in its absurdity: "Beauty will save the world" *(Krasota mir spaset)*.[23] How can beauty save the world? People even laughed at Archimedes[24] when he said: "Give me a lever, and I shall overturn the world" to demonstrate the power of energy. But, then, a lever is an object. A good idea or teaching can save the world, but beauty is babbling as well as *pravda,* and *pravda* is the ultimate truth. Beauty, thus transformed into a universal category, can indeed save the world. For the beautiful *(krasivoe)* is synonymous with the good, the logical, and the harmonious *(lepoe)* in Old Church Russian. Therefore, beauty *(krasota)* in the eyes of the Russian Orthodox Church[25] is a synonym for *pravda.* The expression "divine beauty" *(krasota bozhestvennaia)* does not mean that God has a beautiful countenance, but rather the truth and justice *(pravda)* of God's design of all creation.

From the viewpoint of Russian philosophy, *pravda* is the synthesis of truth and justice. Justice is a moral concept, while truth, in the eyes of positivist philosophy, is an objective concept separate from morality. This different understanding of truth in the East and in the West is not only a linguistic distinction, but also a philosophical one.

In contrast to the path taken by European philosophy – that is, becoming a pure science in the case of Spinoza, Descartes, and Kant – Russian philosophy was always mythopoetic. Hence, we must take into consideration the concept of the holy fool *(iurodstvo)*.[26] The holy fool is a characteristically Russian phenomenon. It is a common occurrence, as well as a metaphor. *Iurodstvo* is not merely eccentricity, but a specific state of the soul connected with the philosophical life. It is unimportant on what social level, high or low, this occurs. *Iurodstvo* is a holistic worldview.

What is the basis of this worldview? In *iurodstvo, pravda* is sought by means of madness. It resembles the ancient Greeks' concept of Cassandra,[27] of visions coming from the gods to the demented. But in Russia a very interesting fusion took place – a fusion of Tibetan, Hindu, Buddhist, and other spiritual schools passing through Siberia with Christianity. These strange states of faith without faith were quite typical of Hindu and Buddhist philosophies. For example, to attract demons a hermit would sit in a pit in total darkness and meditate. When he would finally see a demon, he would make a sign for people to fetch him and would tell them that a demon was sitting with him at that moment. Because he would see demons constantly, the hermit has obviously gone out of his mind. But this state of mind signifies the final stage of enlightenment.

If people ask, "What kind of being is this demon?" and the hermit replies, "The demon came to me because I prayed and waited for him, and that's why God sent him to me," he would receive a low grade, so to speak. And a person who said that the demon was a product of his imagination and came to him in a vision would also be on a lower spiritual level from the viewpoint of these philosophies. It is a very strange dialectical situation, the negation of a negation.

Thus, *iurodstvo* in Russia has enormous power. There is a religious sect in the Ural Mountains known as *dyromoly (dyra,* "hole"; *molit'*, to pray). Members of this sect pray to the holes they have made in the walls of their dwellings and spit on icons. While this act may seem to be unholy, it is one of the rituals of this sect to spit and trample on icons. In Andrei Tarkovsky's film, *Andrei Rublev,*[28] there is a scene where the artist, unable to paint icons and frescoes without a vision, turns to *iurodstvo* as a means of challenging God to battle, as Job[29] did. Rublev suddenly enters a cathedral and begins to smear its walls with feces. Why? To arouse God's wrath, provoke His punishment, and force God to reveal His existence.

In Catholic religious consciousness there is the concept of "doubt," so that a cathedral can contain images of people in doubt. In religion, doubt is not a falling away from God, but a normal state. Another term exists in Christian terminology for being abandoned by God *(bogoostavlennost')*.

Iurodstvo is connected with various religious sects and heresies in Russia. Even Lev Tolstoy was considered a holy fool by the Russian Orthodox Church. The sect of Old Believers was founded on the messianic idea: they believed that Moscow would be the Third Rome[30] and that their observance of old religious rituals would save them, just as Jews believe that they are the chosen people. Thus, the Old Believers thought they had the right to transform Moscow into the Third Rome, and that there would be no other, since that was the end of history, the Last Judgment. And so they went into exile. But, to Russian exiles such as Solzhenitsyn,[31] one must not leave Russia, because the future of the world will be decided there. When I was forced to leave Russia, my friends asked me if I had the right to leave even when I was faced with imprisonment.

Thus, the Russian Orthodox Church won out over the Old Believers, but the latter constituted an enormous movement, especially in Siberia and the Urals. At precisely that time appeared the first Russian dissident, émigré, and social philosopher – Prince Kurbsky,[32] who waged a polemic with Ivan the Terrible[33] on sociological and political problems. Besides the Old Believers, this was the first time in Russian history that we witnessed open discussion of ethical and religious questions.

Secularization took place gradually in Russia. Philosophy was no longer the prerogative of priests and religious sects and became a science in 1685, when the first Academy of Philosophy was created in Kiev. This was the Hellenic-Greek Academy, where Greek, Hebrew, Latin, and philosophy were taught. Grigory Skovoroda[34] was the first brilliant, world-class Russian philosopher. His philosophizing assumed the form of poetry to express his many profound philosophical ideas. Skovoroda was an astonishing personality, for he was a monk, an ascetic, a wanderer, and a holy fool. He was a true holy fool: his only possession was a Hebrew Bible, which he knew by heart, for he had a phenomenal memory. Skovoroda had no need for books: he knew the works of Plato, Aristotle,[35] Epicurus,[36] Plutarch,[37] Philo,[38] and Seneca[39] by heart. Among a circle of friends, he – like Plato – would discuss these thinkers, and his thoughts were noted down by his disciples. Skovoroda created much that was new. Long before Schopenhauer, he introduced the concept of world suffering into philosophy. He affirmed the duality of human consciousness and personality long before the discovery of the subconscious mind by Dostoevsky, Freud,[40] and Jung.[41] In fact, Skovoroda wrote a book on the subject, entitled *Gnosiological Dualism*. When he died, he had inscribed on his grave: "The world tried to catch me, but failed."

Although Russian philosophy developed from the Judeo-Christian branch of European culture through the teaching of a unitary consciousness, it acquired an independent character.

Consequently, there were no philosophers in the European sense of the word in Russia.

Is Vladimir Soloviev[42] a philosopher? Of course, but he was a poet who envisioned a structure of all-encompassing unity. Vasily Kandinsky[43] was a philosopher, as well as an artist. And Lev Shestov[44] was a philosopher of poetic form. The entire Russian school of philosophy is poetical. When Russians are forced to relinquish poetry for positivism, they develop Marxism into a kind of anti-poetry by poeticizing the social sciences and coming up with extreme, maximalist notions in their acceptance of the dialectics of Marx[45] and Engels.[46] This extremism is very Russian.

Philosophy is the foundation of life in Russia. Russians cannot believe in an art that is separate from the whole, any more than a paleontologist can look at a finger and call it a person. So in Russia there were artists, poets, writers, or simply people who aspired to be intellectuals who shared these beliefs. What is a Russian *intelligent?*[47] In my opinion, it is a person with compassion and empathy for all the ills and joys of the world. That is, an authentic Russian intellectual will not be able to sleep nights, as long as people are going hungry somewhere. He or she will feel moral responsibility for the fate of the world and personally feel ashamed and pained. This personal anthropomorphic awareness has left its mark on the messianic tendencies of Russian artists and writers.

But there are simpler explanations, too. If you were to read the manifestoes of Russian artists such as Kandinsky, Kazimir Malevich,[48] or Pavel Filonov,[49] you would be shocked to find that the fate of the world and the whole Cosmos was believed to be decided in their paintings and personalities. They said as much. For Malevich, Suprematism revealed ways of changing not only the social environment of Russia and the world, but also cosmic forms of being. But this is not madness, if you were to look at things from Malevich's viewpoint. The use of Biblical prophetic forms of expression in stating their views is characteristic of Russians more than other peoples.

In recent times one can find a social basis for this phenomenon. In Russia there were no social virtues. Social life was undeveloped. Also undeveloped were social sciences such as sociology, which in Europe had already achieved autonomy as academic disciplines. So Dostoevsky or Tolstoy began to write about those fundamental matters. But there was a vacuum wherever they turned. And they began gradually to broaden the range of their labors. Once outside those bounds, they aroused the demons of sociology and politics, which pounced on them. To protect themselves and create something, they had to create a system, to do something. And so they created some kind of system, a kind of microethics or microaesthetics. Tolstoy created a whole microreligion, Tolstoyanism.

Just imagine a young person (me, for instance, when I began my work as a sculptor), who deliberately or by chance has dreamt up some unusual things, that is, who has exhibited artistic talent. Without suspecting it, I had entered a room where demons lived and suddenly found himself beset by terror from all sides: I no longer belonged to myself, nor was my professional life my own. Young people demanded modern art, but the intelligentsia insisted on progressive art. The Communist Party asked for my allegiance, and the government demanded loyalty. No one would leave me alone. Even my smallest piece of sculpture was looked upon not simply as a work of art, but also as a social and even a magical event. So, to keep from being destroyed, I was obliged to save myself by creating my own microcosmos, which I called the *Tree of Life*.[50]

The poet Osip Mandelstam[51] once said to his wife: "The Soviet Union is the only country in the world that takes poetry seriously. It will kill you for it." The USSR is the only society in modern times that attributes magical powers and meaning to art. And rightly so. Its only mistake is praying to the wrong god. Soviet authorities believe that if a sculptor models a handsome, patriotic, and heroic person, everyone will be transformed immediately into a hero. But, if a sculptor sculpts a deformed person, then everyone will become deformed. According to this logic, if one were to depict trees, then everyone would turn into a tree. Or, if newspapers were to write about happiness, then everyone would become happy. In short, the Soviet state believes in magical incantations and regards the artist as a shaman.[52]

When Solzhenitsyn started writing the *GULag Archipelago*,[53] prophetic intonations began to appear in the artist. He could not help but feel himself a prophet, for he had uncovered a layer of history that no one before him had researched. And Solzhenitsyn felt himself responsible in more than the professional sense of the word. Historical truth had become part of his professional interests. And *pravda* (truth and justice) and *krasota* (beauty) are synonyms. Thus, as we shall recall, beauty will indeed save the world.

[1] Dostoevsky (See Introduction, note 60).
[2] Tolstoy (See Chapter One, note 21).
[3] Honoré de Balzac (1799-1850), French novelist, author of *Eugénie Grandet* (1833) and *Le Pere Goriot* (1834) as part of his vast panorama of French society, *La Comédie Humaine.*
[4] Charles Dickens (1812-70), great English novelist who influenced the writings of Nikolai Gogol' and Fedor Dostoevsky, author of *Pickwick Papers* (1837), *Oliver Twist* (1838), *David Copperfield* (1850), and *Great Expectations* (1861).
[5] Kant (see Chapter 2, note 26).
[6] Baruch Spinoza (1632-77), Dutch rationalist philosopher who held that God is nature.
[7] Plato (c427-347 BC), Greek philosopher, disciple of Socrates , and teacher of Aristotle known for his *Dialogues.*
[8] Homer (See Chapter Two, note 12).
[9] Byzantium, the Eastern Roman Empire with its capital at Constantinople, now Istanbul, Turkey.
[10] Alexander the Great (356-323 BC), King of Macedonia (336-323 BC), and conqueror of Persian Empire.
[11] Eschatology, the study of last things, the meaning of history, and the final destiny of the world.
[12] Solomon, son of David and Bathsheba, ruler of Israel (970-933 BC) known for his wisdom.
[13] Socrates (c469-399 BC), Greek philosopher, teacher of Plato, and exponent of Socratic method of inquiry.
[14] St. Augustine (354-430), Christian theologian, author of *Confessions* (397-401) and *De Civitate Dei* (413-26).
[15] St. Thomas Aquinas (c1225-74), Christian philosopher and theologian, whose *Summa Theologica* attempts to reconcile faith and reason.
[16] Friedrich Nietzsche (1844-1900), German philosopher and classical scholar, author of *Thus Spake Zarathustra* (1833-92).

[17] Arthur Schopenhauer (1788-1860), German philosopher and author of *The World as Will and Idea* (1819), in which will is postulated as the ultimate reality.
[18] Soren Kierkegaard (1813-55), Danish religious philosopher and precursor of existentialism.
[19] Albert Camus (1913-60), French existentialist writer and philosopher, winner of Nobel Prize in 1957 for *The Stranger, The Plague, The Fall, The Myth of Sisyphus,* and other works.
[20] René Descartes (1596-1650), French philosopher, mathematician, physicist, and founder of rationalist school of philosophy.
[21] Andrei Rublev (c1370-c1430), greatest Russian icon painter.
[22] Positivism, a theory of knowledge developed by French philosopher Auguste Comte (1798-1857), who held that sense data comprise the sole basis concerning matters of fact.
[23] From Dostoevsky's notebooks to his novel, *The Idiot.* Alexander Solzhenitsyn refers to this idea in his *Nobel Lecture.*
[24] Archimedes (c287-212 BC), Greek mathematician, physicist, and inventor.
[25] The Russian Orthodox Church was founded in Russia when Grand Prince Vladimir I of Kiev accepted Eastern Orthodoxy from Byzantium as the state religion of Kievan Russia in A.D. 988.
[26] The image of the holy fool or *iurodivy* is dramatized in Modest Musorgsky's opera, *Boris Godunov.*
[27] Cassandra, Trojan princess in Greek legend endowed with prophetic power by Apollo.
[28] *Andrei Rublev* (1966), epic film biography of the artist by Andrei Arsenievich Tarkovsky (1932-86), major Soviet Russian filmmaker.
[29] *Job,* 18th book of the Old Testament suggesting that suffering is not necessarily God's punishment for sin.
[30] After Constantinople fell to the Turks in 1453, Russian theologians proposed Moscow as the "Third Rome."
[31] Alexander Isaevich Solzhenitsyn (1918-), major Russian writer, publicist, critic of Soviet system, and Nobel Laureate in Literature (1970).
[32] Prince Andrei Mikhailovich Kurbsky (c1528-83) defected to Lithuania and became the principal opponent to Ivan the Terrible during his reign of terror.
[33] Ivan IV [the Terrible] (1530-84), grand prince of Muscovy and first Russian tsar (1547-84).

[34] Grigory Skovoroda (1722-94).
[35] Aristotle (384-322 BC), influential Greek philosopher, pupil of Plato, and tutor to Alexander the Great.
[36] Epicurus (c341-270 BC), Greek thinker who propounded a materialist philosophy emphasizing the positive things in life.
[37] Plutarch (c46-120 AD), Greek biographer and philosopher.
[38] Philo Judeas (c20 BC-c50 AD), Jewish thinker from Alexandria who combined Judaic and Greek philosophical thought.
[39] Lucius Annaeus Seneca (c4 BC-65 AD), Roman statesman, writer, philosopher, and adviser to Nero.
[40] Sigmund Freud (1856-1939), Austrian psychiatrist and founder of psychoanalysis.
[41] Carl Gustav Jung (1875-1961), Swiss psychiatrist and founder of analytical psychology.
[42] Vladimir Sergeevich Soloviev (1856-1900), major Russian philosopher and writer.
[43] Vasily Kandinsky (1866-1944), Russian artist, philosopher, and founder of abstract art.
[44] Lev Shestov [Lev Isaakovich Shvartsman] (1866-1938), Russian existentialist philosopher and critic.
[45] Karl Marx (1818-83), German socialist, economic theorist, and critic.
[46] Friedrich Engels (1820-95), German socialist, philosopher, and associate of Karl Marx.
[47] *Intelligent* (collective: *intelligentsia*).
[48] Malevich (See Introduction, note 29).
[49] Filonov (See Introduction, note 65).
[50] Neizvestny's *Tree of Life* is conceived of as an immense architectural monument to human creativity in art, science, and technology.
[51] Osip Emilievich Mandelstam (1891-1938?), eminent Russian Acmeist poet.
[52] Shamanism, primitive religious system based on *shaman* or medicine man possessed by spirits. See Mircea Eliade, *Shamanism: Archaic Techniques of Ecstasy* (Princeton: Princeton University Press, 1970).
[53] Alexander Solzhenitsyn's *GULag Archipelago,* modeled after the *Inferno, Purgatory,* and *Paradise* of Dante's *Divine Comedy,* is an epic account of the Soviet labor camp system as it existed from 1918 to 1956.

CHAPTER FOUR

The Tree of Life

1. Theme

The *Tree of Life* is the apotheosis of the human soul and human knowledge. It is an image of man's inner world that affirms the inseparability of the spiritual principle from the purely logical principle of science. By spiritually uniting art with contemporary science and technology, the *Tree of Life* represents the symbiosis of Faith and Knowledge. In unity they enrich one another and thus impart purposefulness to the spiritualized universe.

The material achievements of humanity have often resulted from base motives: pride, greed, indolence, envy, spite, covetousness, lust. And these vices have engendered human sufferings in the cycle of birth, childhood, old age, and death again and again. But, nonetheless, spirit and faith are reunited to transform all this into the sublime miracle of creative human achievement.

2. Description

In the center of the space will rise a sculpture approximately 150 meters high and 150 meters in diameter situated within a circle of intersecting roads forming a compass rose: north, south, east, west. Ideally this compass rose, like a gigantic goblet, would stand in a hollow of the earth.

It is called the *Tree of Life,* for it is an organism that grows from seven roots descending into the earth, each root symbolizing one of the deadly sins. The roots form a system of tunnels, an underground labyrinth.

In the part above ground, the monument consists of seven spirals or Moebius strips,[1] each of which is a different color of the spectrum, forming the asymmetrical shape of the human heart: *The Heart of Humanity.*

Seven roads converge like rays towards the center of the monument. Walking on them, the visitor approaches enormous letters serving as portals and symbolizing the gates of knowledge, the gates of understanding. After passing through these gates, the visitor will be able to examine the monument in detail.

A Biblical citation of an ecumenical character is engraved on the circle surrounding the structure. It is in four languages: English, Russian, Hebrew, and Chinese.

Elevators ascending along the central trunk stop at each of the seven spirals. They deliver the public into the interior spaces in which are distributed sculptures, frescoes. The latest achievements of science and technology organically enter into the architectural-artistic composition and become elements with emotional impact. Music can be heard. Exhibits, while organic to the whole concept, should be replaced as they become obsolete to preserve the timeless character of the *Tree of Life.* For even as it becomes an antique, the *Tree of Life* should preserve the character of innovation and reflect changes in scientific-technical progress.

The forms are open. The monument is simultaneously both interior and exterior. The visitor is at once both inside and outside and, in fact, by moving within it becomes a constituent part of the monument: each visitor is a blood cell pulsating through the Heart of Humanity. The exterior surfaces are covered with plastic and kinetic works on which I have worked throughout my life and which from the very beginning were designed for this purpose. These surfaces are bathed with changing colors by light projectors. The interior is even more polyphonic: sculpture and graphic art, color and music, people moving about – all this should merge into an image of eternity, into an image of the spiritual world.

An electronic program will direct changes in color, music, and the movements of mechanical elements synchronically to the rhythm of human heartbeats.

The base, the pathetic, and the meaningless are continuously and eternally united by faith to become noble, sublime, and meaningful.[2]

3.

My favorite work of literature is Aleksandr Pushkin's poem, "The Prophet" *(Prorok)*, and the finest sculptor I know of is the six-winged seraphim from that poem.[3] You will recall how Pushkin's prophet was created:

> And cleft he my chest with sword
> And fluttering heart withdrew,
> And a coal aglow with fire
> Into my open chest inserted.

Heterogeneous natural elements are fused together here into a single invisible, living, and essential whole. Plastic art is not merely a reflection of the artist's visual interest in the world, but also reflects substantive problems of human spiritual life. Any attempt to divert the representational arts to purely visual tasks conflicts with their timeless function as metaphysics and a world view.

Creative work is meditation objectified. The greater, broader, and swifter the creative current, the less the artist is attached to the fruits of his labor. That which is materialized is no longer the artist, but something apart from him. Whatever an artist has created no longer exists as such. The artist is only a transformer and conductor of feelings and ideas that take shape in him. The artist is bound to be alone. But that does not mean that he always will be. If the artist has genuinely objectified his state of mind, then this condition will be communicated without fail to someone.

Creative work and life do not necessarily correspond to one another. When I was happy, I produced my most dramatic works. When I was in love, I created my most ascetic works. Journalists often write about my works as opposition to the Soviet regime, never as statements of the universal human tragedy. I am not a rebel, but I am regarded as a rebel because I am a personalist.

The very act of artistic creation, as a spiritual feat unrelated to the solution of practical problems, is an action affirming faith. Without faith creative work is impossible. Faith is the striving, attempt, and means of overcoming humankind's cosmic solitude, as well as a premonition of the ultimate answer that resides both within and outside oneself. While this is not the place to discuss the content and symbols of faith, Christianity – since it encompasses the principle of heroism, freedom of human personality, and the understanding of history as eschatological mystery – is of course closer to my views than impersonal Buddhism or other forms of religion.[4]

The Russian avant-garde exerted a very powerful influence on me, and I consider myself its representative and continuation. But in evaluating the Russian avant-garde, one must not forget that Kandinsky,[5] Filonov,[6] Malevich,[7] and others – it is enough to read their manifestoes – regarded artistic form only as a means and not as an end. Therefore, they were never formalists in the narrow sense of the word. They were metaphysicians. This distinguished the Russian avant-garde from the Western avant-garde with its Positivist orientation.[8] Kandinsky saw the future of art in monumental synthesis or synthetic monumentality, as he put it. I am engaged in the same kind of synthesis. I emerge from the Russian avant-garde in a new historical spiral.

My first works were entitled *This is War*. I perceive war not as victory parades, but as a tragic, contradictory, and unnatural human phenomenon. Hence arose this series of sculptures in which part of a man is transformed into a machine, into iron, which personifies war, which enters flesh as pain. Later this theme developed into the theme of *Robots and Semi-Robots*, where man already consciously struggles against moribund metal. Then this theme developed into the theme of *Gigantomachia* and, after that, into the *Tree of Life*. In these cycles man is objectified by his achievements. He has spawned a second nature of objects as extensions of his hands, brain, eyes, nervous system, and heart. The task for representational art in the modern world is to create certain unifying symbols and metaphors to demonstrate the value and infinitude of the human "I" to people disoriented by a surfeit of information.

Any modernist phenomenon, if it is authentic and powerful, is initially received with shock like an earthquake shaking the very foundations of society. But as time passes, we begin to see its indirect link with existing traditions. Today one can find more classical elements in Khlebnikov[9] or Mayakovsky[10] than in smooth, grammatically-correct, but non-creative writing. At the present time we see that these writers had greater affinity with the vernacular language, or even Church Slavic, than the pseudo-Classical poets of the period. Thus, a link with cultural traditions always exists, for these links are unbroken. The task of my art and modernism is to juxtapose the vertical axis representing timeless, esoteric philosophical problems with the horizontal axis representing contemporary problems to discover a new quality or fusion at the center of their intersection.

Everything I work on now, whether an album of drawings, a series of engravings, or individual sculptures and sculptural groupings, is part of this holistic monumental project, which is at once polyphonic and a single whole. Synthesis is not eclecticism, where everything is assembled by chance. Synthesis in art is an organism in which each part fulfills its proper function and in which these parts comprise an aesthetic whole. For instance, the laws of Egyptian architecture inheres in each fragment of Egyptian sculpture; in the least part beats the pulse of the entire structure, because the ancient Egyptians had a holistic relation to the world.

My fundamental work is an enormous monument that I call the *Tree of Life*. It contains the dualistic and contradictory theme of man and nature, of man and the second nature of machines he has created, and of man himself. This theme in itself is polyphonic, and for that reason the creative works of Dostoevsky[11] attract me. The multiplicity of voices and clash of contradictions in his works are close to my own artistic views.

I have worked on a number of writings by Dostoevsky. In the Soviet Union I was able to publish my illustrations to his novel *Crime and Punishment*.[12] In Switzerland, where I initially settled in the West, the stage director and actor Ingold Wildenauer and I mounted a production of Dostoevsky's *Notes from the Underground*. Despite its apparent anachronism, the *Notes* are astonishingly relevant today. We became convinced of this when audiences would sit without stirring and listen to a four-hour philosophical monologue with minimal stage action or effects.

Pushkin once said that Dante would still be a genius if he had left behind no more than an outline for his *Divine Comedy*. The situation with Dostoevsky is different. He gave us no diagrams. While he did say that he wished to erect a cathedral from his novels, we do not know how he planned to do this. We can only catch a glimpse of his overall plan. I am not a professional literary critic, but an artist whose method consists of a system of analogies. Besides, my literary investigations are localized: I study only those literary works that can be translated into a visual or theatrical experience and disregard all the rest. And, proceeding from this method, I propose to explicate Dostoevsky's artistic design.

It seems to me that Dostoevsky's plan consists of transparent ideas and problems posed in antinomic form and found in all his novels. Since I think in spatial images, one can imagine Dostoevsky's antinomies as an infinite game. Imagine a vertical line coming from God knows where and going somewhere endlessly. These are not the closed circles of Dante, but a vertical line. And we begin to play Dostoevsky's game: we place one hand on this vertical line and say, "Yes." Then we put a hand on top of the other and say, "No." Then "yes" and then "no," and so on to infinity. That's what interests Dostoevsky.

His novels consist of endless dialogues in which all these ideas resound not merely in sequence (yes, no), but occasionally together in chorus, as if a person with many voices were disputing with himself: "God exists, there is no God"; "it is permitted to kill, thou shalt not kill"; "one may rape a little girl, one must not rape ..." Dostoevsky the writer gives us no answer. But, as a publicist and social activist, he does provide answers that are often amazingly primitive. As a writer, Dostoevsky gives no answers, and that is his power as an artist. Dostoevsky resembles a vivisectionist who performs experiments on himself, on his own psychology. He anticipates psychoanalysis precisely for this reason.

In fact I have never illustrated a single novel by Dostoevsky. I have illustrated his ideas instead: murderer, suicide, parricide,

matricide, the whole world, children, doubles, and so forth. But because Dostoevsky's works were published as separate novels, I had to select drawings from various albums and put them in a certain order for, say, an edition of *Crime and Punishment*. I can easily remove any illustration from this novel and insert it into another work by Dostoevsky. Dostoevsky himself did this. His ideas move from novel to novel; they are only formulated differently. Therefore, it is quite difficult to speak of any novel by Dostoevsky, say *The Brothers Karamazov*, as such. All the more because this work is unfinished. But, then, Dostoevsky had no finished novels. *Crime and Punishment* is considered a completed work, but it ends with the words: "But that is another story." Besides, what kind of story is it? The main plot is the spiritual recovery of a murderer. The entire novel is a prologue to this idea, but suddenly Dostoevsky cuts it off. I think he does this for two reasons. First of all, Dostoevsky was a great master, perhaps the greatest in the world, of the art of provocation. He provokes us to talk about him today. Secondly, as a religious person, he had an answer. But, as a subtle and refined artist, he could not formulate this answer in literary terms. He could only pose theses and antitheses. Dostoevsky resembles the father of existentialism,[13] Saint Augustine,[14] who once said: "I believe because it is absurd." To positivists this phrase sounds ridiculous, but it is intelligible to a person with religious consciousness: faith cannot be proven. Therefore, the dispute between believers and positivists is futile. Because there is no positive definition of faith, Dostoevsky cannot positively depict this condition. He can only carry out an experiment in "yes" and "no." But we his readers must draw a conclusion, and that is his power as a writer.

But let us return to my *Tree of Life* project. In 1956, when I was in a grave state and seemed to have no reason to continue working, since it was senseless to work without any hope of exhibiting anywhere, I contemplated my future fate as a sculptor. And one night, all at once, I envisioned the *Tree of Life* in a dream. When I awoke, my decision was made. True, at that time the *Tree of Life* comprised not seven Moebius coils, but only a single spiral. But the general form, the form of the crown of a tree and the form of a human heart, was already chosen. It were as if I had envisioned at night a higher aim that reconciled me with my actual fate and provided me with an imaginary model to enable me to work towards a single goal.

Later, I realized that the same thing had happened to many members of the Russian intelligentsia. The question of messianic tendencies in the Russian intelligentsia arises quite often in the West. It is a legitimate question. I do not wish to say that messianic tendencies are exclusively a Russian trait. Such tendencies exist everywhere. But more than elsewhere this trait is manifested in Russia in a pure form, almost as a caricature. I am not comparing myself to those people about whom I am about to speak. I merely wish to explain the appearance of specific tendencies in Russian social, historical, and spiritual thought.

During the time of Dostoevsky, the epistolary genre or simply the genre of correspondence occupied a lofty position in France. Everyone, even simple folk, exchanged letters. Thus, Dostoevsky, beginning to describe the "insulted and the humiliated,"[15] suddenly discovered that there was little to depict. No matter where he turned, he found virgin soil in the literary treatment of ethics, law, religious and moral problems. Dostoevsky felt constrained by the bounds of pure literature. In order to work as a literary professional, he created the model of a gothic cathedral with his novels as elements or constituent parts. To function as a writer and not be restricted by the traditional bounds of literature, he was obliged to create his own system of microethics, microesthetics, and microsociology.

The same thing with Tolstoy. When being a writer was no longer enough, he began to create a microreligion. If a Russian intellectual takes his professional tasks seriously, he begins to notices that problems related to mixed fields have not been researched adequately. The writer is obliged to fill the vacuum or at least study these problems to preserve his self-respect. The same thing happened with Solzhenitsyn,[16] for an adequate knowledge of Russian history and corresponding professional literature simply did not exist. He had to fill these gaps.

For these reasons prophetic tendencies necessarily arose. If these tendencies were reinforced by talent and reality, then they spawned a somewhat different type of intellectual activity than in the West.

Let's take a Western sculptor by contrast. No one questions his right to be a professional sculptor. But in Russia, when I was working on professional sculpture somewhat different from the generally accepted kind, a whole mass of problems arose. First of all, why make it if no one needs it? And there were indirect problems too. It turned out that there were many elements related to the technology and stylistics of sculpture that had simply not been worked out. I had to research an enormous number of the most diverse problems in order to base my art on a solid theoretical foundation. After all, there were no art historians who could theoretically satisfy these needs and establish a basis for my style. Thus, I began to work not only in the field of sculpture, but also found myself in the crossfire of conflicting demands. The government demanded obedience from me; the intelligentsia, progress; the youth, modernity. Each group thought I should behave in a certain way. I entered into a greater number of networks of people than is usual for a sculptor or artist in the West. Without wishing it, I was responsible for whole levels of phenomena. My behavior was looked upon not as the personal behavior of Ernst Neizvestny, but as the behavior of a particular social tendency. Many people even claimed my sculptures as their own achievements. In such a dilemma there was nothing left for me to do but commit suicide or dream up some kind of universal conception. Thus the *Tree of Life* was born.

What is the *Tree of Life?* It is seven Moebius strips in the form of a human heart. For me symbols and signs are not without meaning. In the Bible "tree" is a synonym for "heart," but "heart" is a synonym for "cross." In this way the *Tree of Life* unites these three concepts. Technically, the Moebius is quite suitable for many effects. The fact is, sculpture, painting, and other forms of representation art are usually displayed on a surface, such as depictions on the walls or ceiling of a temple. The Moebius permits a gigantic number of planar possibilities under natural or artificial lighting. It allows spatial representations in a mathematically almost infinite number of points, foreshortening, and perspectives. It creates visual effects which possibly could be quite significant on a large scale.

The Moebius is also viewed today by many scholars as a scientific and metaphysical model of the universe. For me this is important because all structures that assume the role of a temple are micromodels of the universe in principle. Even the plan or foundation of a temple in all religions is symbolically a map of the universe. Of course, what I propose is not a temple. I have no such aspiration. We do not live in a period of temple culture. I do propose a sculpture, the principle of which is borrowed from temple architecture. And I strive to create a certain synthesis by designing a sculpture in architectural form. At the same time such a structure in the eyes of traditional construction is quite unexpected, since there is no separation of interior from exterior in it. The interior and the exterior interpenetrate one another.

Therefore, my structure had to be sufficiently large. Its diameter of more than 100 meters was dictated not merely by my desire to make something large, though in my firm opinion what is very large or very small is good. Only the average is bad in my view. After all, there are two attitudes towards size in the consciousness of children and great folk cultures. Both are impressed by dwarfs and giants. Only bourgeois culture gave rise to the average in size and scale. It is poetic for average people to experience large and small, for such a person to enter my legend, the *Tree of Life*. The contrast between large and small is a legitimate attempt to transport art out of everyday life.

Hence the great size of my *Tree of Life* is due to technical reasons. If there is no interior and exterior, how shall we enter this body? We shall pass through tunnels in the shape of alphabetical letters or ideograms. The phrase, "People who live at the time of a temple that has been destroyed resemble people who live during the destruction of a temple," will be inscribed in four languages – Russian, English, Chinese, and Hebrew.

The *Tree of Life* is situated at the center of a cross formed by north, south, east, and west. These tunnels-letters will have not merely symbolical meaning (passage through a letter as passage to meaning), but also visual meaning. When we drive or walk up to the monument, it will rise up above these letters, and the small tunnels will not be visible. When we enter a tunnel or letter, we will not see the monument, which will be hidden from our view. And, when we emerge from the tunnel, we shall find ourselves in a space where a gigantic structure is suddenly suspended above us. We shall enter a labyrinth organized by seven roads symbolizing the seven human sins. There will be no representations in this labyrinth, only a naturalistic figure of a blind man walking

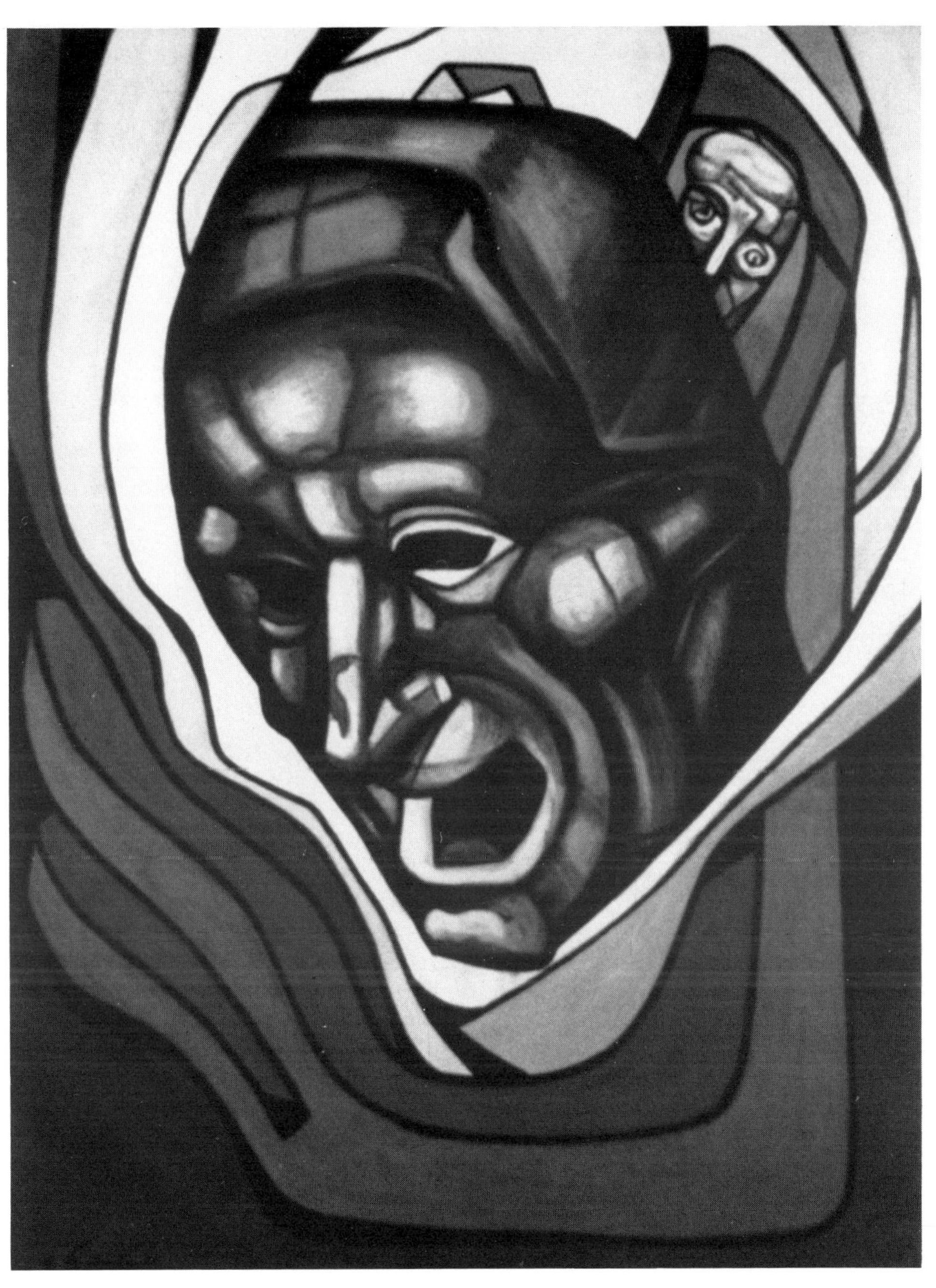

Krik (The Outcry), 1980-85
Oil, 121.92 x 91.44 cm.
New York
Photograph by Albert Leong

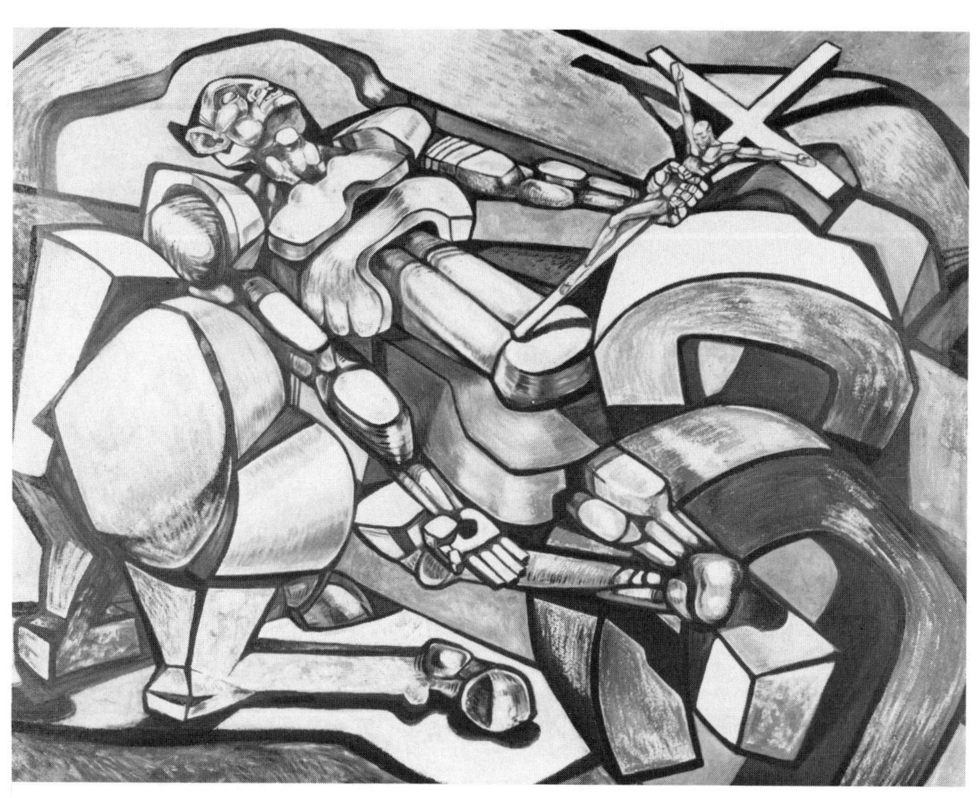

Kentavr i krest (Centaur and Cross), 1980-86
Acrylic/Oil, 152.40 x 203.20 cm.
Tree of Life Museum, Uttersberg, Sweden

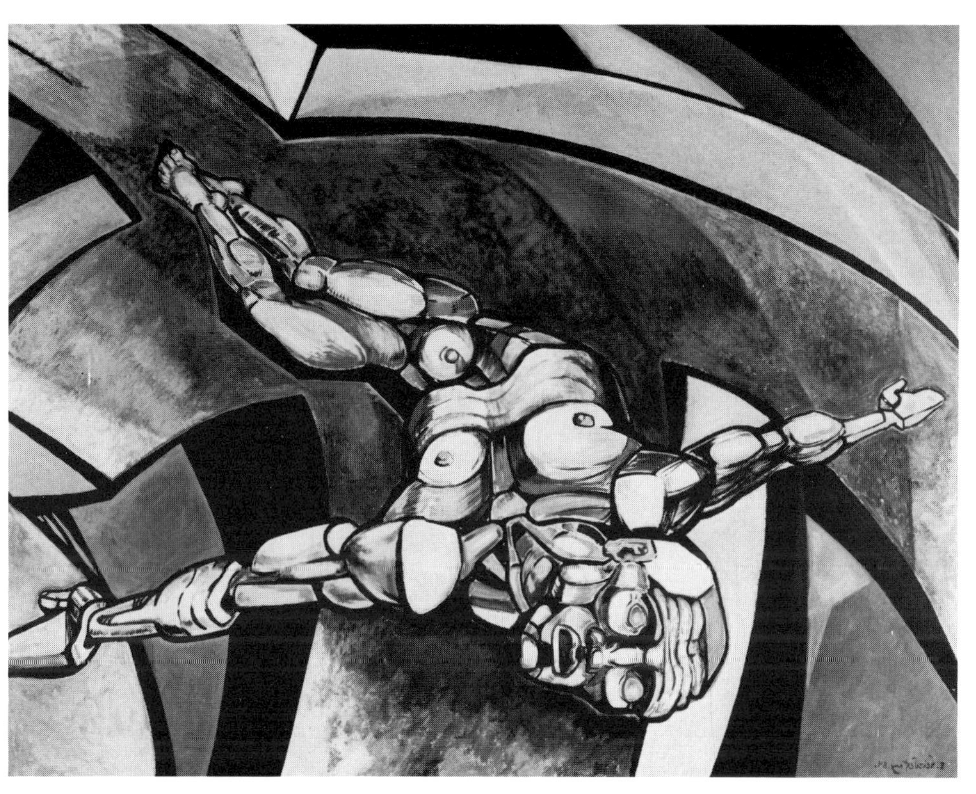

Raspiatie vniz golovoi (Upside Down Crucifixion), 1986
Acrylic/Oil, 152.40 x 203.20 cm.
Tree of Life Museum, Uttersberg, Sweden

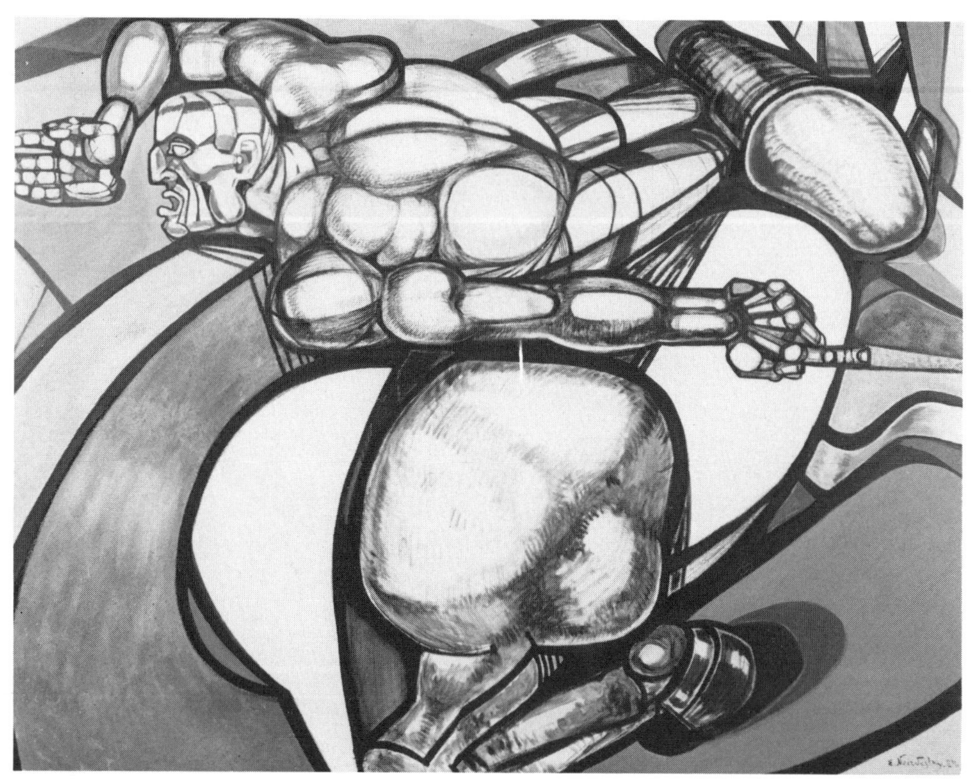

Kentavr (Centaur), 1987
Acrylic, 152.40 x 203.20 cm.
Tree of Life Museum, Uttersberg, Sweden

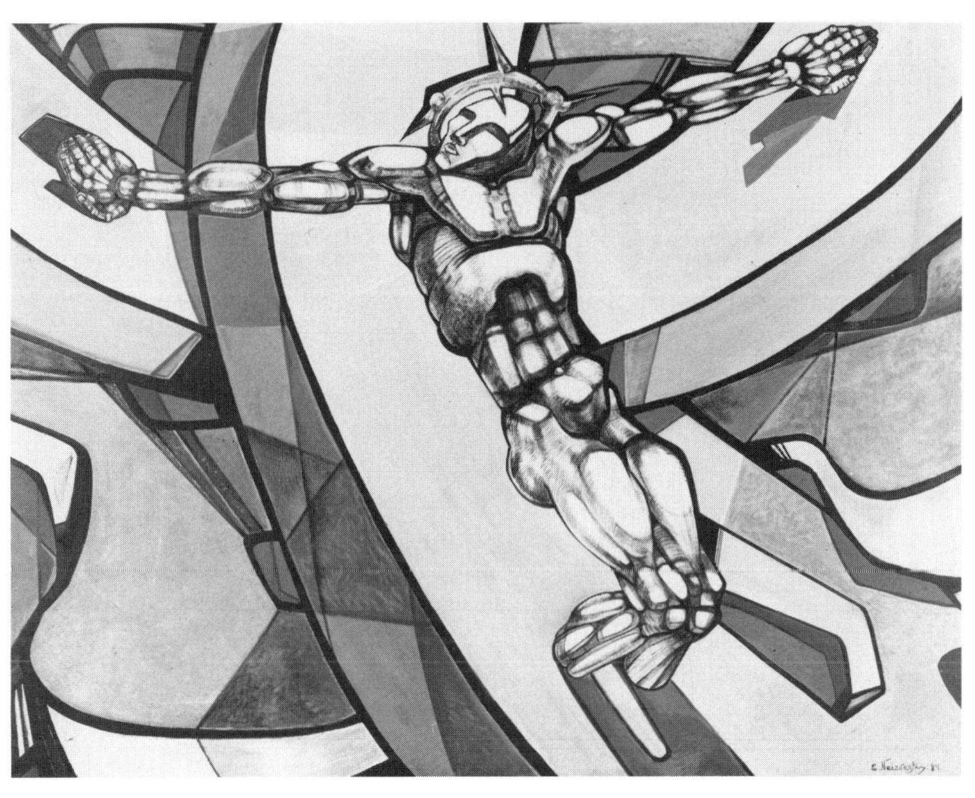

Raspiatyi v tekhnike (Man Crucified in Machinery), 1980-89
Acrylic, 152.40 x 203.20 cm.
Tree of Life Museum, Uttersberg, Sweden

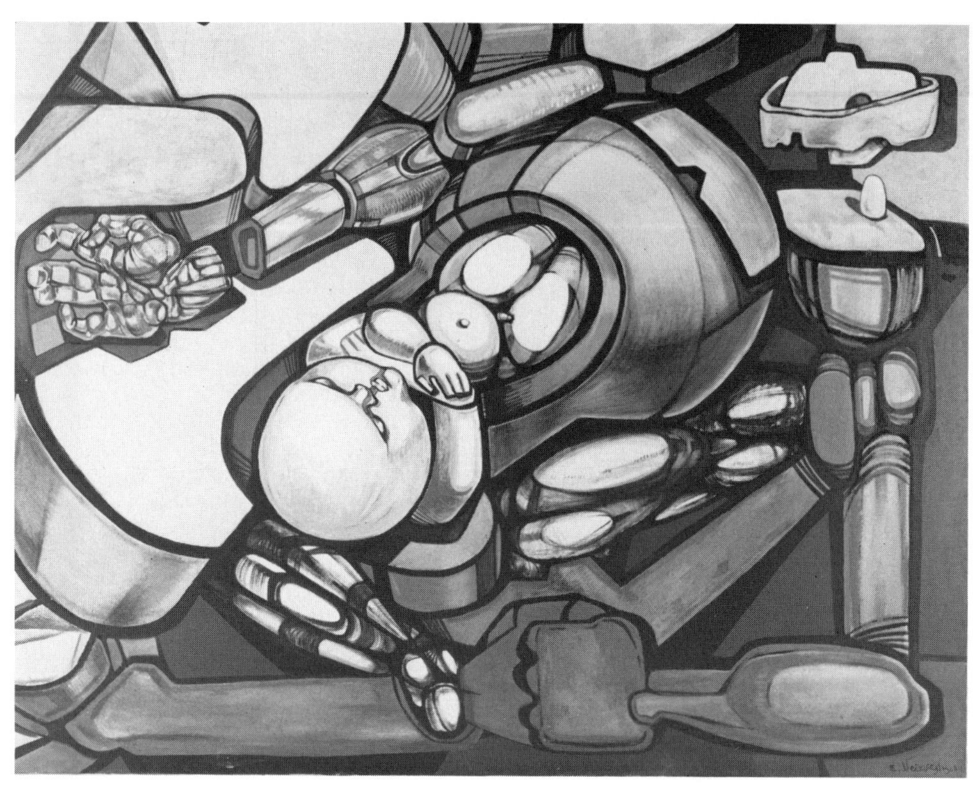

Polurobot ((Semi-Robot), 1980-89
Acrylic, 152.40 x 203.20 cm.
Tree of Life Museum, Uttersberg, Sweden

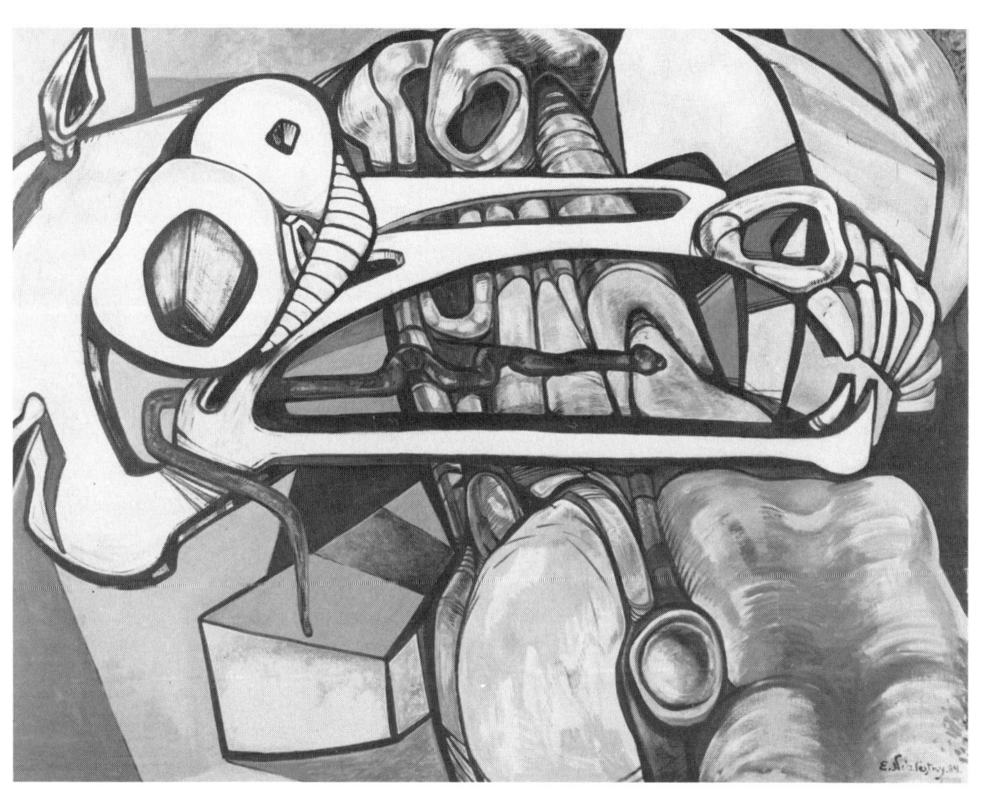

Kosti i plot' (Bones and Flesh), 1980-89
Acrylic, 152.40 x 203.20 cm.
Tree of Life Museum, Uttersberg, Sweden

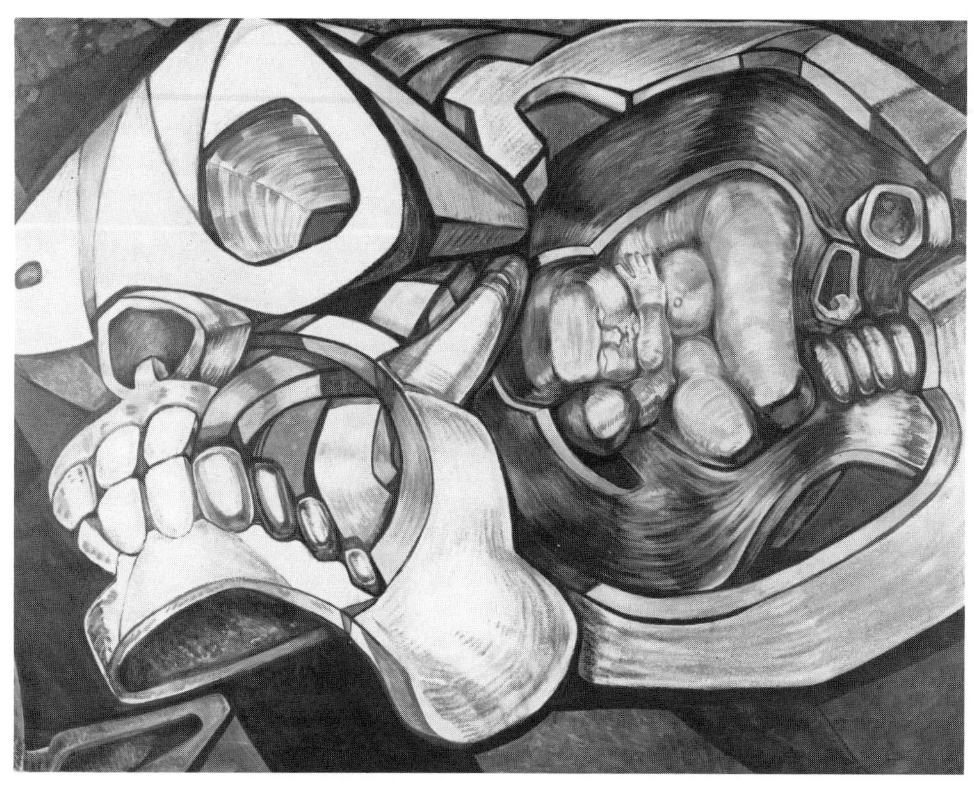

Rozdenie iz smerti (Birth from Death), 1980-89
Acrylic, 152.40 x 203.20 cm.
Tree of Life Museum, Uttersberg, Sweden

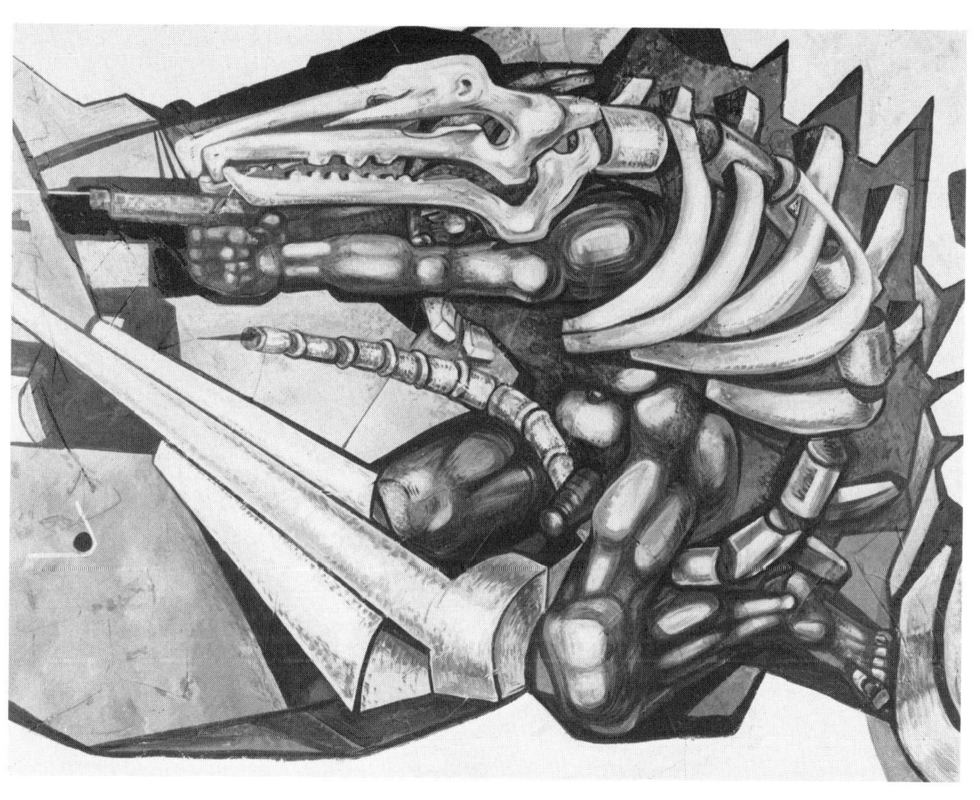

Terrorist (Terrorist), 1980-89
Acrylic, 152.40 x 203.20 cm.
Tree of Life Museum, Uttersberg, Sweden

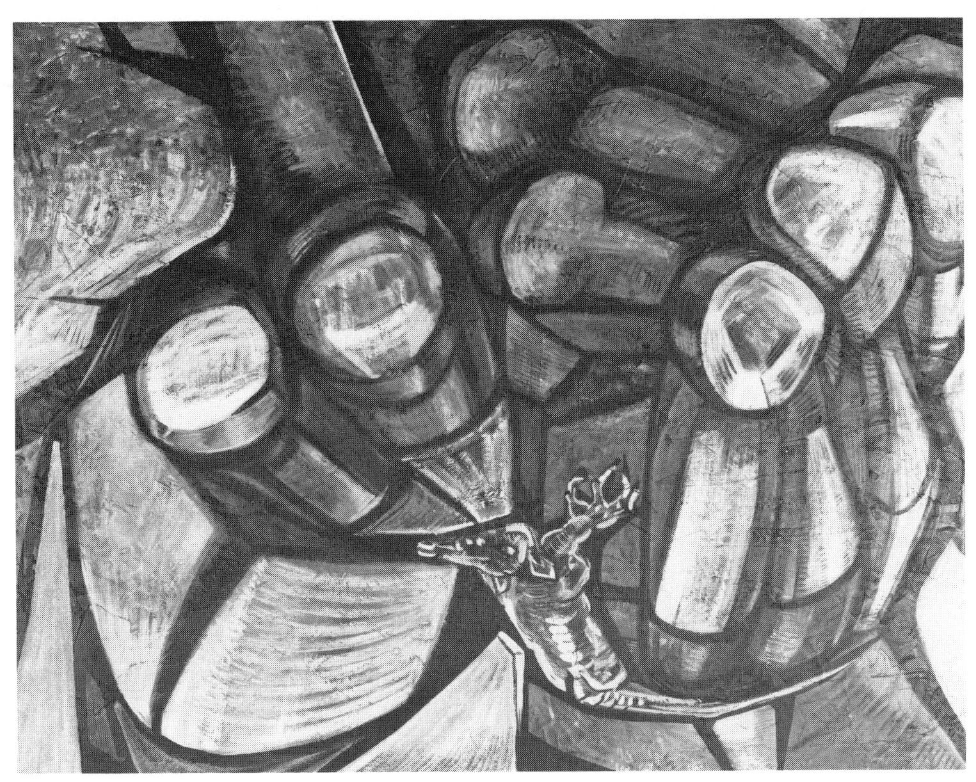

Krysa v zheleznykh rukakh (Rat in Iron Hands), 1980-89
Acrylic, 152.40 x 203.20 cm.
Tree of Life Museum, Uttersberg, Sweden

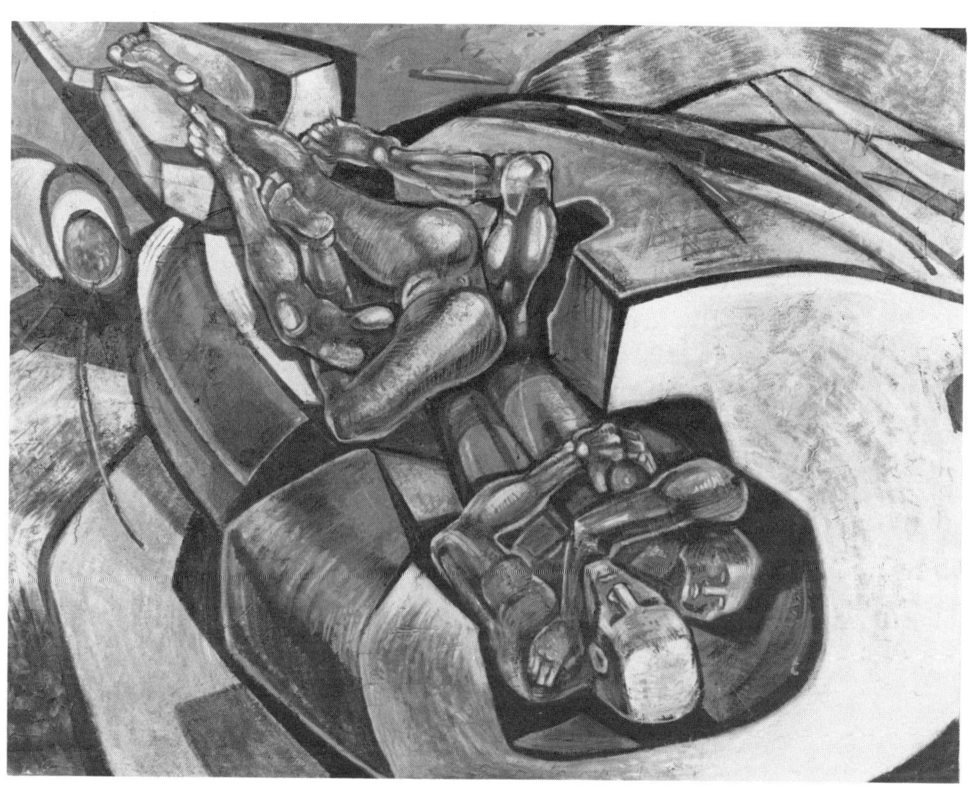

Sarkafag liubvi (Sarcophagus of Love), 1980-89
Acrylic, 152.40 x 203.20 cm.
Tree of Life Museum, Uttersberg, Sweden

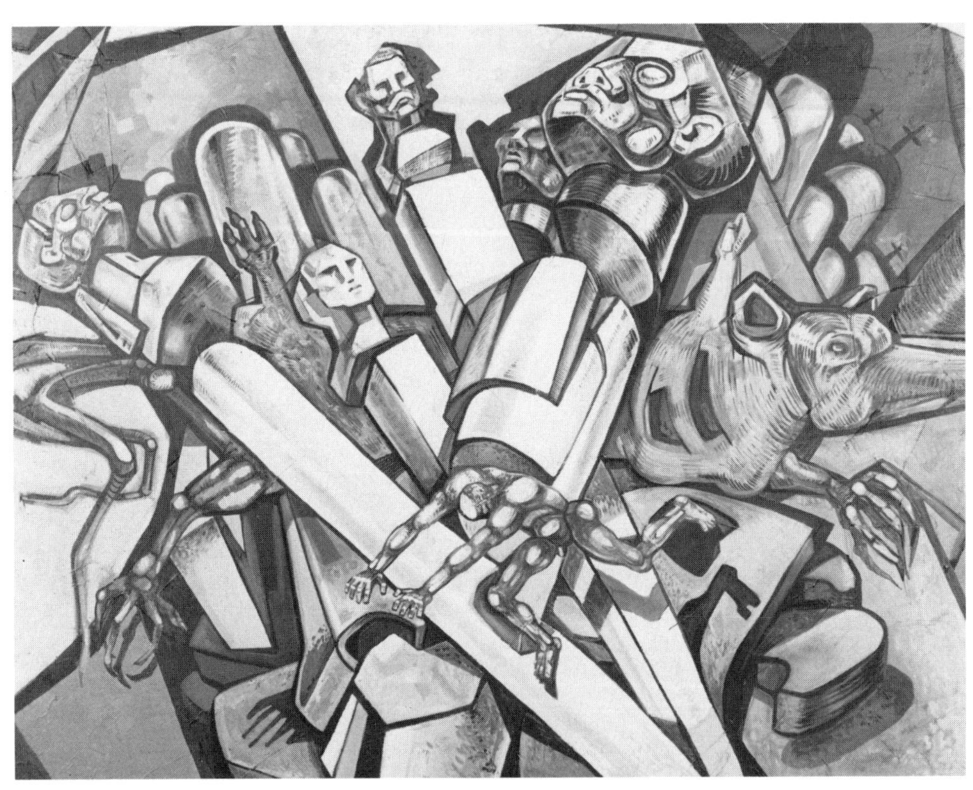

Padaiushchie totemy: Gitler, Stalin, Mussolini, Mao i t.d.
(Falling Totems: Hitler, Stalin, Mussolini, Mao, etc.), 1980-89
Acrylic/Oil, 152.40 x 203.20 cm.
Tree of Life Museum, Uttersberg, Sweden

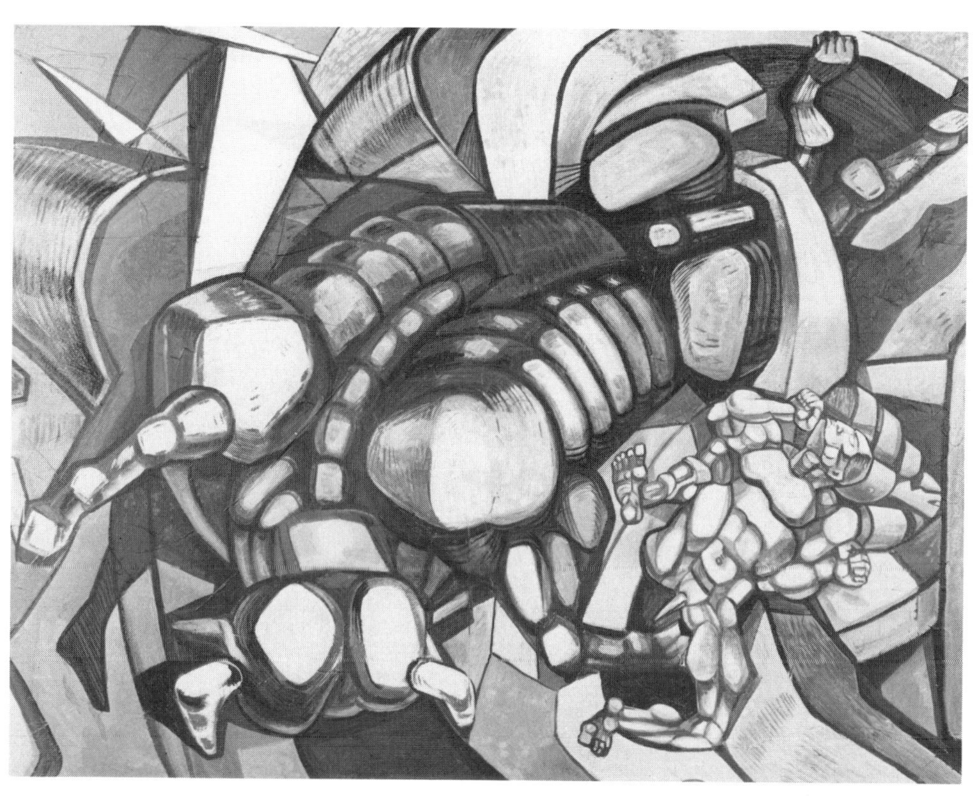

Byk revoliutsii (Bull of Revolution), 1980-89
Acrylic, 152.40 x 203.20 cm.
Tree of Life Museum, Uttersberg, Sweden

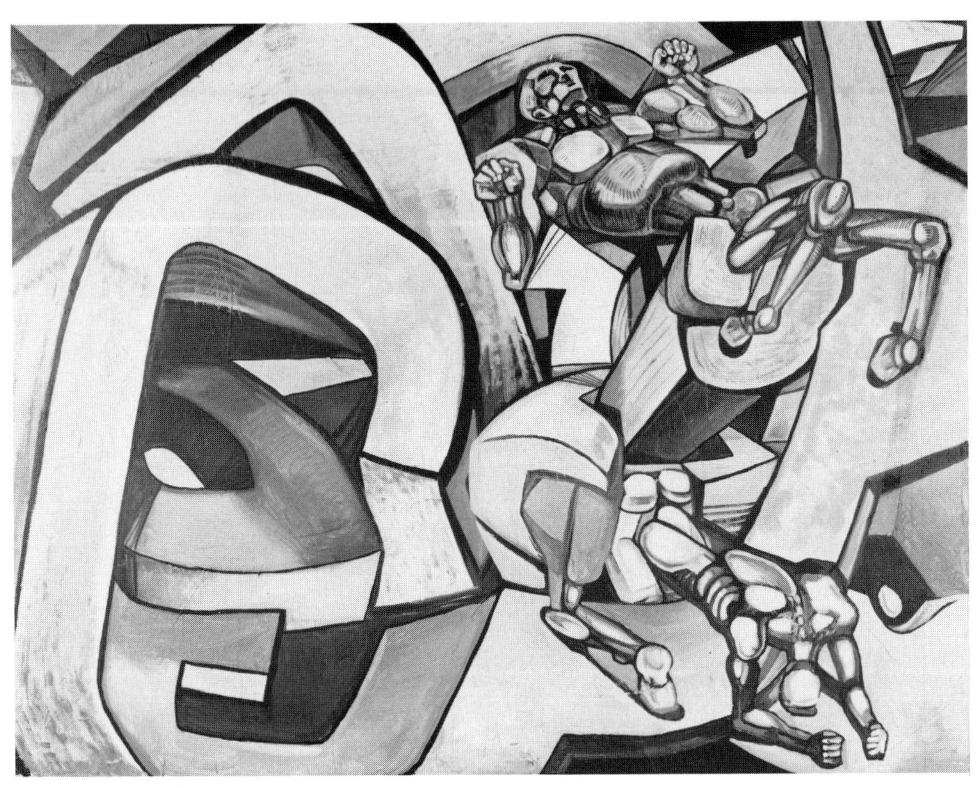

Kentavr i rab (Centaur and Slave), 1980-89
Acrylic, 152.40 x 203.20 cm.
Tree of Life Museum, Uttersberg, Sweden

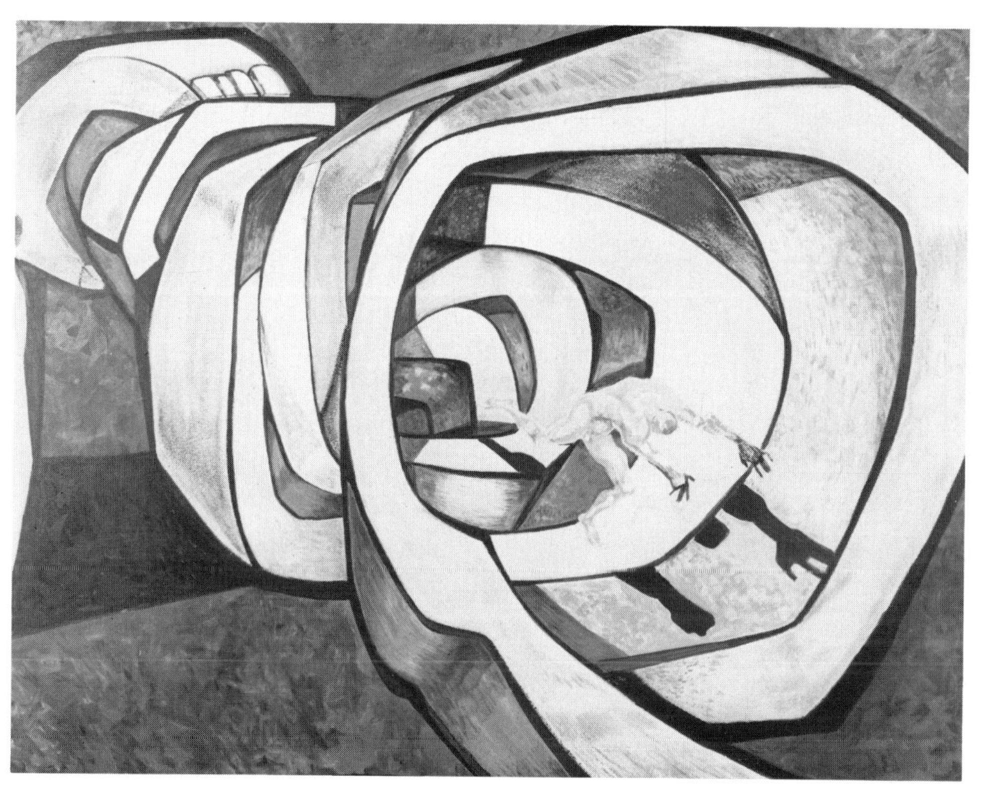

Begstvo iz zheleznogo uzla (Escape from Iron Knot), 1980-89
Acrylic, 152.40 x 203.20 cm.
Tree of Life Museum, Uttersberg, Sweden

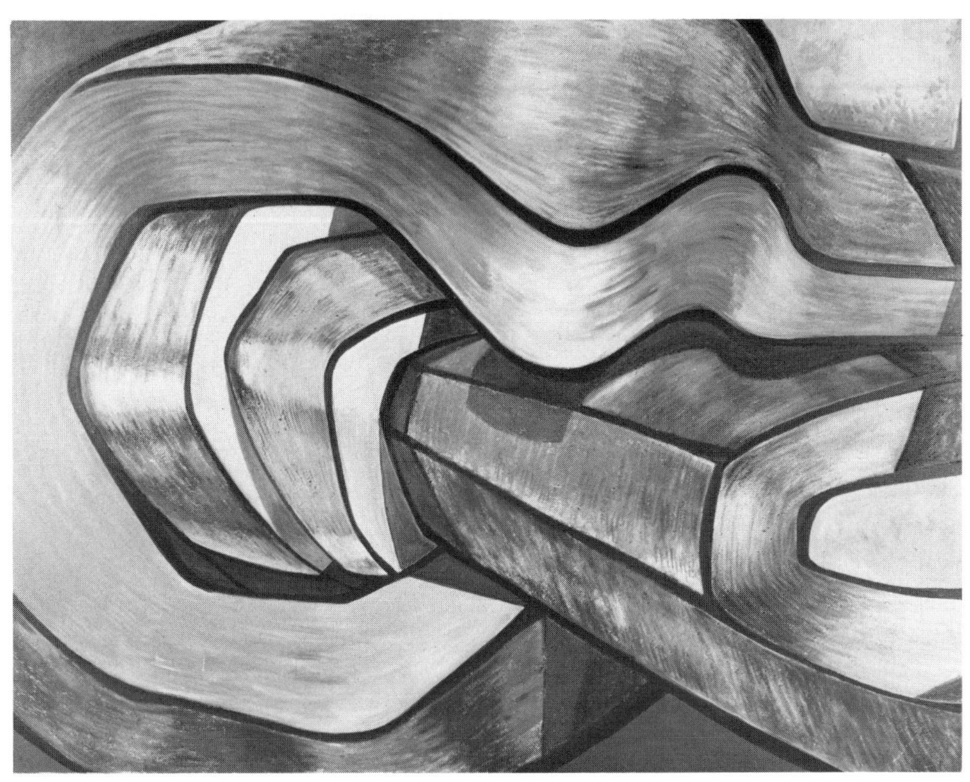

Zheleznyi uzel (Iron Knot), 1980-89
Acrylic, 152.40 x 203.20 cm.
Tree of Life Museum, Uttersberg, Sweden

through this labyrinth with his arms outstretched. He will walk through the labyrinth with the crowd in the most unexpected places: now among us, now on the walls, now on the ceiling. It will be a a figure repeated many times.

After this we enter the central foyer where we step into elevators and ascend to seven levels. How are these elevators designed? In Italy there is an ancient well, where women descend and then come up with water. This well consists of two turns, cut left to right and right to left. The women walk independently, but their movement is opposed. That is how the elevators will move. They shall resemble glass baskets. Moreover, the crest and center of the *Tree of Life* and its elevators shall be designed to repeat the motion of DNA spirals, as well as symbolize the male and female principles. These elevators will move quite slowly, and we shall come out onto seven levels. Glass floors appear in the shape of a fan. The floors allow us to see what is happening above and below without obscuring the representations. Since seven spirals create a completely fantastic number of perspectives and views, we cannot predict all the visual effects that can arise at any given point. I do not strive for these visual effects, which must come about by themselves.

What is depicted on these Moebius spirals? Technically, these spirals consist of reinforced concrete structures resembling honeycombs of the most diverse diameters. These two-sided honeycombs are filled with sculptures, paintings, lighting effects, and moving structures. Since these moving elements will age, they will be replaced. Among them will be different moving machines because modern machines are often more dramatic and refined than works by artists.

Lighting technology, cinema, moving parts, elements from different schools and movements in art – from realism to expressionism, from expressionism to Pop Art,[17] from Pop Art to Op Art[18] – can be exhibited there. What do I have in mind? As machines ought to be replaced, my friends, students, and co-authors can each create objects for the *Tree of Life* I have proposed. These objects can be exhibited, and they can be replaced. Thus, this structure would not only be an attempt at synthesizing various movements and schools in art, at finding a place in the text (because numerous movements in representational art have been torn out of context at the present time), as well as a museum of contemporary technology and various possible hypotheses, but also an active museum of art. When I look upon this structure as a sculpture, the question occurs to me: "How can there be so much in one sculpture?" The *Tree of Life* is indeed absurd, just as works of culture like Dante's *Divine Comedy*, the *Bible*, or many other works are absurd if they are not read from cover to cover. These are all cultural phenomena that are studied. For instance, someone reads *Ecclesiastes*, someone reads another part, some read parts of the *Inferno*, others read the philosophical sections of the *Divine Comedy*. This is multiplicity, but there is unity in this diversity. The shining, pulsating musical face of a heart or a tree is a phenomenon of wholeness. And aesthetically, on the whole, it produces an impression of harmony. When we go inside the *Tree of Life*, we do not need to bring along the expectations we have towards an individual sculpture. The *Tree of Life*, after all, is a building. Otherwise we could just as easily negate the Pompidou Museum and the Louvre in Paris, the Guggenheim Museum in New York, or any scientific-technical exhibition. My attempt here is to combine two principles, as well as many other principles.

Why did I dream up such a severe structure consisting of seven Moebius strips of the seven colors of the spectrum? Why do I fetter my creativity to such strict and mathematical bounds? I have explained my fantasy in terms of the historically determined preconditions of the Russian intelligentsia, of the desire to create a universal system in microcosm. This desire proceeded simply from the very fact of a concrete historical and spiritual situation. But there are broader considerations that can be found not only in Russian culture, but also as an attribute of a definite kind of culture in general.

Relatively speaking, I divide artistic activity (written, musical, and representational) into two types: a tendency towards masterpieces or towards process. The former is when an artist has a definite conception of beauty which he wishes to embody by creating a finished masterpiece; the latter is an existential need when creative work is analogous to breathing, heartbeat, and the activity of one's entire personality. Artists of process usually produce mass works. It is not a question of talent. There are mediocre artists of masterpieces and great artists of process and *vice versa.* For example, Flaubert[19] and Turgenev[20] are artists of masterpieces, while Balzac[21] and Dostoevsky are artists of process. Michelangelo, Van Gogh,[22] Rubens,[23] and Delacroix[24] are artists of process to the highest degree.

Artists of process must integrate their current into a certain system. Their streams must be directed into definite, compressed channels to establish a balance between centrifugal and centripetal forces. The plan of the *Divine Comedy,* which according to Pushkin's words is a brilliant work by itself, was needed by Dante to keep his extraordinarily perfected dynamism and fecundity from disintegrating. It was precisely this mighty inner pressure that produced Dante's striving for self-discipline and self-limitation. Artists of masterpieces in principle do not need to do this because they limit their efforts by their very choice of subject.

For artists of process art is objectified existence, each moment moving, appearing, and dying. And when I want to build my *Tree of Life,* I am almost fully aware of the impossible realization of this project. But I need it in order to work. And its multiplicity does not frighten me because it is reinforced by mathematical unity, because it is self-contained. If someone were to ask me where the center of the *Tree of Life* is, I would reply like the Buddhists, "Everywhere and nowhere." If the project depended on my will, I would extend my representation into infinity: each eye and nostril would contain a new *Tree of Life* and so on into infinity.

I shall say a few words about the light that will be present in this *Tree.* As Father Pavel Florensky[25] liked to say in connection with Russian icon painting, color does not exist; only the light of various oscillations exists. Thus, if it were up to me, I would not paint pictures in the structure, although I paint them for it. But I would create a general program of electronic lighting that would change. At the center of the *Tree of Life* would stand the figure of my *Prophet* with an extruding heart. This heart precisely repeats the form of the *Tree of Life* and the human heart. It would be a mobile, that is, a moving heart that rotates. Inside this heart are set eyes. The whole structure consists of electronic constructions in which a computer program regulates the lighting of the *Tree.* The lighting will radiate from within, and the colors will change in accordance with this electronic program. The rhythm of the *Tree* will be a barely audible heartbeat, and the light within the structure will pulsate in harmony with this heartbeat.

All of this is my effort to combine several principles, to combine the eternal bases of art with its temporary manifestations. The base, the pathetic, and the meaningless are united continuously and eternally by faith to become noble, sublime, and meaningful.[26]

[1] Moebius (See Introduction, note 61).
[2] This section of the essay was published in Russian in Ernst Neizvestny, *O sinteze v iskusstve* (On synthesis in art) [Ann Arbor: Hermitage, 1982], 59-60.
[3] See Chapter One, note 25.
[4] Neizvestny's father was a Russian Orthodox Christian, and his mother is Jewish.
[5] Kandinsky (See Introduction, note 28).
[6] Filonov (See Introduction, note 65).
[7] Malevich (See Introduction, note 29).
[8] Positivism (See Chapter Three, note 22).
[9] Velimir Khlebnikov [Viktor Vladimirovich Khlebnikov] (1885-1922), Russian philologist and Futurist poet.
[10] Mayakovsky (See Introduction, note 74).
[11] Dostoevsky (See Introduction, note 60).
[12] F. M. Dostoevskii, *Prestuplenie i nakazanie* (Crime and punishment) [Moscow: Nauka, 1970].
[13] Existentialism, twentieth-century branch of philosophy which maintains that, since "existence precedes essence," human beings are responsible for what they make of themselves.
[14] St. Augustine (See Chapter Three, note 14).
[15] An allusion to Dostoevsky's novel, *The Insulted and the Humiliated (Unizhennie i oskorblennie).*
[16] Solzhenitsyn (See Chapter Three, note 31).
[17] Pop Art, art movement that arose in 1950s in reaction to abstract expressionism by juxtaposing elements of high and popular culture.
[18] Op Art, abstract art style from 1960s in which patterns and colors are composed to suggest movement on a surface.
[19] Gustave Flaubert (1821-80), French master of the realistic novel, author of *Madame Bovary* (1856).
[20] Turgenev (See Chapter One, note 16).

[21] Balzac (See Chapter Three, note 3).
[22] Vincent Van Gogh (1853-1900), major Dutch post-impressionist painter.
[23] Peter Paul Rubens (1577-1640), leading seventeenth-century Flemish painter.
[24] Eugene Delacroix (1798-1863), foremost painter of romantic movement in France.
[25] Florensky (See Introduction, note 67).
[26] This part of the essay was published in Russian in *Govorit Neizvestnyi* (Neizvestny speaks) [Frankfurt: Possev-Verlag, 1984], 139-55.

CHAPTER FIVE

Discovering the New

Until recently implacable assessment of other artists' creative work and non-acceptance on principle of anything that tends to distinguish itself from traditional norms were among the attributes of a good, authentic artist. Each day our lives brought us new facts about the world. Much of what seemed to us new and indisputable yesterday has already become dated today. The bounds of knowledge have been extended continuously. The world in which we live is expanding with unbelievable speed. The world of the cosmos and the microcosmos is yielding us its astonishing secrets, and there seems to be no end to the stream of information accessible to us.

Our time is a time of spurts and hyperaccelerated motion, and today we seek new connections in life. The contemporary artist is a person whose worldview is as complex as current conceptions of the structure of the universe. The genuine artist has always been equal to the spiritual achievements of his contemporaries. Indeed, can you imagine a modern scientist who accepts, in advance, the absolute truth of theories developed before his time? Would such a person still be considered a scholar? And can you imagine a scientist who is satisfied once and for all with the results of his experiments, who does not attempt to extend his theory further or even to discard it for the sake of scientific progress? Modern man prizes achievements and does not erect monuments to himself.

It is only possible to attain such achievements by acknowledging the possibility of contributions made by co-workers in laboratories and studios, and not just personal discoveries. That is why breadth of view is not only a rule uniting artists and realists, but also a precondition of progressive thought and, consequently, of progressive creative work.

I wish to express several thoughts without any claims to absolute truth. These thoughts are instruments that facilitate my work. Let us agree at the outset that when we speak of the artist, we have in mind an authentic artist, and not a servile hack pandering to what is fashionable. And when we speak of the spectator, we have in mind a person who is prepared to experience any manifestation of creative work seriously and in good faith and who understands that the artist serves society not as a buffoon nor as a popularizer who says "as you all know," but as a stonemason building humankind's aesthetic and spiritual world. When we speak of "form," we mean only that content which has assumed the appearance needed for creative work. And by "idea" we mean the concrete embodiment of the idea that lies at the basis of creative work. There can be no creative work without an idea. Similarly, any idea is born in a creative way.

The scientist and the artist both increase knowledge of the world to an equal degree, although the external form of their contributions differs. Image and intuition, concept and symbol enter into the creative work of artist and scientist in different stages and in different proportions. But the nature of art contains presentiments of scientific truth. Indeed, we artists know that aerodynamic forms were generated by art – though in a rather obvious, impure way – earlier than those forms could be realized practically in theory and in mechanics. Tense curves won a place in art before the trajectory of cosmic flight could be calculated and plotted. The ancient Egyptian pyramids incorporated laws that were discovered by Pythagoras[1] much later. Modern study of the pyramids suggests that the aesthetic experiments of Egyptian architects foreshadowed many discoveries that were made afterwards. The stone masonry of the Kremlin[2] arches in Moscow have been shown to be optimal in light of recent scientific discoveries about the strength of building materials. Forms associated with a reality recently illuminated by science enter our everyday lives. Though the world, both the microcosmos and the macrocosmos, and discoveries made possible by the electron microscope, by telescopes, and by radioastronomy have immeasurably broadened our perception of the wealth of forms in the universe, many of those forms have been long anticipated by artists who embodied them in their works. It was not cold invention, but the multiplicity of forms of existing material and the personal experience of people generalized and condensed by the artist that produced new forms in art. All works constructed "intentionally" and speculatively are moribund. Therefore, the artist must study life. Einstein[3] once said that Dostoevsky[4] helped him to discover the theory of relativity. Why Dostoevsky? Because Dostoevsky profoundly and sharply experienced life, boldly and unsparingly conducted experiments on the human psyche.

To launch a complex circle of associations and depart from dogmas, one must overcome stagnation in oneself before one can actually displace the boulders of outdated concepts. Intuition and imagination are essential for any kind of creative work. And, indeed, did scientists not imagine things they could not see, such as the structure of an atom or the structure of genetic material? A scientist fantasizes and has premonitions. All the more so with artists. From my viewpoint, only a step into the "unknown" is creativity. This step can be apparent, unnoticed at first, or be expressed externally in traditional form. But creativity must be movement into the unknown.

At the present time, when the consciousness of modern man strives towards more general concepts and the elimination of redundant information, there can and should be no place for the endless repetition of commonplaces. Machines have been invented for thinking and computing so that people are now freed from a passive contemplation of the world that is alien to human nature. Humankind was born to create, not to count what already exists. Thought-action, not thought-contemplation, is characteristic of modern man. The program of our Party states that science should become a productive force. The image of the artist as a person reflecting the empirical surface of phenomena, and not as a person creating and transforming the world, is thoroughly scholastic and contradicts the concept of man as a creator. The time has come for the artist-philosopher. It is naive to display, next to endless photo-essays in newspapers, remarks by painters and sculptors about summer, spring, or vases of flowers: "Summer is blossoming, and spring its precursor. A flower embodies the process of growth." Only the art of ideas can inspire the modern spectator burdened by countless facts. The viewer expects the artist to create objectified concepts. A primitive person visually perceives a tree as a trunk with foliage and, palpably, with smooth or rough bark, with a thick or thin form. We artists can also see and experience the tree that way, but for us the tree is much more than that. Any schoolchild knows that a tree is a laboratory producing chlorophyll and that our breathing depends on trees. One can speak of even more complex circles of associations. What is important is not that the tree stands, but that it is growing. A tree is a world consisting of many laws, each of which can become a subject for poetry because the links and laws of the forest can be discerned in the tree. What is important is the thought that becomes the flesh of art. Eternal and contemporary! "The same heavenly stars gladden us . . ." *(Te zhe nas raduiut zvezdy nebesnye . . .)*. Yes, the same stars, but not as they were for Aleksei Konstantinovich Tolstoy.[5] In the age of astronauts the stars remain the same as they were before, but people have already seen the infinite abyss of cosmic space and the blue radiance of the planet Earth.

In the human spiritual sphere the creative activity of the artist and the scientist is necessarily interdependent. The artist broadens the circle of associations and feelings, including those of the scientist. The scientist broadens humanity's concept of the world and reveals new possibilities for the artist's creative work. The artist today needs the scientist's discoveries for his own work. Many modern scientists in cybernetics, physics, and mathematics take a great interest in experimental works of art because thought processes are most apparent in such works. Machines that compose poetry have been invented to anatomize thought processes. Those works of art which exhibit not only the result, but also the process of creation, attract the attention of some scientists most of all. One could say that one of the most obvious attributes of contemporary art is *the artist's desire to integrate the spectator, almost as co-author, into the creative process itself.*

The Soviet art journal *Iskusstvo* has asked me to state my views on "plastic expressiveness in sculpture" and, in this connection, on my present work and plans. Here is what excites me now. If I were asked to define the beautiful, I would reply: "Tension, dramatic forms expressing a great idea intellectually and sensuously." Beauty is what is expressed. The dead is not intense, for it is deprived of the possibility of growth. Life, under tension, overcomes obstacles in itself by moving. Motion and repose are beautiful. The indifferent is amorphous and revolting. Formalism is somnolent feeling and formal indifference to the subject depicted. A sculptural representation is three-dimensional. A spatial composition can arouse aesthetic excitement in a viewer if his vision is trained. For the unprepared spectator space is only extension. Similarly, an uncultivated ear serves only utilitarian aims: to hear what is said.

A sense of three-dimensionality is developed by sculpture. Therefore, I try to make each work not merely an object and thing, but also as "organized" and "conquered" space. Inside the sculpture itself are masses and protrusions. Explosions also create a definite rhythm, now nervous, tranquil, grave, elegiac. I try to accent this rhythm, but the main thing is a striving for compositional unity, since compositional thought is one of the basic preconditions of tension. What is compositional thought? It is clarity and unsparing delimitation of the thought content of the work, as if it were produced in one outburst of creativity. A good sculpture is one that cannot be spoiled, such as the altar of Pergamon[6] or *Nike of Samothrace.*[7] Everything already exists in the rhythm of these works. Therefore, these sculptures bear the original idea, even when they have been destroyed by time or by people.

In the very first quick sketch, in even the skeleton of a sculpture, the idea of its future form should be embedded like an embryo, so that all that remains is to complete its development. But unexpected thoughts and peripheral images arise in the process of creative work. I retain those thoughts and images which accompany the original idea. Improvisation is often closer to truth than *apriori* reflections leading to practical creative work. But I direct this improvisation into the channel determined in advance by the theme. In myths about centaurs, people with wings were fantasies. Now, instantaneous flight through space is an everyday occurrence. I am working on a system of symbols and metaphors consonant with our times. What is a centaur in reality? It is man and nature conjoined. And what is a sphinx? It is a winged person with the power of a lion. Nowadays, however, horses and lions are no longer symbols of strength. Technology and science have given us the power to be as menacing as lions and to fly swifter than eagles. But how can man and technology be linked organically? In the same ideal manner as the Egyptian artists did by combining a human face with the body of a lion, or as the ancients did by fusing the torso of a man with that of a horse.

For these combinations to become plastic art it is necessary to conduct many experiments on the organic linkage of the hard, the artificial, and the metallic with what is real, soft, and human. These are new linkages. But one must overcome habitual associations in oneself to discover new linkages in art. It does not take much strength to overcome vulgar scholasticism. But it is extremely difficult to overcome fixed notions of good and bad taste, to overcome the snob in oneself. Ultimately, good taste is nothing to brag about. What is important is not how an artist perceives someone else's creative work, but what he creates himself. Acquiring good taste is just as hard and easy as learning good manners. An artist who possesses good taste, but who does not attempt to develop anything new or extend the boundaries of his own creative work, is making use of the sufferings and quests of other artists who are in essence canonized, albeit unofficially. Thus, what constituted good manners in the past petrifies the artist as to the content of art. It seems to me that this is a rather provincial attitude, but it was developed as the antithesis to tedious academic stories and pictures about various occasions, to reportage illustrated with pictures. But the content, not the plot, comprises the work itself. For that reason, a person – unless he is a bourgeois – has no need of a notion of plastic art freed from complex philosophic content and designed to afford only pleasure.

I think quite often about the viewer. I have come to the conclusion that an artist has the right to be incomprehensible, but to make this his slogan would be a transgression. The artist always wants to be understood by as many people as possible. It is always a tragedy for an artist to be misunderstood. Moreover, the spectators have the responsibility to look actively, without bias, and with as much attention as they listen to a concert or read a complex modern novel. I know what joy awaits a person when he or she comprehends not only the external form of a symphony, but also understands and senses the inner beauty of its unifying idea. Joy of perception, then, equals the joy of creation.

Modern metaphors and the search for tension in sculpture have helped me greatly in my work on specific projects of urban construction. In monumental art the idea of a work commissioned by society is expressed with greatest directness. For that reason, one of the main problems is clarity and emotional impact on the viewer. Here, all the accumulated experience of the artist ought to be activated and his whole arsenal of techniques ought to be used, so that a protracted complex project can proceed towards clarity without losing the tension stemming from the intellectual content of the original idea.

At the present time notions of aesthetics have changed sharply in urban construction. We artists are obliged to reflect on the problem of contemporary monumentality. Architects help us to overcome many prejudices and moribund schemas, but our link with architects and scientists is reciprocal and interdependent. Nowadays, Soviet architecture frequently addresses merely applied problems of decor and nonwhimsical design. But synthesis anticipates the content of both arts. Synthesis is complex interrelation, when the representation not only expands the idea of the structure, but also is an independent work that often contrasts with the architecture. Subordination of representation to architecture occurs when even a sculpture taken from the structure contains the pulse of the scale and image of the architectural ensemble. Ideological art, not design, is a constituent part of an architectural ensemble. Multifaceted experiments in artists' studios should not only adorn a modern building, but also assist in its construction as rational and aesthetic links of one whole. In practice they are unfailingly interchangeable, with one leading to the other. The qualities of cement have been known since the sixteenth century, but cement did not seem to be a material beautiful enough to replace stone. However, cement was considered not only rational, but also beautiful in the aesthetic sense, in the experiments conducted by Le Corbusier[8] in the twentieth century. I doubt that this could have happened without Le Corbusier's experiments as an artist or the achievements of Picasso[9] and his circle. Rhythm, texture, tension, the complex and organic understanding of space, the study of the variegated world of natural forms – from intricate human anatomical constructions to tortoises, sea shells, and one-celled animals – this multiformed world of the artist enables builders and engineers to find more rational and, at the same time, beautiful forms. The line of tension of the Eiffel Tower[10] and its construction correspond to the lines of tension and construction of the human skeleton. An experiment in the studio of an artist enters into the workshop of an architect. It is much easier to conduct searches in the quiet of a studio than in architecture itself: a building is enormously expensive. Because architects enable us to overcome the present vulgarity of art that depicts everyday life and the snobbery of pseudo-aesthetic art, we ought to help them shape the plastic appearance of the modern world.

It is hard today to draw a line between representational and applied art. In the field of industrial aesthetics it is no secret that the Soviet Union learns from foreign countries such as Czechoslovakia, where industrial designers are allowed to experiment more boldly. To create an indigenous school of industrial aesthetics, it is necessary to encourage experiments by artists who work not only in the field of applied art.

We have little personal experience in this area. There is tradition, the accumulated experience of centuries. But which tradition should we turn to? It seems to me that medieval Russian art, ancient Greek art, and the art of ancient Mexico and Egypt are near to us.[11] It is hard to imagine the building of a modern cosmodrome decorated with reliefs in the spirit of sculpture from the period of the decline of monumentalism at the beginning of the twentieth century. It is difficult to imagine a lyrical monument to commemorate the conquest of Mars.

Our life demands generalizations and great philosophical ideas that can stir enormous masses of people today. Therefore, close to us are the arts of intense, complex, and holistic folk cultures of the past – that is, philosophical arts and not arts serving petty castes, whether descriptive or entertaining. I, for instance, like the experience of Mexico.[12] I do not mean that we should work like the Mexicans do, but their approach to things is instructive. Let us make use of the traditions of our forebears, multiplied by the experience of what is most modern and progressive in art. Naturally, this is not a mechanical, but a complex process in which the personality of the artist who assimilates these traditions plays a vital role. We have temple paintings, the wood sculpture of the Perm' region,[13] reliefs on white stone, and many other traditions. We have a holistic world view and an enormous young state. We can erect new cities according to plan. Is it not for us to create progressive monumental art?[14]

[1] Pythagoras (c570-c500 BC), Greek philosopher and founder of Pythagorean School, which formulated the concept of the soul and affirmed a life of moderation.
[2] Kremlin, walled citadels characteristic of medieval Russian cities
[3] Albert Einstein (1879-1955), German-born Swiss-American theoretical physicist and author of theory of relativity; Nobel Laureate in Physics (1921).
[4] Dostoevsky (See Introduction, note 60).
[5] Aleksei Konstantinovich Tolstoy (1817-75), Russian poet, novelist, dramatist who wrote collective works with cousins under the name of "Koz'ma Prutkov."
[6] Altar of Pergamon (Turkey), sculptural frieze (c200-150 BC) for great altar to Zeus.
[7] Nike of Samothrace, Greek sculpture of goddess of victory.
[8] Le Corbusier [Charles-Edouard Jeanneret] (1887-1965), Swiss-born French architect and a founder of the international style of modern architecture.
[9] Picasso (See Introduction, note 26).
[10] Eiffel Tower, Paris (1887-89), created by French engineer Alexandre Gustave Eiffel (1832-1923).
[11] Neizvestny cites ancient metaphysical cultures that celebrated monumental art.
[12] A reference to great Mexican muralists of the twentieth century, such as Diego Rivera (1886-1957) and José Orozco (1883-1949).
[13] Neizvestny was profoundly influenced by the wooden folk

sculptures of Perm'.

[14]This essay, first published in Russian in *Iskusstvo,* No. 10 (1962), was reprinted in *Posev,* No. 13 (29 March 1963) and in *Govorit Neizvestnyi* (Neizvestny speaks) [Frankfurt: Possev-Verlag, 1984].

CHAPTER SIX

Bronze

For a sculptor the history of bronze is the history of civilization. We encounter bronze in the earliest epochs: Egyptian, Assyrian,[1] Phoenician,[2] Etruscan.[3] The Bible tells us about King Hiram of Tyre[4] who cast bronze for the Temple of Jerusalem during the reign of Solomon.[5] The basic principles for the technical art of casting statues were developed during the time of Kir[6] and Krez in the sixth century B.C. From that time on the principles of casting bronze have remained the same as those used on the isle of Samos.[7]

Bronze is formed from alloys of copper, tin, and zinc, along with other metals and metalloids such as lead, magnesium, silicon, phosphorus. Bronze is a unique material for sculpture. Melted, it seeks to fill space. Like lava or a fiery river, it surges into a form and, cooling, assumes the contours of a sculpture. Each time I cast a sculpture, I see something cosmic in this process of transforming fire into form. Bronze is extraordinarily sensitive. It reproduces the smallest irregularities on the surface of a sculpture – the touch of an instrument and even the sculptor's fingerprints. Without exaggeration one can say that we can discern the sculptor's temperament and moods by the surface of a bronze sculpture. While cooling, sensitive bronze becomes mighty and powerful. It resists destruction, breakage, rupture. It is hard, resilient, viscous. It is severe. It was no accident that cannon balls were cast from bronze. In the Soviet Union bronze was declared a strategic raw material and could be used by a sculptor only with permission from the Council of Ministers, and only by those sculptors whose works were regarded as ideological weapons, that is, as cannon balls. That is why Nikita Khrushchev[8] and Shelepin,[9] head of the KGB,[10] accused me of unauthorized use of bronze for sculpture. Bronze in their opinion was a material for war, not for art. But this terrifying bronze can also be pliable and malleable in the skillful hands of a sculptor. After casting, the small jewel-like bronzes of Benvenuto Cellini[11] were painstakingly engraved. The tiniest details were meticulously refined. The form of a bronze work is related not only to sight and touch, but also to sound. The various tones of bells, percussion instruments, and Chinese cymbals exploit these qualities of bronze. One feels like composing poems in honor of bronze. At the present time I am completing a bronze model of my "Tree of Life" monument that will measure sixteen meters in height. In this work I shall utilize all the possibilities of bronze, including the musical. I would like this monument to be my poem in honor of bronze.

In everyday work the fusibility of bronze and its commanding aggressiveness in seizing space stir me most of all. I once had to work as a foundry hand in a factory that built railway cars in the Ural Mountain city of Sverdlovsk[12] where I was born. Secretly, at night after work, I would try to make sculptures from scraps of leftover metal. There being little time, I would press out a future sculpture in the casting sand, improvising without a model. A counter-relief would be produced, that is, the deepest part of the relief would become most prominent after casting. While I was pressing out the form, I tried to imagine it as an enormous landscape with mountains, plateaus, plains, and rivers. Looking upon the flow of bronze in the form of a negative, I came to understand that the current of this fiery lava and river had its own systematic laws and attempted to create the form in which this irresistible bronze would freely and organically spread out. Imagine the eruption of a volcano, and imagine the landscape and the region around it. Lava, erupting and pouring forth, courses organically along the contours of the land, naturally filling voids and cavities. But the area, the landscape relief I created by the flow of molten metal was not accidental. I opposed a sculptor's might against the might of metal, that is, I entered into a dialogue with unadorned bronze, attempting to extract the most expressive qualities from it.

My fundamental attitude towards sculpture was formed by the end of the 1960s. In 1960-61 I wrote an essay entitled *On Synthesis in Art*.[13] Since my basic approach to sculpture has remained the same, the following passage on sculpture from that essay remains pertinent:

> In this connection I would like to say a few words about sculpture, which we shall provisionally describe as dialogical.[14] Or, more precisely, we shall speak about the possibility of developing the synthesis inherent in sculpture. In speaking of dialogical sculpture, it is difficult to think about the beautiful while proceeding only from the classical monological notion of the human body. Rather, what is beautiful about it is the state of soul of a person, that is, what is indifferent and under tension as manifested in the form of a sculpture. But it is not merely what is under tension as physical form, but form and space in their interaction that express psychology and, more than psychology, the spiritual life of a person. In this instance, sculpture is not simply a quantity of surrounding physical material, organized according to the external form of a person, animal, or other natural or geometrical forms and situated in space: the sculpture contains within itself a dialogue between spirit and flesh. The sculpture is one, but it is not homogeneous.
>
> . . . .
>
> A sculpture has appeared in which heterogeneous elements, realistically existing parts comprise the whole in the conflict, engulfment, and collaboration of many principles, where everything is fraught with contradiction, a sculpture

caught up in Heraclitean flux,[15] a form emerging into space or engulfing it, one part restraining the other or repelling it. The metallic and the softly organic appear in combat and interlocked: the soft flows into the hard, the hard compresses and transforms the soft. A sculpture, its volume as if compressed from all sides by an external force, but resisting this force or expanding from the center, as though someone were tugging it apart from without, while the central nucleus keeps it from rupturing.

In this manner the dramatic quality of the sculpture is conditioned by the presence within it of heterogeneous principles and impulses, and its movement becomes not only a pose or a form in space, but mainly motion inside the form itself. This kind of sculpture can contain within itself the Apollonian principle of perfected form (man) and the Dionysian principle of movement (destruction of man). In its movement it implants the man in man, the child in an old man, and a person into stone. Machinery containing both male and female principles and a tree contain in themselves people, just as people contain in themselves the whole evolution of earthly creatures and the most complex products of their hands. In this manner a sculptural composition is created in which all things exist everywhere and the least part is just as great and intense as a large one.

And only the sculptor's will, the flow of the composition's rhythm magnifies or diminishes the scale of what is depicted. But each part of the representation is a titan finished in its form and breaking out of its small dimensions, a giant attempting to part, broaden, and fill everything. Such a sculpture, obviously, cannot be contained within the bounds of Euclidean or Kantian space and does not look upon space in general as homogeneous. In this way the parts of a sculpture make up a whole in struggle, engulfment, and repulsion. Such a sculpture is not a static object, but an object embodying a contradictory process of being, where each thing, fraught with its very opposite, has not one but several meanings.

Of course this is only my goal. In each individual sculpture it is impossible to realize one's concept fully. This is true of my monument, *The Tree of Life,* on which I have been working my whole life. Separate bronze sculptures represent only a part of this project, which on principle is intended to be polyphonic and monumental.

Monumentality

Monumentality is not a function of size. Not everything large in scale is monumental, nor is the small necessarily a miniature in effect. Monumentality is a rhythm embedded in the interrelationship of forms. Of course an authentically monumental piece of sculpture that is enlarged only gains in impact. Enlarged, it becomes expressive. But we can see the same principle and melody at work in a small bronze sculpture. It is as if a small-scale model of a monumental sculpture genetically embodies all the elements of its larger counterpart, and *vice versa.* There are sculptors who work well only on a small scale. It is absolutely impossible to enlarge their works and transform them into monuments. It would be just as ridiculous and useless to expect a miniature poodle to turn into a Great Dane someday. We often destroy their merits by enlarging these small-scale sculptures.

Similarly, the sense of hearing is better developed in our times than the sense of sight. What do I mean? Almost anyone can hear the difference between chamber music and a mighty symphony, between the sounds of classical and rock music, between a lyrical melody and a military march. The musical imagination of contemporary man is more highly developed than his sense of space. Space is often perceived as a practical category – far/near, high/low, wide/narrow – but not an aesthetic one. Therefore, the expression, "what a disgusting sound!" is often heard as an aesthetic judgment, but almost never "what a disgusting space!" And even if you do hear this, it is in the sense of something uncomfortable in practice. The sense of space, the sense of sculptural rhythm is rare in our times. Therefore, we monumental sculptors are grateful to our collectors who understand the intended scope of a monument in a small-scale model and who are not afraid to adorn their homes with models of future monuments.

In many of his essays Henry Moore[16] remembers people who made it possible for him to work. I share his sentiments, since collectors have become our friends and share our thoughts. Any small bronze sculpture of Henry Moore's is monumental. It conquers space and emanates from natural forms. Pebbles chiseled by the sea, the outlines of wind-shaped mountains, and mysterious caves are the basis of his sculptures. They are pantheistic, and the rhythms of the ocean are inherent in them. Although these sculptures were crafted in our age, they emanate something altogether ancient, pre-Christian, and infused with elementally natural emotions. Their tectonics are compact and stone-like. Moore masterfully utilized the unique qualities of bronze. For the most part he sculpted and chiseled his works directly in plaster, polishing large rounded surfaces and leaving traces of his chisel on the transitional planes to create tension. We see the same play of texture in nature in animal bones and sea stones. But Moore's principal power is apparent in his three-dimensional vision of sculpture. Once, in a conversation with him, I asked him about the meaning of holes in sculpture. He replied, "A hole in a sculpture creates the sensation of three-dimensionality and makes it possible for one to sense its volume without walking around it." "And why do you have holes in your sculptures?" he asked me. "Because I have a hole in my body," I jested, referring to my loss of three ribs on the Ukrainian Front in World War II. Moore thought about this and said, "It turns out that I am a classicist and you are a romantic." To a certain extent he was right, because for me a hole in a sculpture is an element of psychological expressiveness, rather than a formal one. However, the one does not exclude the other. Henry Moore sought epical rhythms and always aspired to large size and scale. He once told me that he suffered his whole life from the impossibility of reproducing his models on the size and scale that his concept demanded. I understand this quite well. I do not tire of repeating that the artist is always a Gulliver[17] who lives and befriends giants and dwarfs. The artist always tries to tear himself away from the mundane and to pass into another dimension. The very small and the very large are poetic in our awareness if we have not lost a child's spontaneous, wise way of seeing or the lofty wisdom of great folk cultures, the plastic music of which is always based on the contrast of great and small.

Monumentalism

The purest examples of monumentalism, one could say its formula, are the Egyptian Pyramids[18] and the Sphinx.[19] A monumental sign is enbedded in the very contour and rhythm of these forms. No matter how we break up a pyramid by cutting off one segment after another, its form remains in our consciousness. It is all the same even if we destroy a pyramid to its very foundations, for by the direction of the foundation stones we can outline the pyramid's entire volume up to its uppermost stone. We cannot annihilate the pyramid's monumental rhythm. Similarly, the passage of time cannot destroy the Sphinx. Eroded by the desert sands, the surface of the sculpture does not hinder us from seeing the sign of a reclining animal with a human face. A severed paw or another part of its body is restored in our consciousness and occupies its intended place, just as a lizard in nature regenerates a severed tail. Look at the Greek *Nike of Samothrace*.[20] Although it is not as generalized as the Sphinx, although it is more baroque and lacks arms and a head, this figure of Victory moves forward swiftly and absolutely. The sign of motion is powerfully embedded in this sculpture. That is why I study the great sculptors of the past and present. That is what I am striving for in my small bronzes, which I look upon always as models of larger sculptures. I aspire towards archetypes, signs, and rhythms. A cross by itself, in its lines of tension, has the vertical axis of a human body and the horizontal axis in the outstretched arms of a crucified person. The sign of the cross is so expressive in itself that it would be possible to stop at the frame, barely outlining the figure of a human being, as Giacometti,[21] one of my favorite sculptors and an artist of astonishing purity of mystery, has done.

Giacometti

Giacometti's bronzes are drawn out in the gothic manner. Shadows, signs as if crushed and pushed out by space, reach upwards, emaciated until the frame and skeleton of the sculpture are revealed. These are tragic signs of life. These are no longer bodies, but rather the idea of a body and its parts. The idea of a nose or hand, the idea of people walking or standing. His bronzes are emaciated and reduced to the face or profile of a human figure. Giacometti makes maximal use of bronze's ability, unlike that of stone, to be strong even in a very thin mass. The surface of these bronze bodies and shadows are extremely agitated and lacerated, reminding us of impressionistic modeling, but in no way repeating its striving for illusory effects or attempting to imitate painting. The surface of Giacometti's sculptures appears to be bitten off by space, which compresses these figures, emaciated to immateriality and attempting to depart from life. These ideas and formulas were developed by Giacometti to the level of the hieroglyphs[22] of Egyptian sculpture. Giacometti worked on a small scale. But he is monumental. Looking at his works, you understand that monumentality of sculpture does not depend on whether the work is large or small.

I love and respect Giacometti and Henry Moore. Once, in Austria, an exhibition of works by Moore, Giacometti, and myself was in preparation under the title, "Three Men in the Same Jeep." Alas, the moguls of Soviet culture did not let me ride in that jeep.

But my temperament, my life experience, and my sense of time and space naturally are somewhat different from theirs. I deviate from their terseness. The most important thing in art for me is tension. The tension of the material is the tension of metal, of the geometrical forms of machines, or of the organic forms of anatomical bodies. These tensions are generated by the spiritual life of the sculptor. The more intense the inner life of an artist, the more this intensity is expressed in the tension of the form created. This tension can be expressed both in the dynamics and statics of the work, in minimalism and in maximalism. There is a certain mystery here. When we look at the polished surface of a bronze by Brancusi[23] or Arp,[24] we sense the pressure pressing against these sculptures from within. When we compare a real apple with an exact wax copy of it, we sense the energy radiated by the living apple and the lifelessness of the wax replica. If we use time-lapse photography to film the ripening of an apple day by day and then project this film in real time, we will see the dramatic growth of this apple from the center to the surface. A ripening apple is filled with energy pressing against its skin to the point of bursting. An apple is brimming with the life force or *vita* given us by God.

A sculpture is energized by the will and spiritual experiences of the sculptor. If an artist does not have these experiences, no matter how you polish the surface or mimick spiritual life in the work, no matter how you cut into it to break up its surface, the sculpture will not be looked upon as a living apple, but a replica. It is possible to steal and reproduce anything but intelligence, temperament, and talent.

Ever since I began to sculpt bronze, I always wanted to create my sculptures, like apples, from the inside, as if pressing out its form. When I work, I usually look at my sculpture and intuitively (or is it something else besides?) take measure, coordinating my inner feeling of tension with what I see in my sculpture. And almost never does my inner feeling correspond to what I see before me. "Some more tension?" I ask myself, "Still more?" And I begin to add to or reduce the form of the sculpture, but always as if I were working from within the sculpture itself. I want to feel like a fetus of a pregnant sculpture pushing against its mother's womb: I press out, spread out, pull in, make holes, even out, bend out – but only from within.

Because I wish to say so much, my sculptures are overgrown with extra elements that complicate my general idea. But I always strive to have the fundamental melody contain the improvisations and caprices departing from this center. This is precisely why the idea of a sign or archetype is so important to me. The additional elements and details are only instrumentation, counterpoint, and pauses intensifying the expressiveness of the whole work. They should enter into the sign of a cross, the sign of a totem, the sign of a centaur, the sign of a heart. They create multiplicity in unity. They help to develop the tension inherent in me which I attempt to transmit to my sculptures.[25]

[1] Assyria, ancient Near Eastern kingdom situated in Mesopotamia.
[2] Phoenicia, ancient territory (c3000 BC) situated in coastal region of present-day Lebanon.
[3] Etruscan civilization of Etruria (6th century BC).
[4] King Hiram of Tyre, a friend of David and Solomon who provided material for the Temple of Jerusalem.
[5] Solomon (See Chapter Three, note 12).

[6] Kir, unidentified land and home of the Aramaeans cited in *Kings*, *Isaiah*, and *Amos*.
[7] Samos, Greek island on which lived Aesop, Anacreon, Pythagoras, and the sculptor Rhoecus.
[8] Nikita Sergeevich Khrushchev (1894-1971), Ukrainian-born Soviet premier (1954-64).
[9] Aleksandr Nikolaevich Shelepin (1918-), head of KGB (1958-61).
[10] KGB (Committee for State Security), Soviet political police.
[11] Benvenuto Cellini (1500-1571), Italian goldsmith and artist known for his *Perseus with the Head of Medusa* and his *Autobiography* (1558-62).
[12] Sverdlovsk, formerly Ekaterinburg, Ural Mountain city named in 1924 after Russian politician and revolutionary leader, Iakov Mikhailovich Sverdlov (1885-1919).
[13] See Chapter One.
[14] Neizvestny's concept of dialogical art is based on the work of Bakhtin (See Chapter Two, note 44).
[15] Heraclitus (c540-c480), Greek philosopher who believed in universal impermanence and the interrelation of all things.
[16] Moore (See Chapter One, note 17).
[17] *Gulliver's Travels* (1726) by Jonathan Swift.
[18] See Chapter One, note 10.
[19] Sphinx, mythical monster combining a lion with a human head, symbol of Egyptian pharoah.
[20] See Chapter Five, note 7.
[21] Alberto Giacometti (1901-66), Swiss-born sculptor and painter known for his elongated, skeletal figures expressing human isolation.
[22] Hieroglyphs, pictorial characters found on ancient Egyptian monuments.
[23] Constantin Brancusi (1876-1957), Romanian sculptor known for simple, polished forms such as "Bird in Space" (1919).
[24] Jean Arp (1887-1966), Franco-Swiss artist and poet associated with the Blaue Reiter and co-founder of Dada in 1916.
[25] This essay was composed by Neizvestny as the introduction to his exhibition catalog, *Ernst Neizvestny: Bronze* (New York: Eduard Nakhamkin, 1989), 1-12.

CHAPTER SEVEN

Dante

The plan alone of Dante's *Inferno* is the fruit of high genius.
–Aleksandr Pushkin[1]

1. Dante's *Inferno*

The space of Dante's *Inferno*[2] is not Euclidian space,[3] just as the time of Hell is not real time. The spherical space of Hell is like a sculptural negative. The naturalism and precise three-dimensional descriptions of discrete details of the dreamlike landscape merely intensify the general dreamlike quality of the poem. These are assemblages of reality unconnected to the perspective of Hell, sometimes reversed as in a Russian icon,[4] sometimes diffused as in Chinese and Japanese art.

Nor does time develop according to the laws of natural time. It is interrupted, it is psychological time – sometimes static, sometimes accelerated, sometimes retroactive, as in dreams or memories. Space and time contain premonitions.

Horizontal spirals, the structure of Hell, are pierced along the vertical axis by gigantic bodies. Their legs, torsos, and arms are parts of the horizontal cross-sections of the circles of Hell. Tormented souls, centaurs, serpents, furies, and demons become small against the background of immense flesh. But, as in modern cinema, the montage of frames and the shift in scale of what is depicted create the poetics of small and large. Great art, like a child's imagination, attempts to escape the quotidian. The artist is always a Gulliver:[5] he befriends only giants or midgets. Dante, while visiting the circles of Hell with Virgil,[6] synthesized various cosmological myths. He also foresaw the travels of Gulliver.

2. The Din of Hell

Dante's suffering and deformed bodies are plunged into the din of Hell's dialogues. The convex planes and spherical acoustics of Hell form an enormous organ in which the rhythm of voices, the rhythms of deep breathing, the rhythms of ecstasy, elegy, laughter, and weeping expand, grow, take over space, and then recede. It is as if someone were shutting our ears and then opening them once again in the ebb and flow of sounds. The chaos of sounds and its echoes in the spaces of Hell are contained by Dante's orderly *terza rima*[7] and mathematical structure. And, as in everything, the madness of destruction is controlled by the power of creation. Centrifugal forces are held in the center by centripetal forces. The center will hold.

3. Word and Body

In his words Dante approached the representational symbolism of today and perhaps went beyond it in many ways. Words could depict the deformations[8] and transformations of the body long before artists could acquire these techniques. Even Michelangelo[9] is closer to us in his poetry than in his sculptures. It was only after surrealism and the achievements of the avant-garde in the twentieth century that artists could use the representational metamorphoses of the body described by Dante. In other words, Dante's body is in dialogue between the body and the soul, the mundane and the divine. Dante's Hell consists of speaking bodies, bodies that are disjointed and deformed, bodies that incorporate heterogeneous elements. Every part of the body is pregnant with its opposite. Dante's body is a perfected form – Apollonian[10] man and Dionysian[11] motion destroying man. The body, like all the circles of Hell, is pierced by spherical energy.

Bodies are extruded from other bodies. Tree branches are intertwined with anatomy. People as stones or animals taken apart and put back together grow and penetrate one another. Dante is a great executioner: the Marquis de Sade[12] is just a child by comparison. But Dante's cruelty is the cruelty of compassion and mercy.

Dante is a great anatomist. His sculptural bodies – writhing, moaning, screaming, contorted – are dissected by a powerful and knowledgeable hand. His bodies are anatomical. His anatomy is symbolical and cosmological at the same time. The intertwining of bodies, the tension of listing space, the multi-voiced and motley chorus create a powerful polyphony of chaos and order, uncontrollable temperament, and cold mathematics.

For the illustrator every individual stroke and representation connected with Dante is a window into that strange world, simultaneously mobile and immobile, in which all things exist everywhere, and small parts are just as significant and full of tension as large ones.[13]

4. Dante, Dostoevsky, and Beckett

My illustrations to the works of Samuel Beckett are a continuation of the graphic art I have always created.[14] The earlier drawings for works by Dante and Dostoevsky were done in connection with my *Tree of Life* project and with my own study of Dante. I think that my recent Beckett illustrations are no worse and no better than my earlier work, but merely different. My Dante drawings were inspired by his theme of the "tortured body." At present I am discovering not only the visual, but also the spatial and musical essence of Dante. Dante is a person who creates a sculptural and spatial complex in his *Inferno.* Separate representations, at times extremely precise, are perceived as local collages or collections of realia immersed in mystical, spiritual, and spherical space. Dante creates a metaphor of the body. Moreover, he defines time in a visual sense. Earlier illustrators of Dante did not have the opportunity to follow Dante's verbal metaphors, because the word, which is always a verbal representation of the body, in Dante surpassed his visual metaphors. His transformations are physical. Severed bodies, bodies penetrating one another, and bodies as trees in essence constitute Dante's world of the body, which contains outcries, moans, laughter, dialogues, monologues, and, on the whole, a polyphony of the body.

No artist illustrating Dante in his lifetime, not even Botticelli,[15] possessed these technical means of representation. This is not surprising, since even the greatest sculptor in the world, Michelangelo, did not have visual metaphors, for instance, for his own poetry. In a sense Michelangelo's poetry, in the somewhat free meaning of the word, surpassed his visual representations because verbal metaphors were generated before visual ones, at least in European art. Only after the discoveries by twentieth-century avant-garde art as a whole and by surrealism in part – was it possible for artists to depict Dante's verbal metaphors. Because Dante is infinitely great, I, of course, have not exhausted his metaphors. I think he has even conceived of things that I still cannot create. And this limitation forced me to return to Dante.

The history of humanism is a very strange phenomenon. The fact is, humanism from its very beginning always seemed to be anti-human and cruel. Authentic humanism was never sweet. Michelangelo was called "divine" and "terrifying" because he was cruel. To their contemporaries Rembrandt[16] and Goya appeared to be insufficiently humane. Dostoevsky was called a "cruel writer" because humanism at first often seems to be anti-human. In reality Dante is a grandiose executioner: the Marquis De Sade is a rank amateur by comparison. Those teachings which Dante attributes to God's enemies (or, more often, to his own enemies) surpass everything written before or after him in their cruelty. But the fact remains that he is a great humanist who illuminates everything with unbelievable goodness and personal compassion. Occasionally he simultaneously hates and suffers for those whom he torments. Because Dante thinks like a philosopher, poet, and visual sculptor of genius, because he models his own body as a man of his time, as a topical journalist who cannot forgive God's or his own enemies, the only people he despises and does not forgive are those who are indifferent. Dante personally considers himself so obligated to God, so exposed to God's power, that he would punish his own enemies as he would God's enemies. But he was the forerunner of lofty humanism, so that in his cruelty could be heard the strains of authentic Christian compassion. In general I think that genuine humanism is not sweet, rosy lisping, but total fearlessness before the real truth of human suffering.

There are cultural phenomena that sunder the bounds of the purely national and become universal. Ultimately it was Judeo-Christian civilization that produced Christ and the Bible. But the Bible delights and inspires people of all races and colors despite the fact that it was created in Israel. Similarly with Dante. Dante, being national, is simultaneously universal. This is always the fate of the mightiest discoveries of the mind. The same with Dostoevsky and Tolstoy. I am deeply convinced that the more universal a national genius, the more international he or she is. Therefore, anyone can illustrate the works of Dante, because he is no longer a part of Italian culture, but of world culture. You will recall what Pushkin said about Dante, "The plan alone of Dante's *Inferno* is the fruit of high genius."

5. Space and Time

In visual representations, space and time are not neutral. There are different temporal categories in the space and time of literature. Lev Tolstoy's space unfolds according to the laws of Euclid. Space and time are real: real characters move in real space. Horses are running, trees are standing over there, birds are flying. And, at the same time, people, in accordance with physical and psychological laws, undergo change in real space. Thus, Pierre Bezukhov[17] in *War and Peace* changes his mask, his body, and his character in accordance with real time. There is none of this in writers such as Dante, Dostoevsky, Kafka,[18] and Beckett. For these writers Euclidean space does not exist. Their concept of space resembles the reversed space of Russian icons, or the scattered space of Chinese and Japanese art. The same thing happens to time, which is interrupted or reversed, as in a dream, moving from the past to the future or *vice versa*, the time of recollections and dreams. Occasionally, the boundaries between the past, present, and future are effaced. Thus, the concept of time and space dictates the form of a representation.

6. Samuel Beckett

For me the names of Dante, Dostoevsky, and Beckett are inseparable. In his *Notebooks to Crime and Punishment,* Dostoevsky wrote: "I wish to create a novel like Dante's *The Divine Comedy.*" And, in fact, Dostoevsky made use of allusions to Dante such as fire and water. Dostoevsky is close to Dante not in his poetics, but in his method of thinking. Beckett has been called the Dante of the twentieth century, and this is absolutely true. In Beckett's works there are Dantesque characters who are linked by a common sense of time, space, and description of their physical suffering. Beckett is just as merciless as Dante in his depiction of the anatomy of the human body in sickness and agony. Beckett might appear to be more refined and, perhaps, more cynical, but this is merely a question of different epochs. In his creative power and humanism Beckett approximates Dante. While Beckett has never spoken directly about Russian culture and its influence on him, I can discern direct echoes of Russian ideas in his works. For example, Beckett's play, *Krapp's Last Tape,* embodies an idea that goes back to ancient Greek philosophy, namely, that it is impossible to step twice into the same river. I believe that Beckett's use of the idea of flux and irreversibility of time is opposed to Dostoevsky's static hero in the *Notes from the Underground,* where time has indeed stopped. What Dante, Dostoevsky, and Beckett have in common is neither the poetics of language or images, but the more fundamental concepts of time and space in which their characters are placed.

7. Rhythm

Osip Mandelstam[19] once called Dante a journalist, and he was right in a sense. Dante and Dostoevsky were always topical in their references to actual people and political events. They simply were not visual artists. I personally have never indicated time by depicting clearly recognizable individuals in my work. Although the men and women I depict in my paintings have no external temporal attributes in their dress or hair style, my characters and situations nevertheless embody the rhythms of contemporary life.

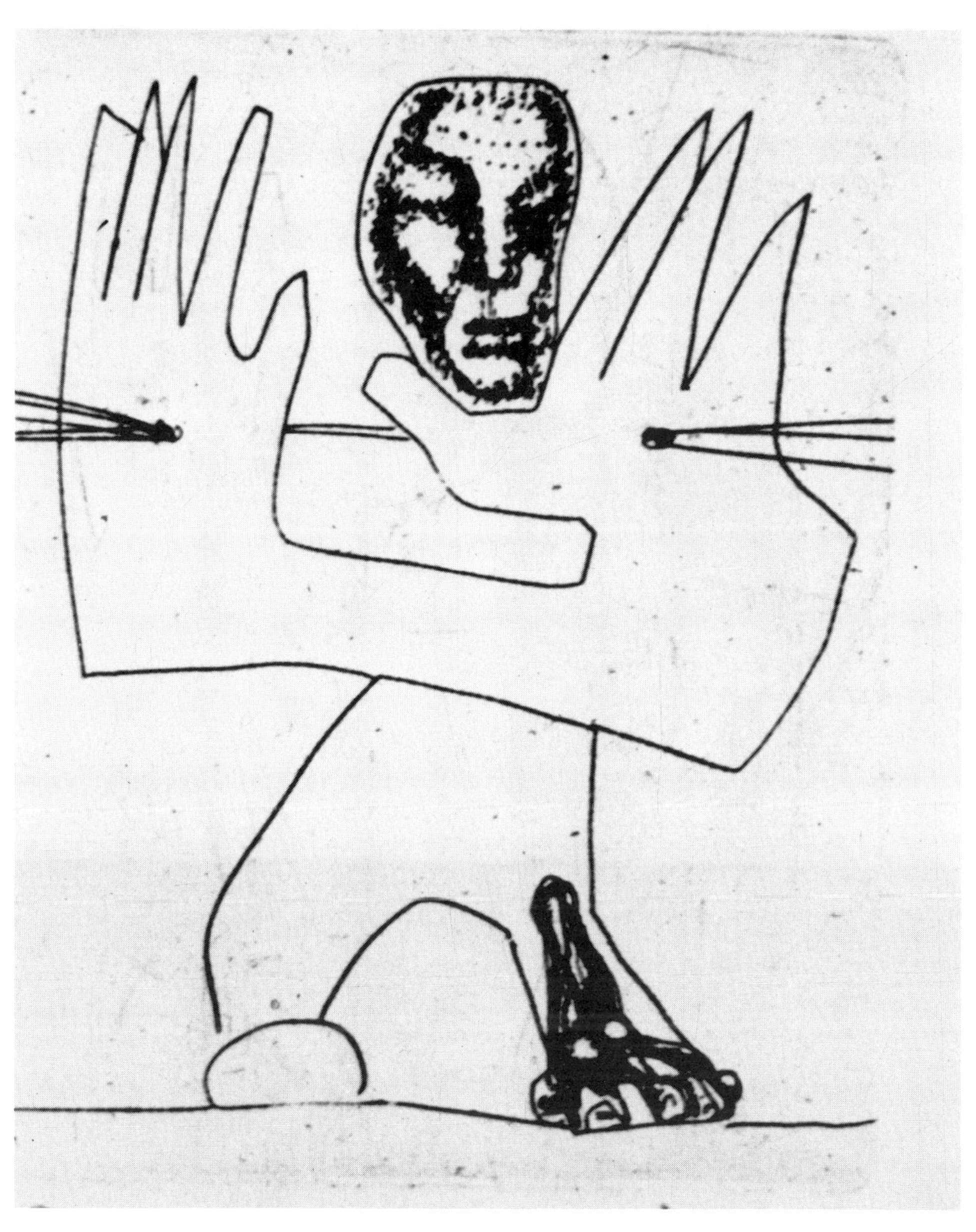

Ptitsa iz tsikla "Sud'ba" (Bird from Cycle, "Fate"), 1973-75
Etching, 17.78 x 12.70 cm.
Tree of Life Musuem, Uttersberg, Sweden

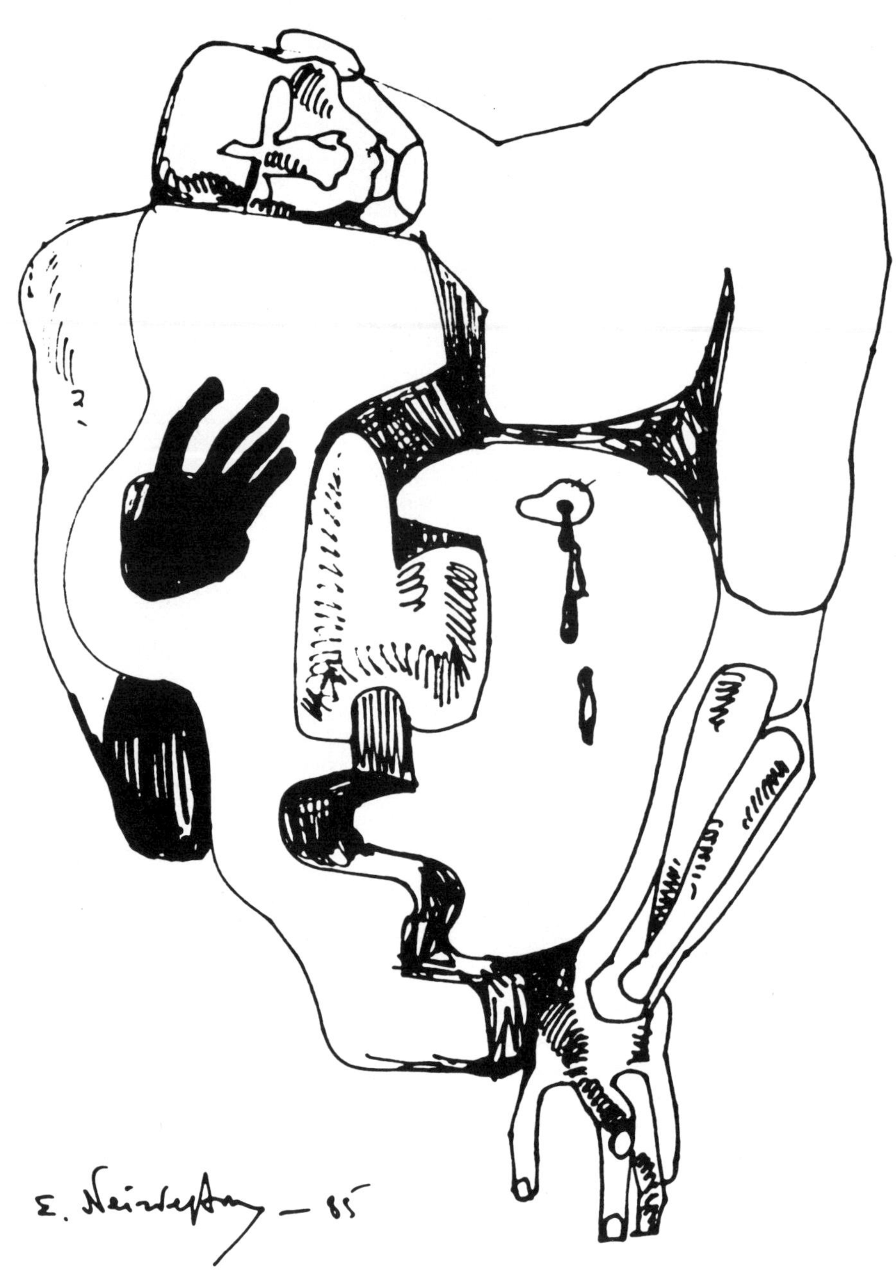

Chelovek – Maska (Man - Mask), 1985
India ink, 30.48 x 22.86 cm.
Tree of Life Museum, Uttersberg, Sweden

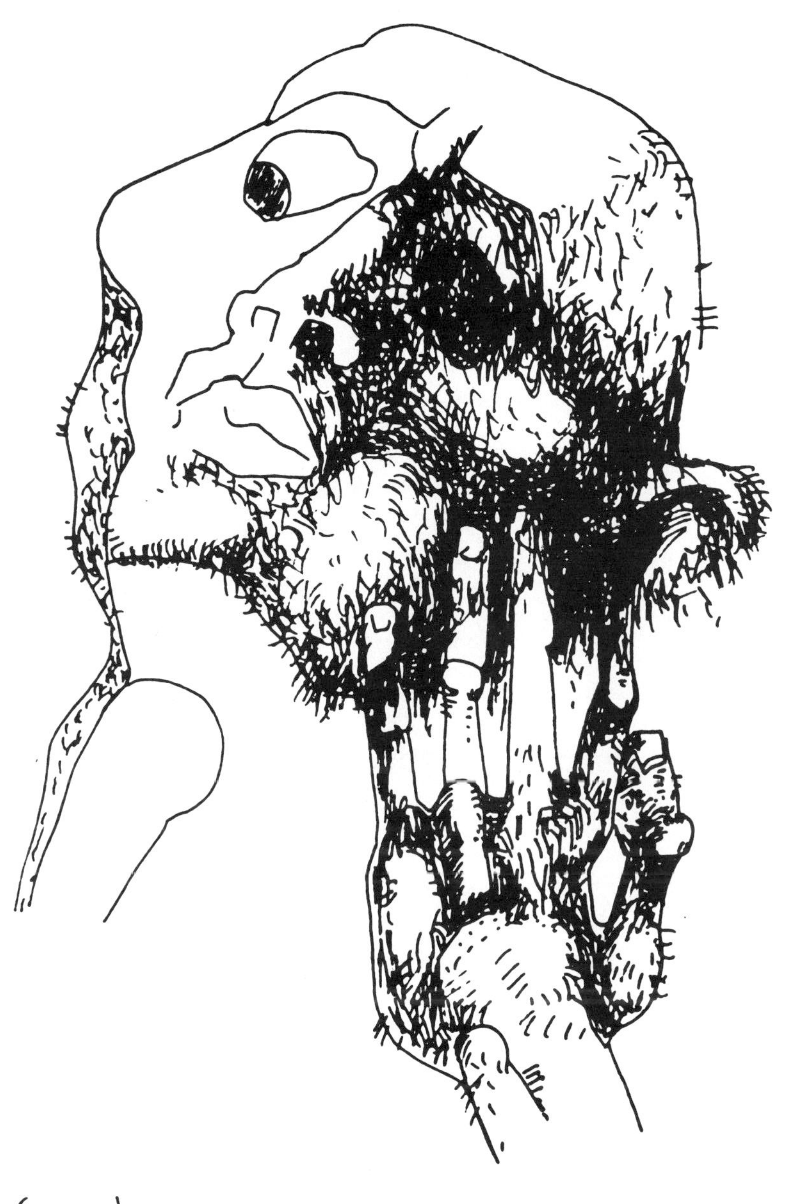

S. Beket (Samuel Beckett), 1987-89
India ink, 30.48 x 22.86 cm.
Tree of Life Museum, Uttersberg, Sweden

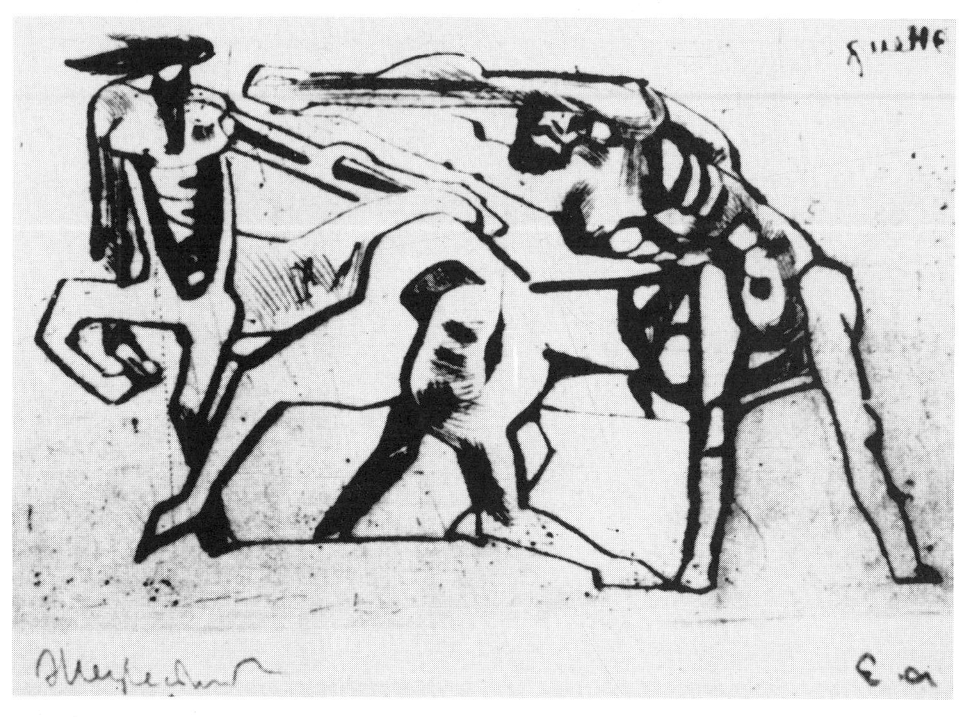

Kentavry (Centaurs), 1975
Dry point etching, 12 x 20 cm.
Tree of Life Museum, Uttersberg, Sweden

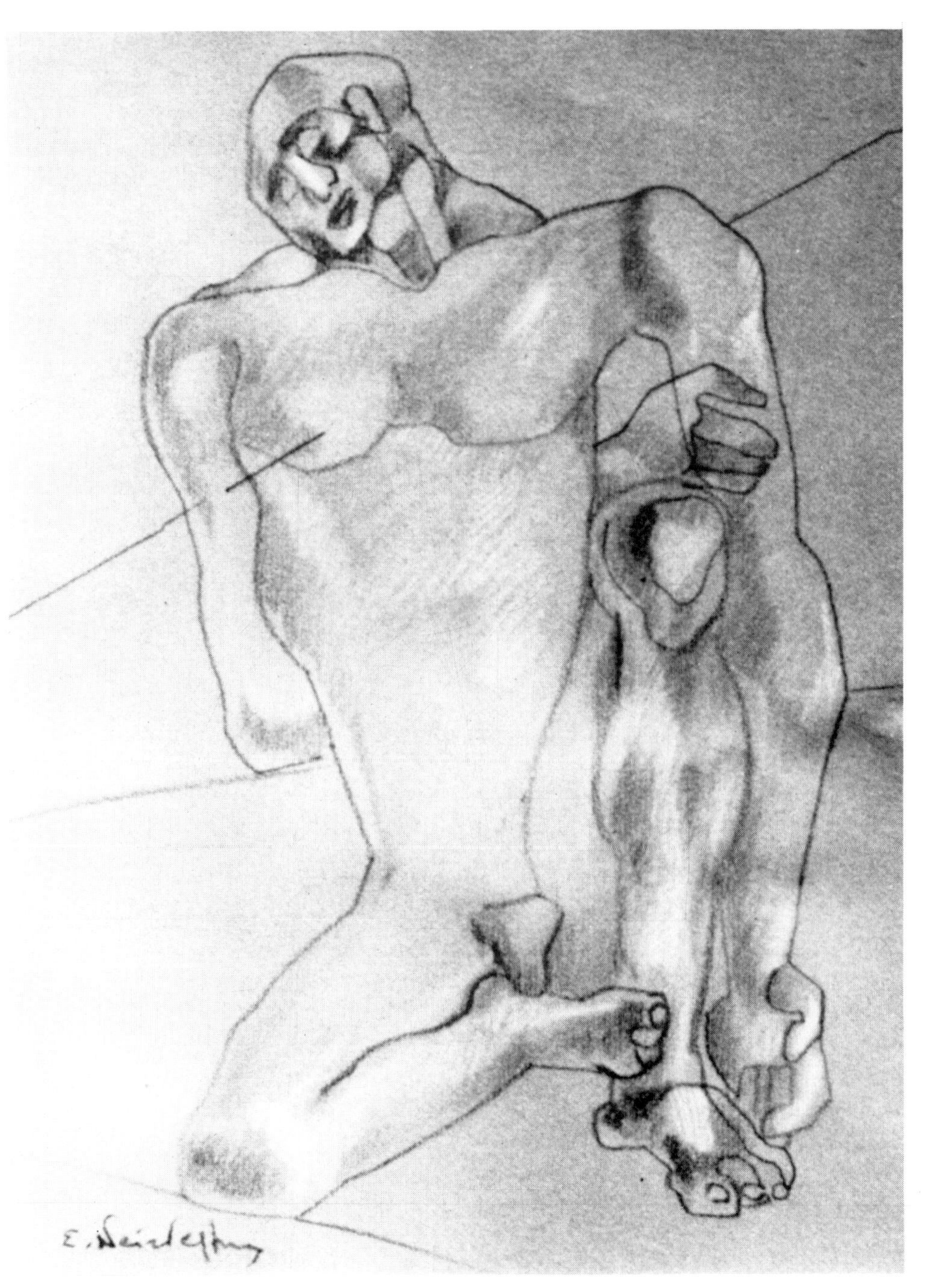

Sviatoi Sebastian (Saint Sebastian), 1989
Pastel. 99.06 x 69.85 cm.
Tree of Life Museum, Uttersberg, Sweden

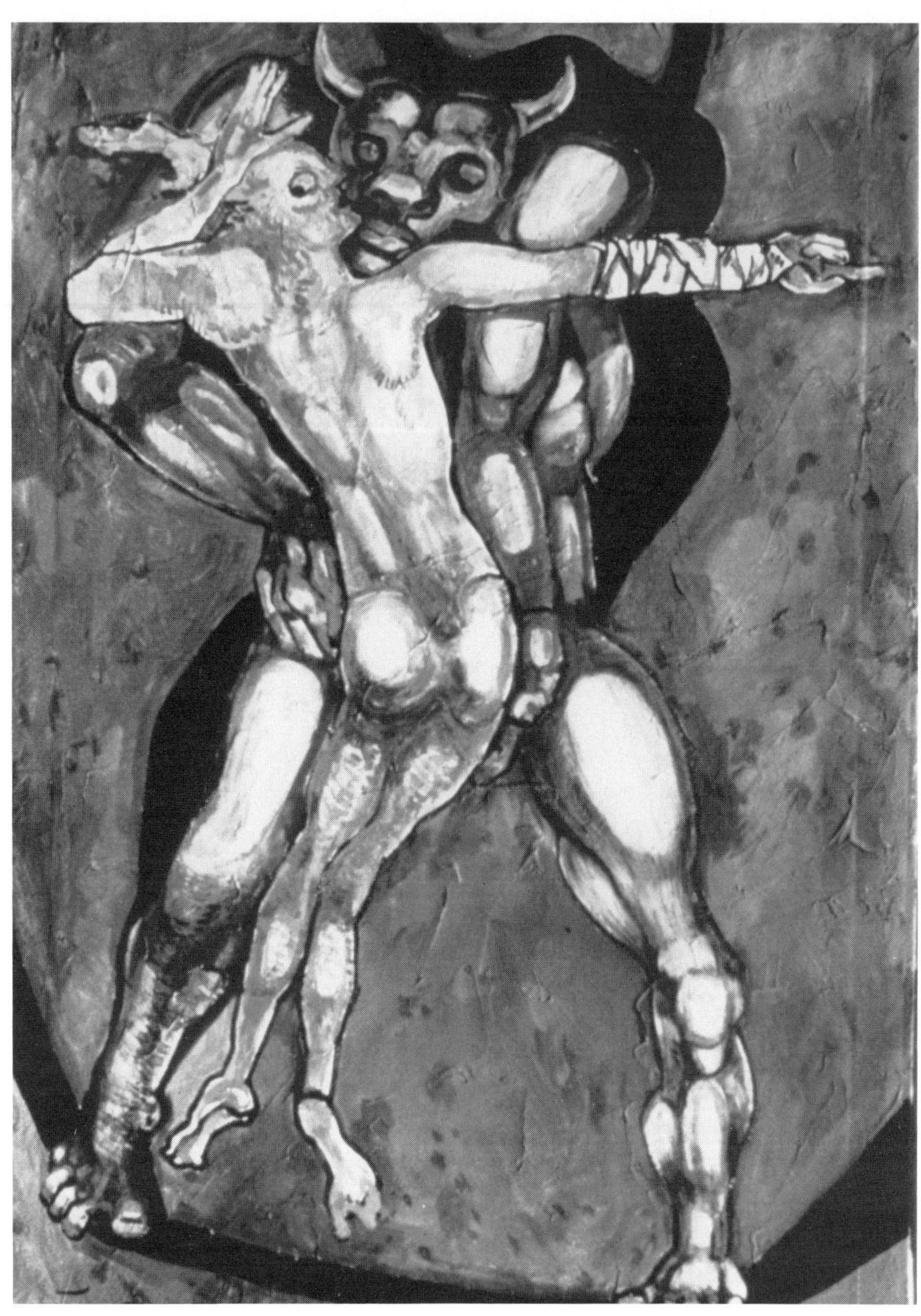

Minotavr (Minotaur), 1987-89
Acrylic, 203.20 x 152.40 cm.
Tree of Life Museum, Uttersberg, Sweden

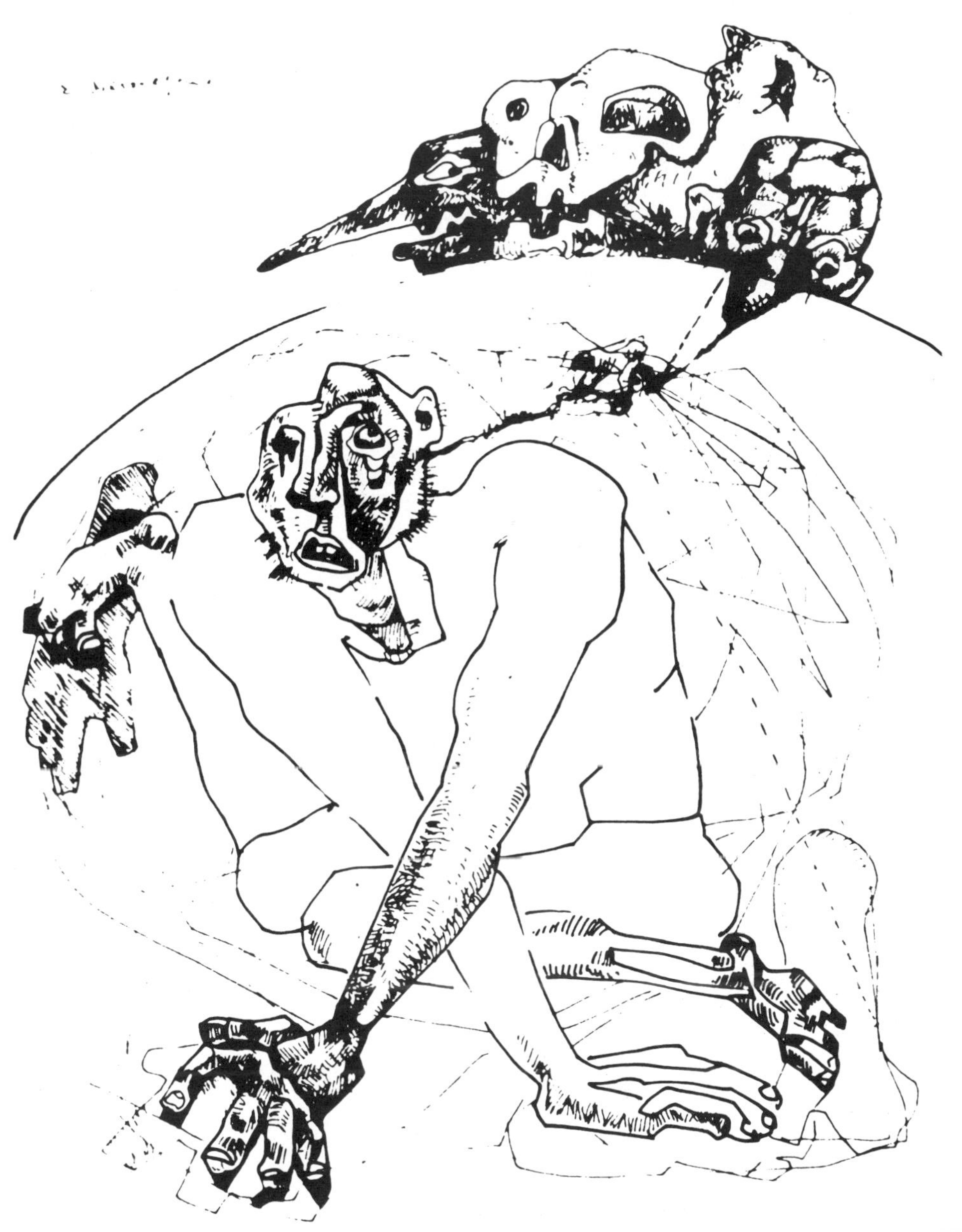

S. Beket: Khromoi (Samuel Beckett: The Cripple), 1987-89
India ink, 30.48 x 22.86 cm.
Tree of Life Museum, Uttersberg, Sweden

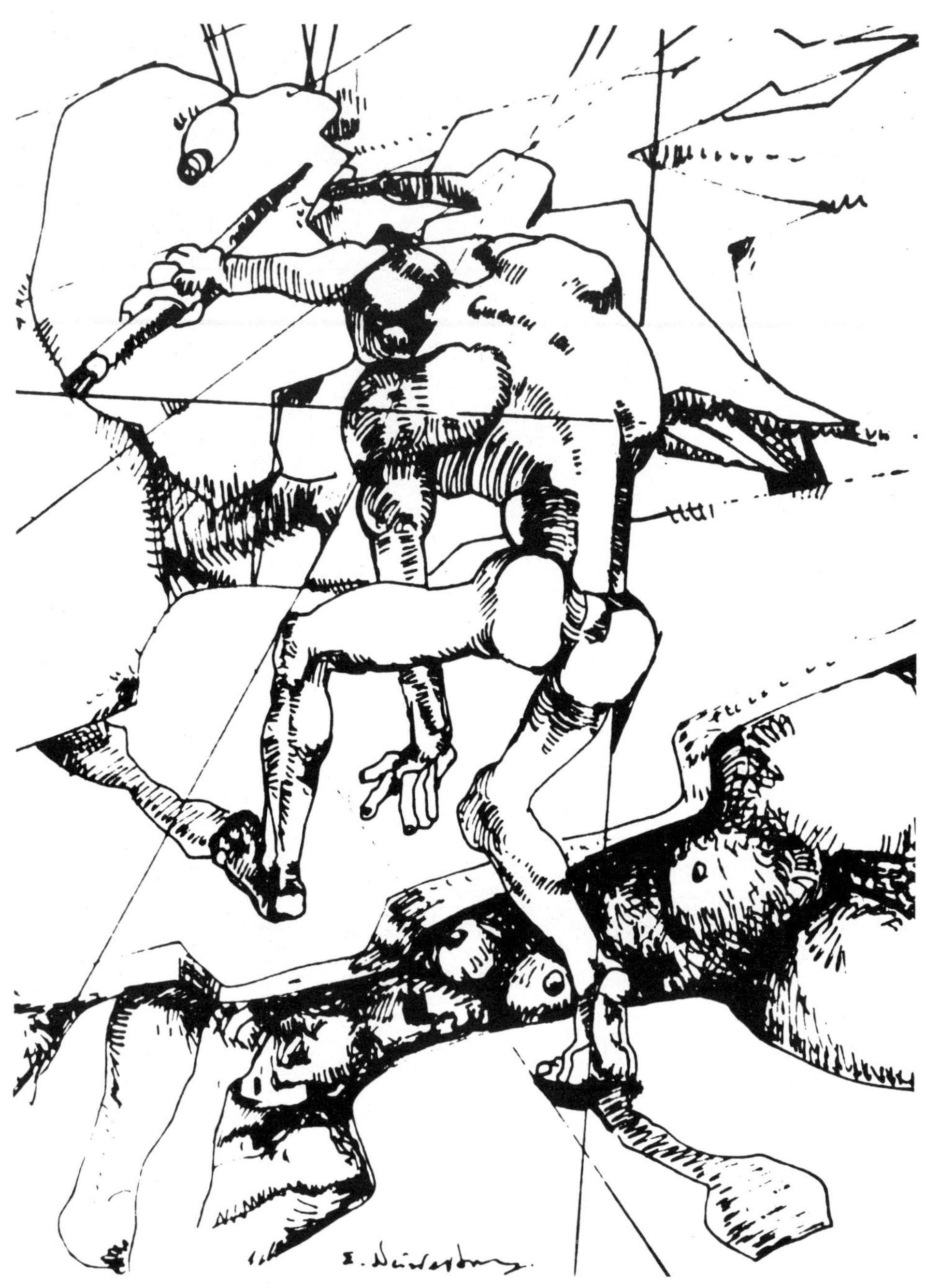

Shag cherez liubov' (Stepping Over Love), 1987-89
India ink, 30.48 x 22.86 cm.
Tree of Life Museum, Uttersberg, Sweden

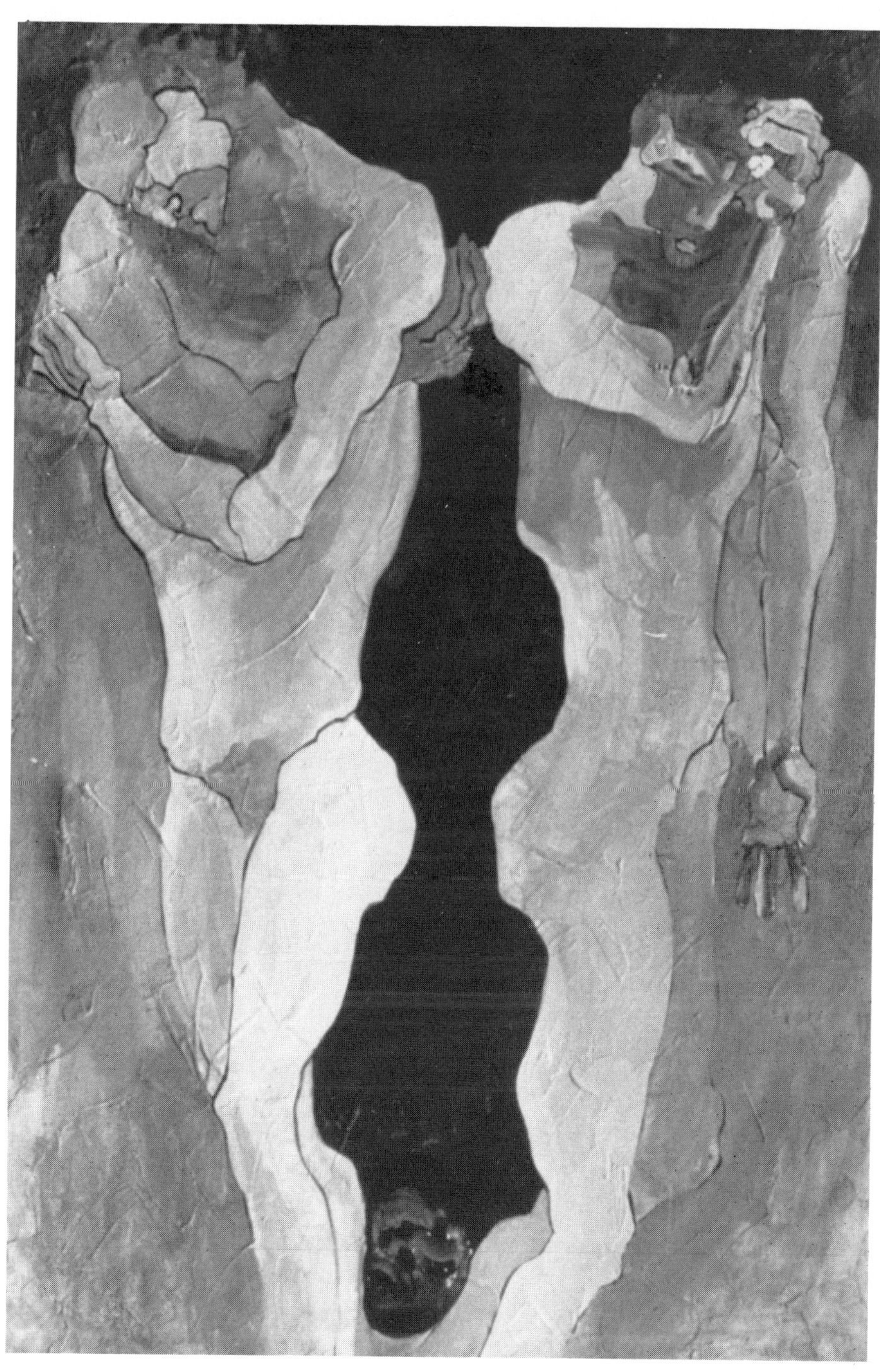

S. Beket: Ten' (Samuel Beckett: Shadow), 1987-89
Oil/Acrylic, 91.44 x 45.72 cm.
Tree of Life Museum, Uttersberg, Sweden

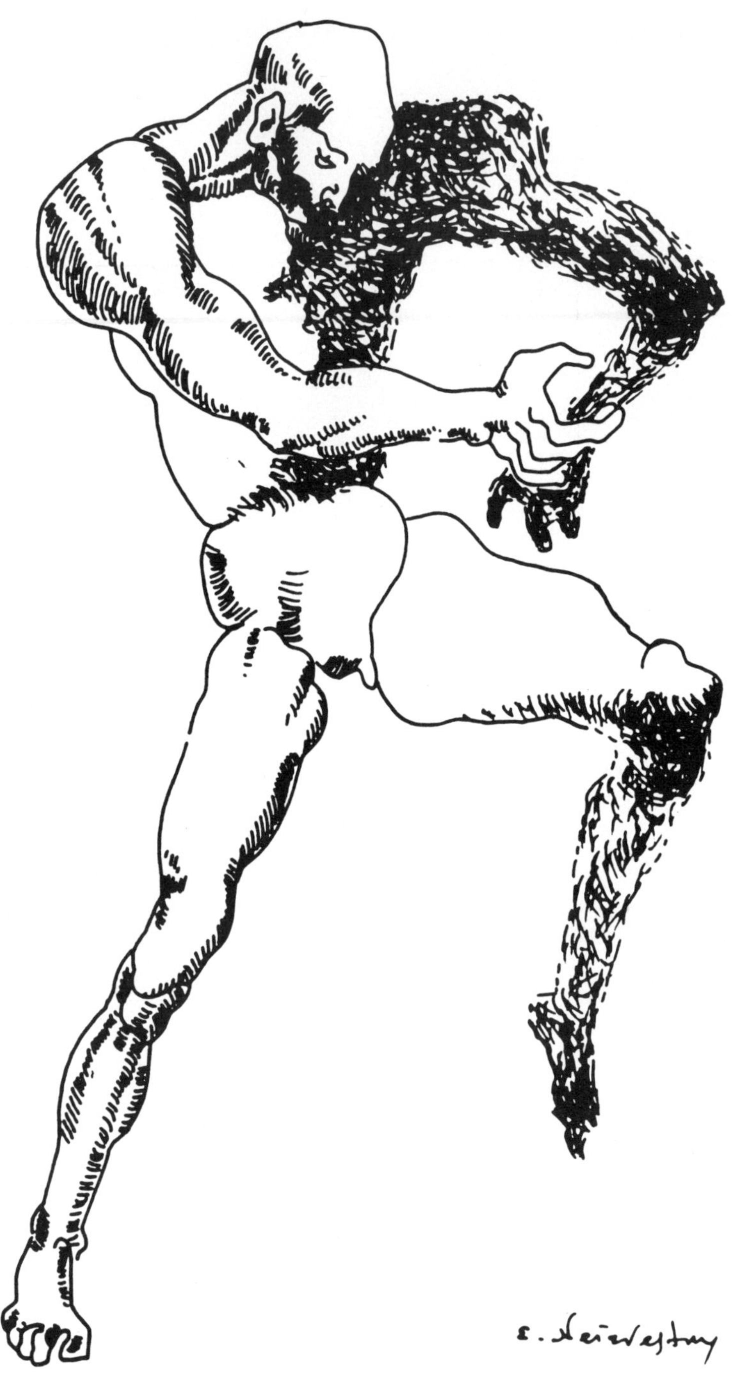

S. Beket: Dialog s ten'iu (Samuel Beckett: Dialogue with a Shadow), 1987-89
India ink, 30.48 x 22.86 cm.
Tree of Life Museum, Uttersberg, Sweden

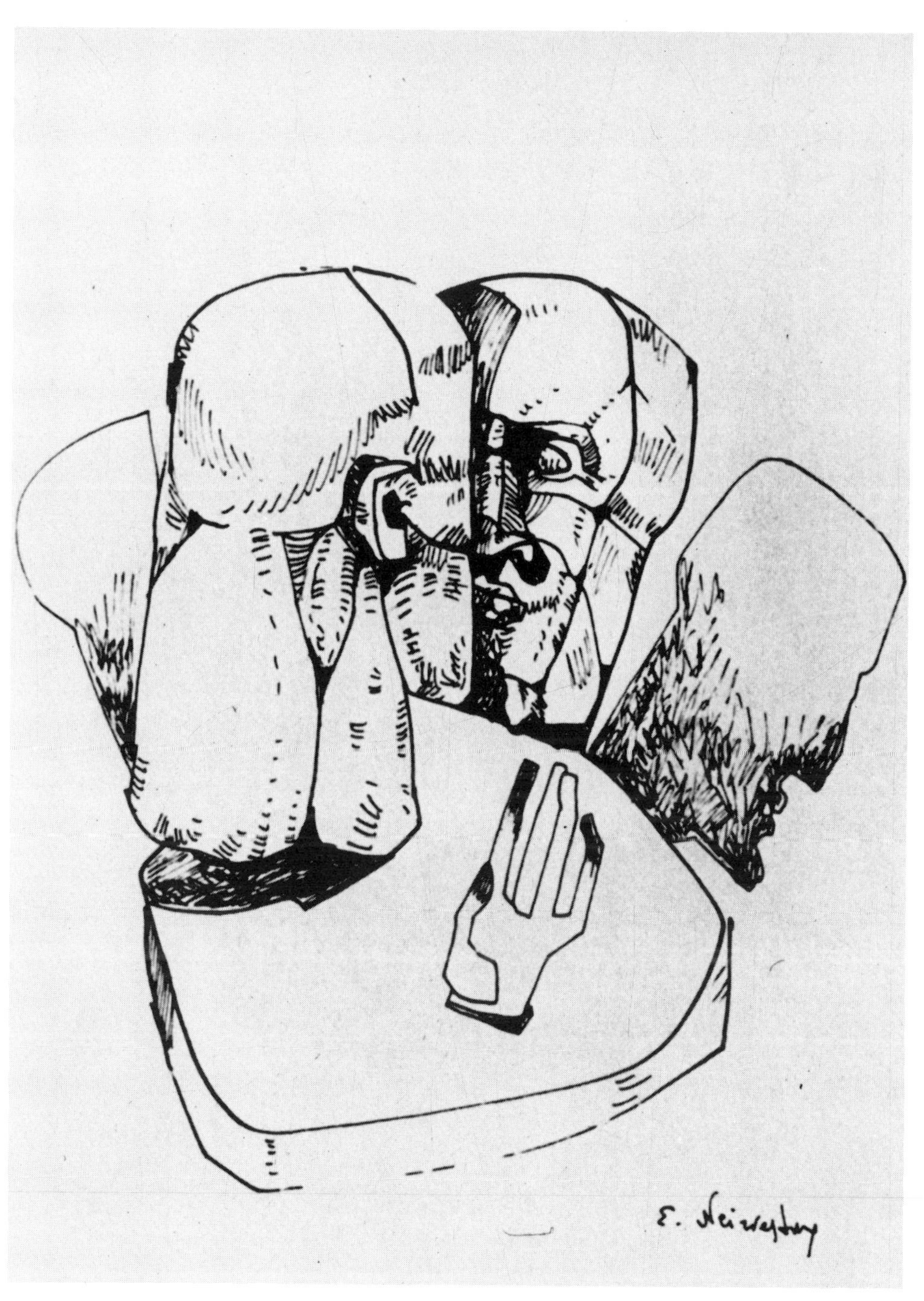

Stol Beketa (Beckett's Table), 1987-89
India ink, 30.48 x 22.86 cm.
Tree of Life Museum, Uttersberg, Sweden

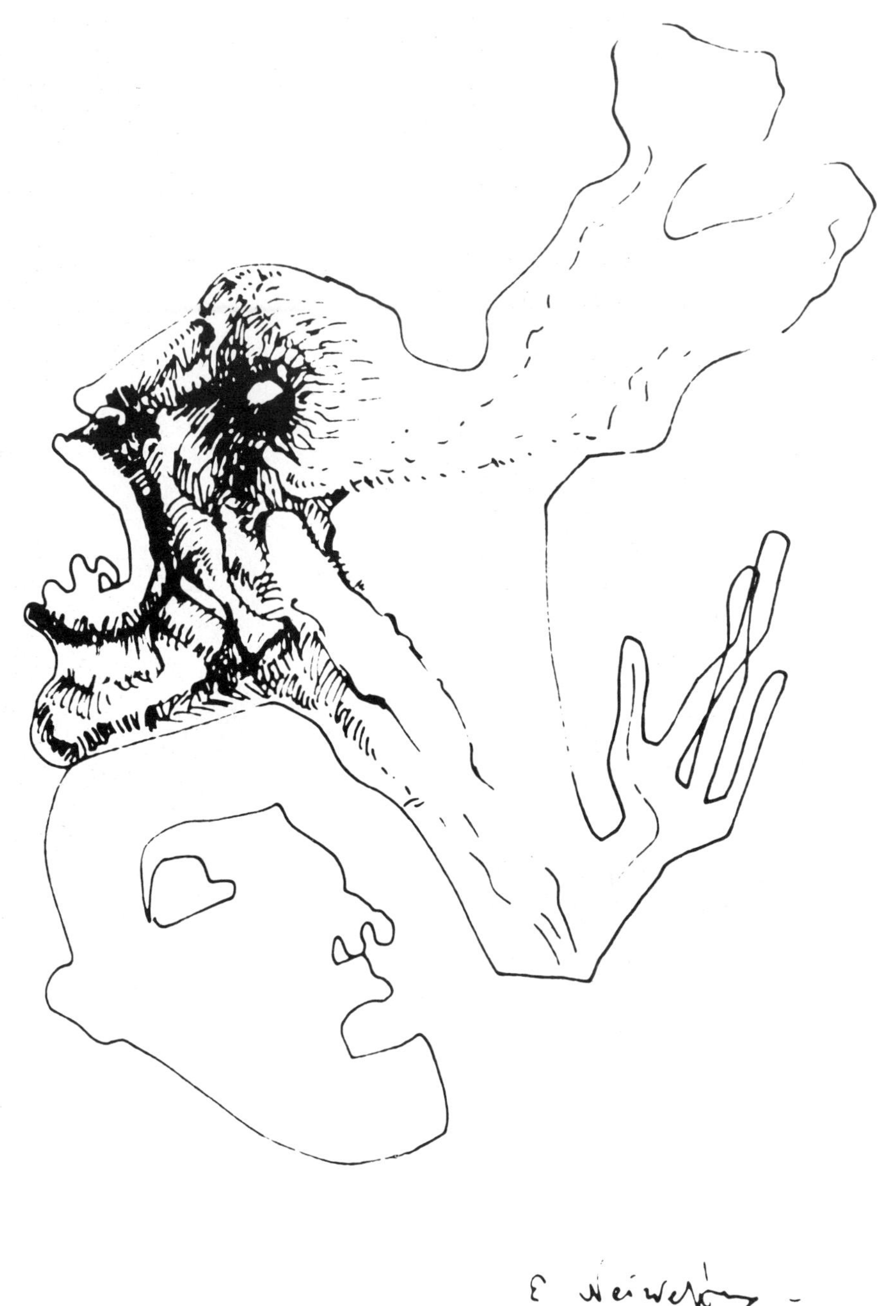

S. Beket: Dialog s ten'iu (Samuel Beckett: Dialogue with a Shadow), 1987-89
India ink, 30.48 x 22.86 cm.
Tree of Life Museum, Uttersberg, Sweden

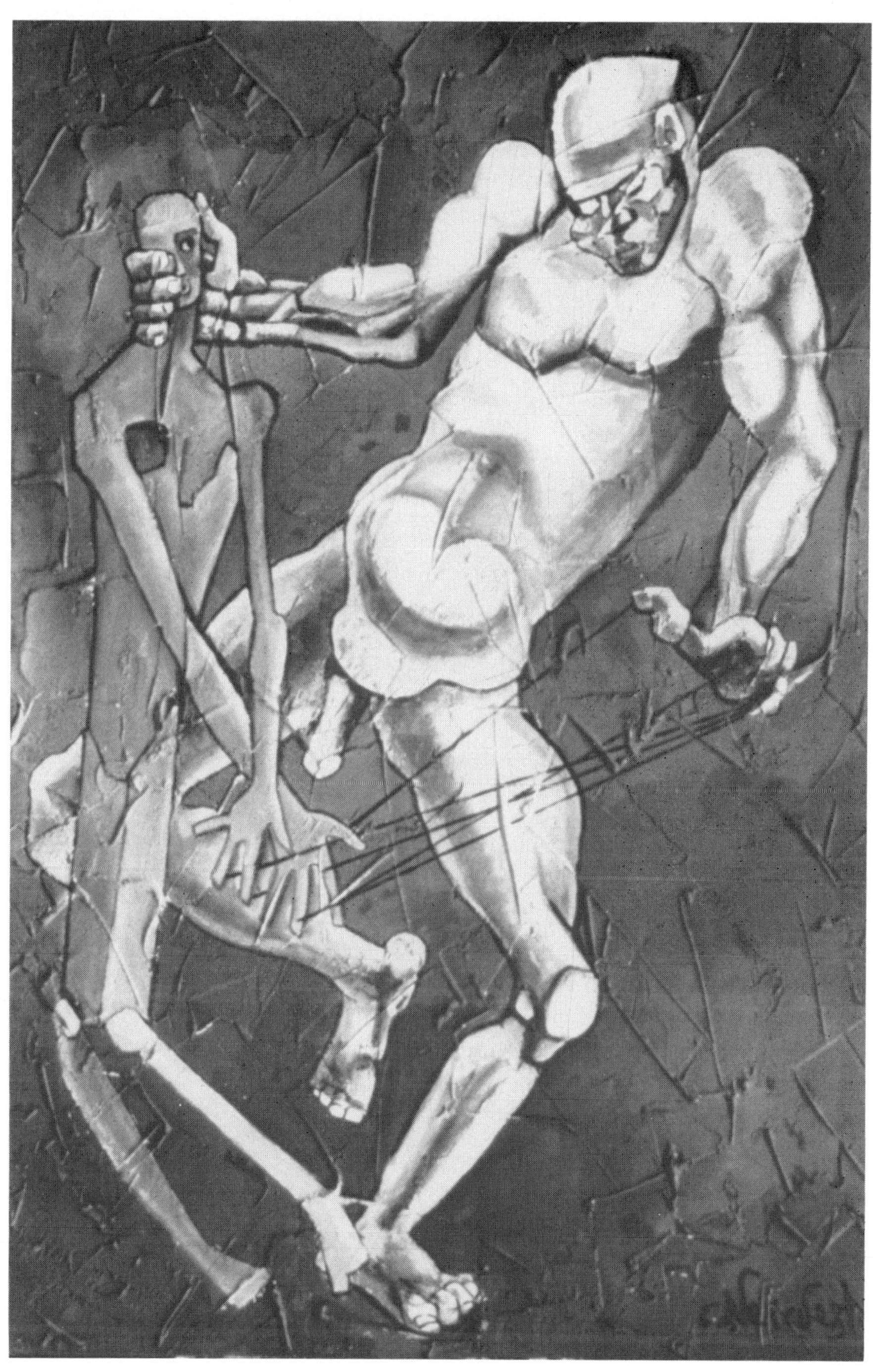

Tanets s kukloi (Dance with a Puppet), 1987-89
Oil/Acrylic, 203.20 x 152.40 cm.
Tree of Life Museum, Uttersberg, Sweden

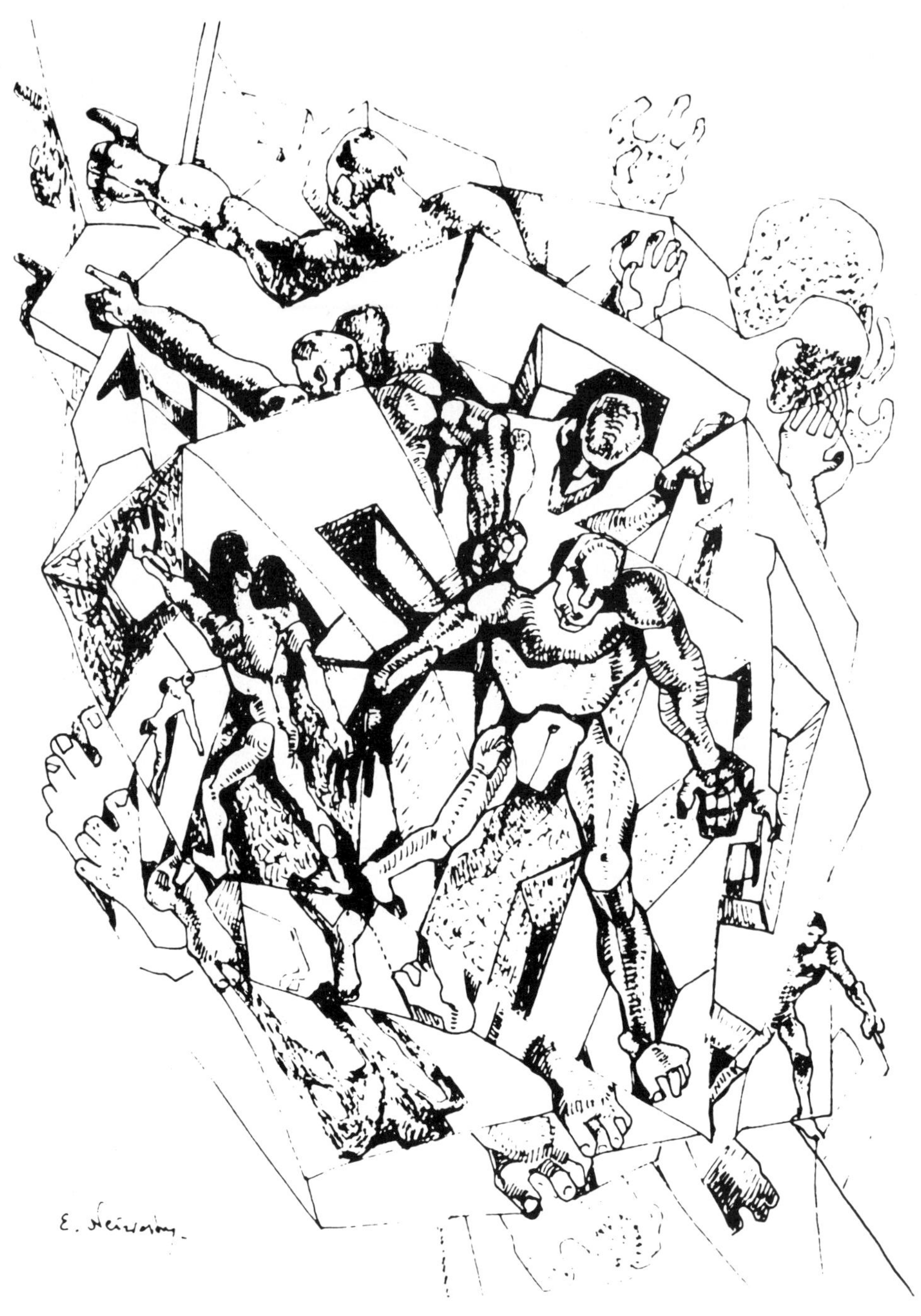

S. Beket: Labirint (Samuel Beckett: Labyrinth), 1987-89
India ink, 30.48 x 22.86 cm.
Tree of Life Museum, Uttersberg, Sweden

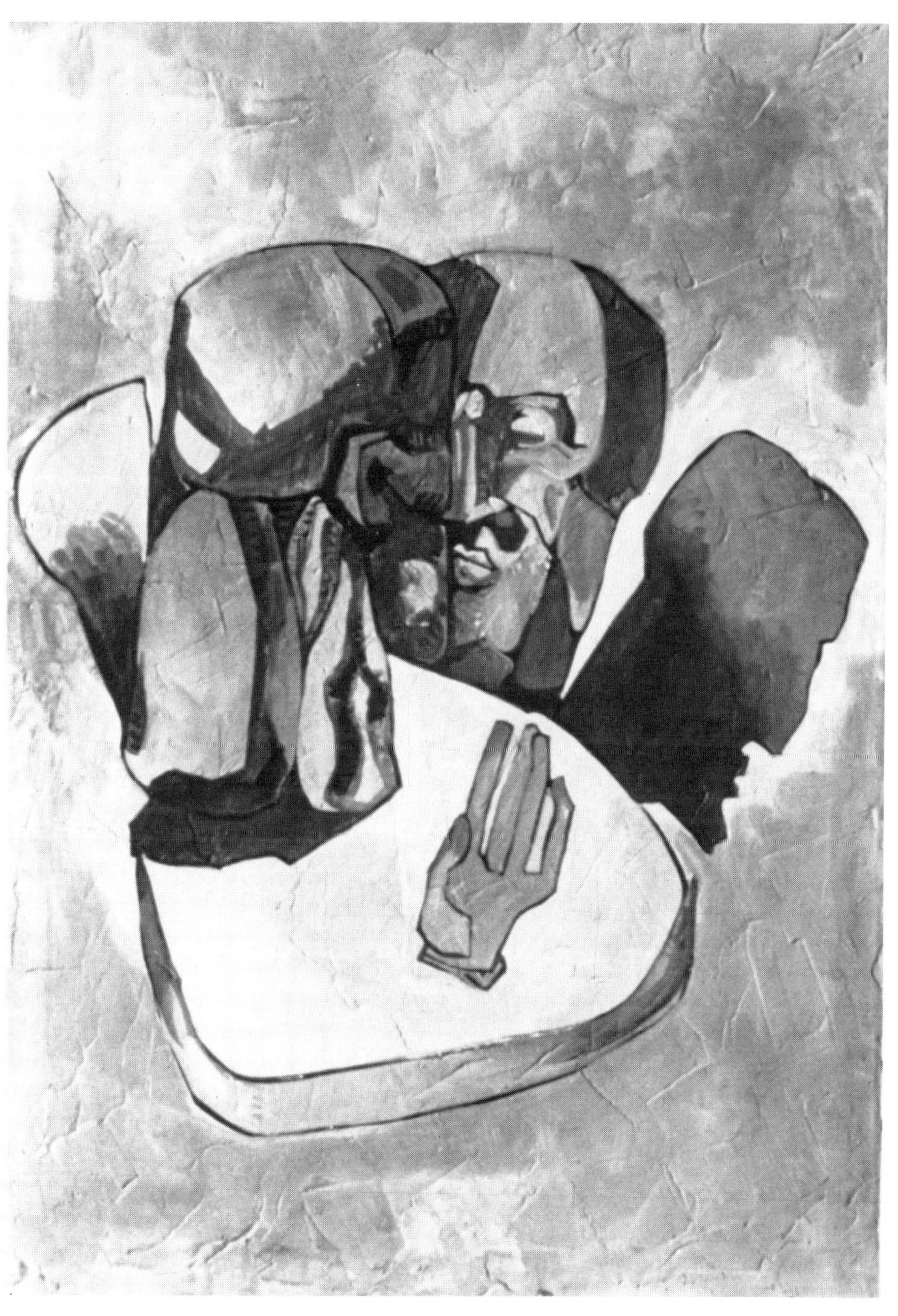

Stol Beketa (Beckett's Table), 1987-89
Acrylic, 121,92 x 91.44 cm.
Tree of Life Museum, Uttersberg, Sweden

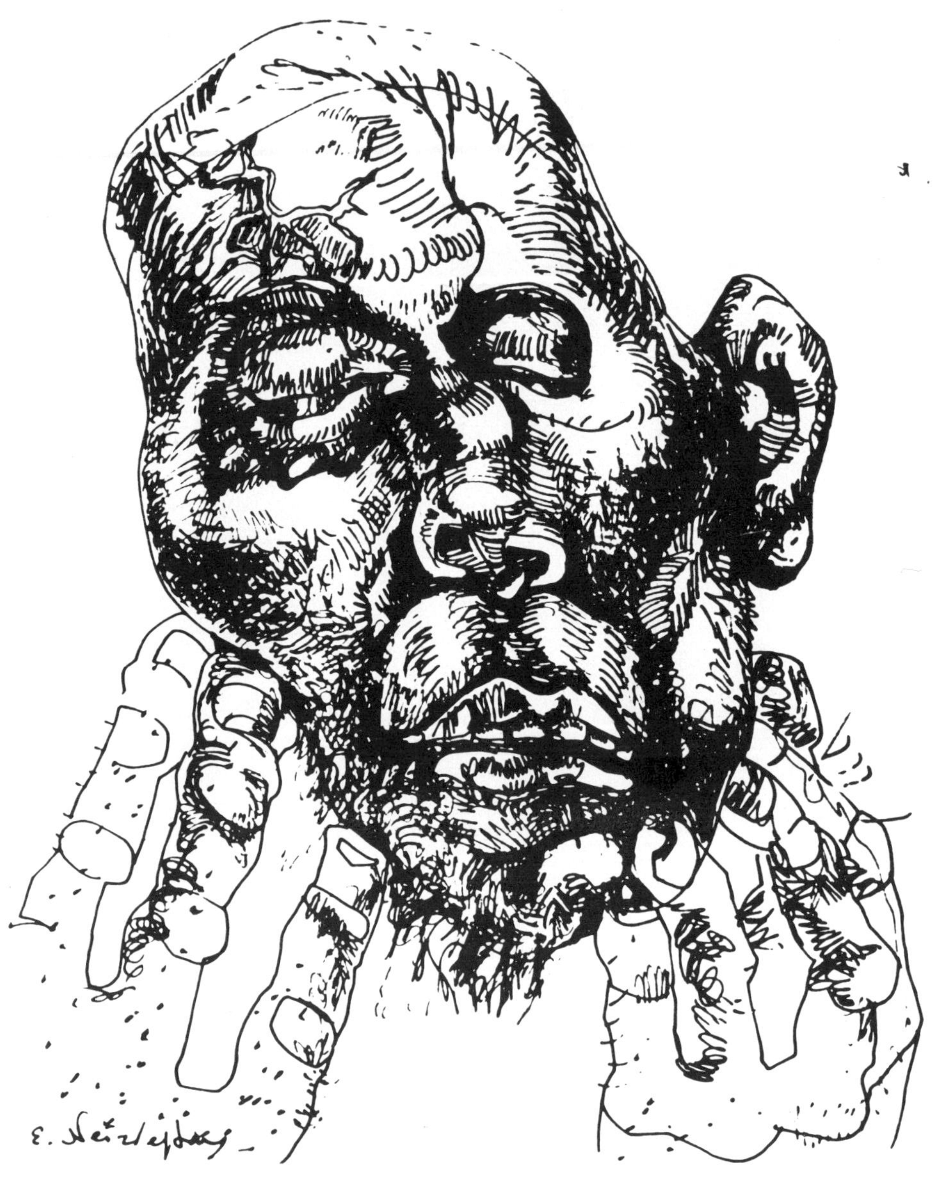

S. Beket: Maska (Samuel Beckett: Mask), 1987-89
India ink, 30.48 x 22.86 cm.
Tree of Life Museum, Uttersberg, Sweden

When people ask me how I can continue the traditions of the Russian avant-garde without creating purely abstract constructions, I reply: "Look at the rhythm. This rhythm is concealed inside a leaf, or inside the sculpture." Or, when I am told that there is nothing Russian in my work such as churches, beards, or bast shoes, I explain that such details are unnecessary when authentic Russian rhythms permeate my works. What is important is the rhythm. When we listen to jazz, we do not hear the words that accompany the music: we can figure out the time period from the rhythm. Similarly, when we hear Russian revolutionary or urban songs, rock music, or art songs, it is not essential to understand the words. In the final analysis, rhythm is higher than words in representational art and in music. The most subtle investigators of my creative work such as Albert Leong have understood that my linkage with the Russian avant-garde is the use of common rhythms of composition, and not visual or semantic concepts.[20]

Mandelstam was absolutely correct when he spoke of Dante's creative process as an outbreak of images. I have spoken of the buzzing and humming of his *Inferno*. This is none other than the chorus of definite rhythms, voices, and music which resounds and echoes in Dante's spherical space. It is the kind of echo one can hear in a train station or a bath house, in a large enclosed space where a multitude of voices is buzzing and one can interrupt these pulsations at will by cupping and uncupping one's ears. This echo – like the roar of tides coming in and going out – is chaos.

8. Centrifugal and Centripetal Forces

In Dante the formation of this sound is fettered by the mathematically precise rhythms of his *terza rima*. In this way chaos is controlled by mathematics, a process typical of great, grandiose talents such as Dante's. The fact is, a mighty artist of flow and process like Dante requires a centripetal force to balance his centrifugal tendencies. Otherwise, his innate temperament would sunder his works, and his inner chaos would gush forth as if the core of his personality had burst. For that reason, powerful talents usually display the greatest self-discipline. Great visionary madmen create for themselves cages in which they can safely express their madness. Dante created such a cage for himself in the very structure of *The Divine Comedy.* Within these *terza rima* resound the incredible roar of chaos, unbelievable howls, outcries, moans, and laughter. But all of this is counterbalanced by the mathematical structure of the work. Thus, what is mobile becomes still; what is dynamic becomes static. The true sign of grandiose talents is their ability to restrain themselves. In Michelangelo's case it was the Pope who placed the artist in a cage – the Sistine Chapel[21] – to enable him to create *The Last Judgment.*[22] Michelangelo possessed such a powerful talent that, without this cage, he would have completed nothing, but would constantly begin and discard work after work, because his mighty imagination far outstripped the material production of sculptures and paintings. But Dante created his own constraints: he was both Pope and visionary madman.[23]

[1] Pushkin (See Introduction, note 34).
[2] Part One of Dante's *The Divine Comedy.*
[3] Euclid (c300 BC), Alexandrian mathematician whose *Elements* established the basis of geometry, which treats the properties of three-dimensional space.
[4] Sacred images painted on wooden panels.
[5] The hero of *Gulliver's Travels* by Jonathan Swift (1667-1745), major Anglo-Irish journalist, poet, and satirist.
[6] Virgil or Vergil (70-19 BC), great Roman epic poet and Dante's guide in *The Divine Comedy.*
[7] *Terza rima,* the verse form devised by Dante for *The Divine Comedy* and composed of iambic tercets (aba, bcd, etc.), in which the second line of the first tercet supplies the rhyme for the second tercet, the second line of the second tercet supplies the rhyme for the third tercet, and so forth. Dante's *terza rima* may be a symbolic allusion to the Holy Trinity.
[8] Neizvestny applies the Russian Formalist concept of deformation to sculpture.
[9] Michelangelo (See Chapter Two, note 4).
[10] Apollo, son of Zeus, god of justice, and leader of the Muses in Greek mythology.
[11] Dionysus, son of Zeus and Greek god of wine and fertility.
[12] Marquis De Sade (1740-1814), French writer who justified sexual deviation and criminal acts as natural.

[13]This section was composed by Neizvestny as the introduction to his exhibition catalog, *Ernst Neizvestny: Dante's* Inferno (New York: Eduard Nakhamkin, 1987), 2-3.
[14] Beckett commissioned 100 drawings from Neizvestny for the jubilee edition of his collected works, *Concepts and Representations* (See Introduction, note 58).
[15]Sandro Botticelli (c1444-1510), major Italian Renaissance painter.
[16] Rembrandt van Rijn (1606-69), greatest Dutch painter.
[17] Pierre Bezukhov, the central male protagonist in *War and Peace.*
[18] Franz Kafka (1883-1924), German-language writer of Jewish origin known for fictional treatment of theme of alienation and nightmarish situations confronting protagonists.
[19] Osip Emilievich Mandelstam ((1891-1938?), outstanding Russian Acmeist poet and essayist.
[20]See Albert Leong, "Ernst Neizvestnyi i russkaia kul'tura" (Ernst Neizvestny and Russian culture), *Kontinent 61* (1989): 273-83 and "Ernst Neizvestny and the Russian Avant-Garde," in *Proceedings of Summer 1986 Intensive Workshop in Chinese and Russian*, edited by Albert Leong, 237-52 (Eugene: University of Oregon Press, 1988) [Reprinted in *Studies in Chinese and Russian Culture*, edited by Albert Leong (New York: Peter Lang Publishers, 1990)
[21] Sistine Chapel, papal chapel in the Vatican named for Pope Sixtus IV and known for its magnificent frescoes by Michelangelo.
[22] *The Last Judgment* (1536-41): Pope Paul III commissioned Michelangelo to paint a huge fresco depicting the Resurrection on the end wall of the Sistine Chapel.
[23] These sections were translated from taped interviews with Neizvestny conducted in New York and Uttersberg, Sweden, by Vladimir Bondarev in 1988-89 in connection with the Soviet documentary film, *V otvete l' zrachii za sleptsa* (Will the visionary answer for the blind?) [1989].

CHAPTER EIGHT

Creativity in Disgrace

Everything significant in Soviet artistic culture has been created despite the will of the authorities, while everything insignificant has been supported. What is the reason for this? Why was it precisely those who sincerely, uncompromisingly, and devotedly served their calling and, therefore, society who were subjected to the most degrading insults? The list of shattered fates, ruined talents, or people who were simply annihilated physically in the Soviet Union is disproportionately great. What is the cause of a nation's suicide: the destruction of the most valuable group of people in society? These people were killed not by an army of occupation, nor during periods of revolution or war, but day-by-day – regularly, routinely, as an ordinary occurrence.

I have shared the fate of those persecuted: I was a guinea pig in an experiment to extinguish my innate desire to create. But I lived through the experiment, refused to undergo a lobotomy, and survived without losing the gift of thought and speech. There was never a moment when I could have been forced me to forget the past or to refrain from drawing conclusions from the past for future reference. Geography and the present placement of my body have no meaning. Culture has always been a migration of people and ideas. I not only have the right, but also the duty, to think and speak. In the history of humanity there have been no underground sculptors, but only unrecognized ones. There have been no sculptors who were recognized and persecuted at the same time. This dubious lot was mine.

A monumental sculptor by nature cannot be found in the underground. The sculptor throughout history has come to terms with authority. Theocracies and democracies, monarchies and republics all have need of chronicles in stone. The sculptor has linked his fate with all kinds of tyrants, and therefore the history of the creation of the arts of Egypt, China, Mexico, as well as Europe from ancient Greece to the present day is the history of the relationship between the sculptor and authority. Because sculpture is material, it requires financial and political support from the authorities. In this respect, the sculptor is conservative by nature. But sculpture is not only material, but also spiritual. And every significant sculptor has been revolutionary: his creative work, revealing new paths, sunders the commonplace. It was precisely the authorities who defended the sculptor from the tyranny of democratic guilds, from the ordinary. The authorities made it possible for Phidias[1] and Michelangelo[2] to create the works they created. Pericles[3] and the Pope in essence were co-authors of masterpieces. Can you imagine what would have happened to the Sistine Chapel[4] if its fate depended on the consensus of fellow artists, and not on the will of the great man who commissioned it? Democracies, monarchies, and even tyrannies understood that their social mission was to defend culture from the forces of chaos and entropy.[5] A ruler is only human. There were mistakes, and tragedies occurred. But the authority of religious, state, and financial power has always defended and created civilizations.

In the Soviet Union power for the first time in history has sided with anti-culture, with mediocrity against talent, with idleness against diligence, with destruction against creation. My own personal example is sufficiently minor in comparison with the scale of the tragedy, but it is quite eloquent precisely because I am a sculptor. I do not consider myself unique and inimitable, but truth is truth. The tendencies in art I defended have finally won out, but with what unnecessary losses! At what cost! Why?! Where is the root of this evil? The usual answer is: the post-revolutionary Thermidor[6] created the rule of the worst people. But this is no answer; it is only a hypothesis. The worst in what sense? In contrast to Cesare Borgia,[7] Nero,[8] or Peter the Great,[9] Brezhnev,[10] I think, was simply a "nice guy." But for some reason those "bad" tyrants after their demise left not only ugly memories, but also a powerful mark on the history of art.

But what can Brezhnev boast about? Only those works that happened to slip through due to negligence. The vulgarity and incompetence of the upstarts and the ignoramuses of the Brezhnev period were flagrant, although there were devotees of music, poetry, and literature among the ruling elite. Every now and then a member of the elite would sincerely attempt to patronize art, while the worst of them would usually – according to the laws of social and psychological necessity – learn to do so and, when they replaced the old elite, would undertake the defense of culture.

But why didn't this take place? What kept it from happening? "The lack of alternatives is what is unfortunate," the foes of centralization would say. "There is only one patron – the State." That is a possible explanation. But, after all, it is precisely through the efforts of the State or of a group of authorities commanding centralized resources that the finest models of art have arisen. It is possible to rationalize and raise one question after another endlessly by noting only the external characteristics of the process, but not its motive force. My own experience suggests another answer, one that rests not on the personal qualities of those in power, nor on organizational structures, but on the ideology of culture itself.

Soviet power did not attempt to destroy culture, for mere mortals cannot carry out such an evil idea. A politician proclaiming evil as his goal is unimaginable. No, even the most unbridled tyrant is "altruistic." Force is his means of making others happy. The inner cause lying at the basis of the misfortune that has overtaken Russian culture was that an attempt was made after the 1917 Russian Revolution to create a new culture on the rotten and illiterate basis of a class approach to art.

Art was considered to be the direct continuation of the social and economic structure of society. The Marxist notions of "base" and "superstructure" are well-known. According to this theory, progressive art is born in the depths of old foundations. When a new base is established, progressive art blossoms and becomes dominant. After the October Revolution of 1917 every artist claimed that progressive role. The Russian Association of Proletarian Writers (RAPP) and other groups of the 1920s represented new (i.e. "proletarian") art, but in the socialist realism of the 1930s it was discerned that, while they were far from the highest models of "reactionary" art, nonetheless historical "truth" backed them up. This error distinguished not only the "victors", but also the "vanquished": Aleksandr Blok,[11] Boris Pasternak,[12] Osip Mandelstam,[13] Sergei Esenin,[14] and even Vladimir Mayakovsky[15] considered themselves fragments of a vanishing past.

Psychologically the same thing happened when early Christian values replaced Hellenic ones. Inept and semi-literate (from the viewpoint of Greek canons), the masters of early Christian art had a sense of a higher truth, and the most farsighted representatives of Hellenism sensed that beyond those flat "barbaric" representations stood an invincible work of the spirit. This spirit indeed did stand behind Christian art, but it is not present in Soviet socialist realism. God and the Devil, Life and Death, Good and Evil – those were the subjects of art. Everyday scenes and even objects were permeated with a spiritual sense of life. In works of art the pulse of the cosmic whole, the pulse of Being, pounded.

Why couldn't socialist realism, then, develop simply a style, if not a civilization? Because art is not just a social phenomenon. Although art, of course, can be used for propaganda, that does not exhaust its essence. Can a culture develop when it believes that the plastic arts of music and literature are only the continuation of material demands? Can there be a civilization of art and ritual that is liberated not only from lofty idealism, but also from magic and the esoteric as primary characteristics of art objects? A civilization that takes the shell and surface of past ages can only imitate the external appearance of spiritual work without faith in the spiritual nature of art and culture as a whole.

Because socialist realism[16] was spiritually barren and theoretically and practically emasculated, it immediately became petty and flat. Quite soon it turned out that there was no proletarian art, nor could there ever be, that proletarian art was a phantom serving talentless cynics. "I may be a worse artist than you, but I am right because I am a proletarian" became the first slogan of a careerist.

Later on the slogan was changed to: "I am better because I'm in charge." This created a favorable atmosphere for the mass mediocrity of Salieris[17] to be directed against the few Mozarts.[18] Thus, Shchigalev's proposal in Dostoevsky's *The Possessed*[19] was realized: Mozart should have been killed in his cradle. Consciously, for the sake of the happiness of the mediocre, a crime against humanity was committed.

During the period of its existence, the mighty Soviet state squandered enormous amounts of money with which the beginnings of a new civilization could have been established. By killing and eliminating in a centralized way any competition against a talentless army of bootlickers usurping the right to represent the culture of a great people and basing themselves on the theory of socialist realism, not a single original work could develop, nor make anyone happy, not even a worker. Mayakovsky, Maksim Gorky,[20] Mikhail Sholokhov,[21] and even Aleksandr Fadeev[22] were sacrifices! And in what way were they socialist realists? How were they essentially different from any good writer from another culture? Everything that socialist realism takes pride in has no relation either to its theory or practice. There have always been bad and talentless artists, but there is no reason to call dullness a proletarian style. In the final analysis this is unfair to the proletariat! Soviet art is whatever you wish – from futurism[23] to realism, from modernism[24] to naturalism.[25] The phantom of socialist realism is only materialized non-being. And, like any vampire, it needs blood from the living in order to simulate life.

At the present time the vampire of socialist realism is sucking the blood of the Russian Silver Age[26] that it killed, the fresh blood of the art of Nikolai Gumilev,[27] Andrei Platonov,[28] Boris Pasternak, Osip Mandelstam,[29] Mikhail Bulgakov,[30] and other writers, and the same thing is happening in art, music, theater, and film. If we, untouched by this phantom, are worth anything, it will drink our blood too. It is possible that I, too, will be transformed after death into a socialist realist. Alas, once bitten by the vampire, we ourselves, against our will, will become like it.

Yes, I know that some of my friends in Russia might say: "Why are you pounding on an open door? Everyone – both the artists and the authorities – knows that the best works of Soviet culture have been created in spite of socialist realism and its theories. People work and pay no attention to that phantom." I don't believe that. Cursing socialist realism creates an atmosphere of danger. If proponents of socialist realism don't kill you, then they deprive you of your will and force you to lead a humiliating existence.

Everything bad, talentless, and moribund rests on falsehood struggling against the living. In its day Russian society found the strength to say to those opposed to genetics: "Stop lying!" Is it not time to forbid the theoreticians of socialist realism from lying? And, pounding in the aspen stake, to say to that vampire: "Rot!"

[1] Phidias (c500-c432 BC), great Greek sculptor who idealized the human form.
[2] Michelangelo (See Chapter One, note 27).
[3] Pericles (c495-429 BC), Athenian general and statesman.
[4] Sistine Chapel, papal chapel in the Vatican known for its frescoes by Michelangelo, Perugino, and Botticelli.
[5] Entropy, dissipation of energy in thermodynamics.
[6] Thermidor, eleventh month of the calendar adopted by the French Revolution and in effect from 1793 to 1805. The downfall of Robespierre (July 27, 1794) is referred to as the coup of 9 Thermidor.
[7] Cesare Borgia (c1476-1507), Italian patron of the arts.
[8] Nero (37-68 AD), infamous Roman emperor.
[9] Peter I [the Great] (1672-1725), tsar of Russia and founder of St. Petersburg (1703).
[10] Brezhnev (See Introduction, note 39).
[11] Aleksandr Aleksandrovich Blok (1880-1921), foremost Russian symbolist poet, author of *The Twelve*.
[12] Boris Leonidovich Pasternak (1890-1960), major Russian poet, translator, and author of *Doctor Zhivago;* Nobel Laureate in Literature (1958).
[13] Mandelstam (See Chapter Three, note 51).
[14] Sergei Aleksandrovich Esenin (1895-1925), Russian lyric poet of peasant origin.
[15] Mayakovsky (See Introduction, note 74).
[16] Socialist realism, Soviet state aesthetic system that affirms the concrete representation of reality in its revolutionary develop-

ment and the transformation of workers in the spirit of socialism as the aims of art.

[17] Antonio Salieri (1750-1825), Italian court musician in Vienna, rival of Mozart, and teacher of Schubert, Beethoven, and Liszt.

[18] Wolfgang Amadeus Mozart (1756-91), Austrian composer and musician of genius.

[19] Dostoevsky's political novel *The Possessed [Besy]* (1873).

[20] Maksim Gorky [Aleksei Maksimovich Peshkov] (1868-1936), Russian author and exponent of Socialist Realism.

[21] Mikhail Aleksandrovich Sholokhov (1905-84), Soviet writer and Nobel Laureate in Literature (1965).

[22] Aleksandr Aleksandrovich Fadeev (1901-56), classic Stalinist author of *The Rout* (1927) and *The Young Guard* (1945).

[23] Futurism, twentieth century art movement in Italy and Russia celebrating the speed and dynamism of the machine age.

[24] Modernism, theory and practice of modern art.

[25] Naturalism, realistic rendering and conformity to nature in the arts.

[26] Russian Silver Age (1890-1914), a period of Russian culture marked by an apocalyptic mood and a remarkable flowering of the arts.

[27] Nikolai Stepanovich Gumilev (1886-1921), Russian Acmeist poet associated with the journal *Apollon*.

[28] Andrei Platonov [Andrei Platonovich Klimentov] (1899-1951), Soviet writer, journalist, poet, and author of *Kotlovan* and *Chevengur*.

[29] Mandelstam (See Chapter Three, note 51).

[30] Mikhail Afanasievich Bulgakov (1891-1940), Russian writer and playwright, author of *The Master and Margarita*.

CHAPTER NINE

Art and Society

I.

FREEDOM. What is it? Perhaps only space and time have as many contradictory interpretations as the apparently simple word FREEDOM. There has never been a single political or religious movement in history that did not make freedom one of its basic aims.

From the infinite series of definitions of freedom we shall examine only two. Karl Marx defines freedom as "necessity consciously understood." But what kind of "necessity" was he speaking about?! Then there is the following explanation of the word FREE in the children's *Sesame Street Dictionary:* "When you are free, you can move in any direction" – a definition intelligible in its naiveté and without any claims to wisdom. Yet the central question remains: But where do you wish to go?

The life of each individual human being is complex, enormous, and enigmatic. A countless number of drives and desires are compressed within our finite corporeal envelope. MAN CONSISTS OF CONTRADICTIONS.

A foot soldier breathes freely in the ranks. Collective breathing, movement, rhythm, goals. And only dust and more dust from shuffling boots. FREEDOM.

Sweet freedom from responsibility. It has been decided for you where to go. And you are not alone: you are a part of something directed at a common goal. And even when you sleep, you and everyone else in the collective are moving towards this goal.

A SOLDIER SLEEPS, BUT HIS JOB GOES ON.

An American pioneer breathes freely in the prairie. He can move in any direction. He can choose any goal. He can structure his life as he wishes. Because everything depends only on him, on his mind, strength, dexterity, and will. He is absolutely free.

But on him weighs the heaviest burden of all – RESPONSIBILITY FOR CHOOSING THE DIRECTION OF HIS OWN FATE. And he is responsible even when he is asleep.

In each person stirs a striving for both tranquillity and initiative: a desire to live in peace, even in prison, clashes with a drive for limitless expanses.

Claustrophobia and agoraphobia alternate and conduct an endless dialogue in everyone's heart.

Precisely these innate qualities of the human soul comprise the background and, quite possibly, the foundation of the drama of human history unfolding in time.

Being in a position to know and compare the USSR and America first-hand, I speak as a creature on whom a social experiment in totally different concepts of freedom has been conducted. Not theoretical reflections, but practical knowledge is the basis of my conclusions.

As the epigraph to these conclusions I would take the words of Francisco Goya: "These things I have witnessed."[1]

In my Moscow studio I once debated for six hours the concept of freedom with Jean-Paul Sartre.[2] Sartre, evidently, had forgotten that the possibility of going where one wishes is a basic human need and one of the fundamental elements of freedom. He spoke about the absolute philosophical concept of freedom. But, in the context of my own life and life in general in the Soviet Union, Sartre's words sounded simply indecent. It would be as if I were to prove to a starving Hindu that his hunger would pass, if only he acknowledged its necessity.

In the context of my personal experience, human freedom is a relative concept. Different societies have different degrees of freedom. Different peoples have different degrees of freedom. A single person, even in the course of one day, experiences different degrees of freedom. In prison I possess one degree of freedom; in the Soviet Army, another degree of freedom. A soldier and an officer have different freedoms. I was a Soviet sculptor and became an American one. And these are all different levels of freedom.

How a person speaks about freedom in the context of actual circumstances reveals his true character. Because there is always a moral aspect concealed in definitions of freedom. FREEDOM FROM WHAT AND FOR WHAT?!

MOZART[3]

When we speak of the power of light we use the concept "watts." How many watts? I would propose the concept "Mozarts" to define the level of talent.

We all are born talented. In each child slumbers a particle of Mozart, a certain quantity of talent. The question is: what kind and how much?

Let us present these mysterious potentialities in the form of zeroes. In one child slumbers ten zeroes, or Mozart units; but in another, just one. But if a person were to put a one before this zero (10), but none before the ten zeroes (0000000000), then it turns out that the number 10 is greater than ten or even an infinite series of zeroes (000000000000000...).

Potential, creative energy is inherent in us. It is that inner freedom given to us by God. This creative energy strives to pour forth freely. It is spiritual pressure. An implacable craving to create and understand. But this inborn, inner, mysterious potential can manifest itself only in external real space provided us by life. Circumstances of birth constitute the digit 1 added to the zeroes of creative potential. Where and when were you born? At what period of time and in which country?

When I speak of freedom, I am speaking of these circumstances. Because freedom is essential for creativity. Creativity is the happy combination of inner freedom given by talent with external freedom given by society. CREATIVITY IS THE PRODUCT OF FREEDOM.

Anyone faced with the impossibility of developing one's energy suffers. And the more gifted the person, the more he or she suffers. For certain people the chance to create is the most important need, a need which often is more important than life itself. Such people are ready to die fighting for the right to create.

SOURCES OF UNFREEDOM

Contemporary culture is the fusion of two cultures: the Judeo-Christian culture of the Bible and the humanistic Greek culture of the Renaissance.[4]

This duality we sense constantly. And not only in the reflections of philosophers, in social institutions, and in codes of law. We sense this duality even in relation to ourselves, to one's corporeal and spiritual identity. The dramatic interaction of two principles – the physical/material and the spiritual – constitutes the basis of art.

Since the time of Machiavelli[5] – scion of the Renaissance and Francis Bacon,[6] the forefather of modern philosophy – our inner vision has become dulled. Ontology[7] was exiled from the Cosmos, as well as from the human microcosmos. The primacy of spirituality was pre-empted by materialism. Philosophy, science, and art were no longer means of knowing the secrets of existence, but practical instruments for extracting material goods from nature to satisfy the human body and belly.

We try to ignore the chief element in the visions of Sir Isaac Newton,[8] creator and prophet of modern science, who understood that the universe is no mere mechanism and that matter constantly experiences the influence of other layers of being. The artist has detached himself from fundamental problems and is being transformed more and more into a technician producing goods. In the East, there is socialist realism,[9] subject to ideology and propaganda; in the West, there is hedonistic socialist realism and sensual conformity, subject to market demands.

Let us quickly take a look at these two phenomena, both arising from the same root of anti-spirituality.

Socialism,[10] the legitimate child of the ideology of anti-spirituality, adopting the slogans of Humanism,[11] loudly proclaimed that changing material, economic conditions were the basis of universal human liberation.

The Russian artistic avant-garde sided with the Revolution of 1917 precisely for this reason. But the angel of revolutionary freedoms in Russia has expired. And the Soviet ruling elite has become a closed supersect totally repudiating the goals that produced it.

UTOPIA[12] was not achieved. A limited petit-bourgeoisie and a dissolute lumpenproletariat took the place of the enlightened philosopher and representative of the people. The State machine did not need revolutionaries, poets, or philosophers. Boldness, imagination, and intelligence became negative traits. Servility, cowardice, and absence of initiative were the qualities valued by the State machine.

The mechanical structure of Soviet society itself was an organized striving for entropy[13] and death.

The graveyard of Soviet art is monumentally and strictly hierarchical. Marshals and generals of art are ensconsed in expensive crypts. In rather nice ones are entombed colonels and captains of culture. Privates of art are interred in small graves. But every private in the coffin of his fantasies waves the baton of a marshal. Everyone in the Soviet Union has the chance to be a marshal. All one needs to do is to stamp out in oneself everything alive, every last trace of talent and be submissive. And the more one succeeds in so doing, the higher one's place in the Soviet hierarchy. Benefits are distributed according to rank: who will get caviar, meat, chicken, fur hats, and who will get nothing; whose wife is entitled to birth-control pills, and whose is not; who can see foreign films, and who cannot; who can travel abroad, and who cannot. Permission to travel abroad is a reward for good behavior.

From the viewpoint of the Soviet social pyramid-graveyard or, especially, if one has become weary of active competition in the West, it might seem that Soviet reality is not so bad.

History has known the artist-priest, the artist-philosopher, the artist-revolutionary, the artist-madman. But socialist realism has spawned a monster: the artist-bureaucrat, a concept as unnatural as "fireman-arsonist" or "physician-murderer."

True, the Soviet artist is a member of a bureaucratic society. Well, what of it? Everyone in the USSR is a bureaucrat, and so is the artist. The ruling powers guarantee the artist work. The Soviet artist is not alone. The Ministry of Culture, the Union of Artists,[14] and art enterprises work together with the artist on projects. They all carry out the instructions of the Central Committee, the Communist Party, and the KGB,[15] where whole sections are engaged in executing directives, instructions, and resolutions aimed at controlling artists. There is even a section in the Soviet Army engaged in art. In all Soviet republics, regions, cities, and villages such organizations controlling the Artist are duplicated. Tens of thousands of bureaucrats wear out their trousers supervising Art.

Can a person born in America imagine the President, his cabinet, Congress, the FBI, and the CIA stopping their work to punish an artist like the late Andy Warhol?![16] It would be a surrealistic situation. But this took place not only in the grotesque times of Nikita Khrushchev.[17] It is sufficient to recall the instructions of the Central Committee and the personal directives of Comrade Stalin.[18] But this is not love for culture. The Soviet Ministry of Culture bears the same relation to culture as Orwell's Ministry of Love to love.[19]

Terror underlies the entire State apparatus. The terror of the Bureaucrat before the creative power of Mozart. The Soviet State is a police department created by the many-faced collective of bureaucrats-Salieris[20] in order to kill the Mozart in man, to defend Marxist materialistic ideology from the ontological principles inherent in art.

Their battle against art is waged logically and cunningly, like their campaign against religion. Soviet ideology sees art and religion as its principal internal enemies. For Soviet ideologists free art, like faith in God, is a fifth column.

The struggle against religion is waged by socialist atheism; the struggle against art, by socialist realism.

SOCIALIST REALISM

The so-called "theory of socialist realism" is simple to the point of stupidity. The Soviet artist is obliged to see, in present phenomena, sprouts of the future. And since the future is communism, this future must be beautiful. The hungry is depicted as well-fed; the ugly, handsome; the unhappy, happy. This is the socialist part of the teaching.

But since falsehood ought to resemble truth, the artistic representation must be realistic. Socialism plus realism. That's how they got "socialist realism."

In Stalin's time socialist realism was vulgar, provincial naturalism glorifying the handsome Soviet leader, the beautiful Soviet Man, the beautiful Soviet cow, and beautiful Soviet nature. Smooth, sweet, and accessible. But gradually even this primitively propagandistic function vanished.

Socialist realism, as a style of art, did not and does not exist. There were and are individual artists, writers, and musicians working in various manners and styles – from futurism to realism – whom Soviet power persecuted, murdered, forced to commit suicide or to emigrate. And after their demise, or degradation during their lifetime, they were proclaimed "socialist realists" by the Soviet state. These artists were so designated because socialist realism needs the appearance of cultural achievements, if only for the outside world. But there can be no socialist realist among truly great artists because the basis of socialist realism is a psychological state incompatible with creativity: submissiveness, art as you please.

It is the servile readiness of the Soviet artist-bureaucrat to submit to any demands from a bureaucrat-functionary. Everyone should be alike. If Soviet artists were ordered to become abstractionists, they would all be abstract painters. And the Academy of Arts would be renamed the Academy of Socialist Realist-Abstractionist Art of the USSR.

Socialist realism, then, is not a style of art; it is a style of behavior. To be a socialist realist means to be mediocre. Mediocrity has become the standard, because talent presupposes personality. But personality and individuality are deviations from the ranks of an army heading nowhere.

In contemporary Soviet culture even the pose of propaganda has been extinguished. Only negative goals remain. This pseudoculture has been created so that there would be no other. Even monuments to Marx are erected not to depict his greatness, but merely to occupy space that might be filled by a monument to some less desirable person.

In the USSR even functionaries, at times, complain: "What dreary propaganda we have . . ." They might, perhaps, prefer more vivid and convincing propaganda. But it is precisely the dreary that is **not** dangerous, since the temperament and will of an artist are revealed in vivid, convincing works of art.

This negative function of Soviet culture has spawned a huge army of people whom I call the tribe of NO. These people understood the basic idea of socialist realism: the negative, non-creative meaning of everything produced by official Soviet culture. This tribe demands material benefits and prestige from Soviet society not for what they have created, but for the fact that they have created nothing, that is, nothing ideologically incorrect, and that not once have they behaved badly in the eyes of Soviet power. These people demand rewards for not exhibiting talent, for being irreproachable and, therefore, harmless. The more adroit and accommodating members of this clan often become critics of so-called bourgeois ideology and hatchetmen killing everyone and everything talented that happen to appear in Soviet art.

All of Marxism and all Soviet academic culture are founded on these principles of negativism. Marx[21] was a powerful critic of the capitalist system of his time. But his positive principle for restructuring the world is utopian. Marxism, at best, is political poetry. As a result, Soviet people are masters of accusations and denunciations.

Soviet philosophical science basically consists of volumes of denunciations of what should **not** be. Marxists are masters of the NO, of the negation. This, then, is the theory and practice of the great NOTHINGNESS in the Soviet Union.

SOCIALIST REALISM IS NOT ART.

When we speak of style in art, a certain image, sign, or symbol occurs to us. When I utter the word GOTHIC,[22] you will mentally outline or trace tension directed upwards. An archetype. A sign. A vivid indication of the existence of a distinct style. This is obligatory not only for a culture formed over a long period of time.

Various tendencies in art today exhibit vivid attributes: impressionism,[23] abstractionism,[24] Pop Art.[25]

Now I ask you to concentrate and to visualize socialist realism as a whole, not as a discrete social phenomenon, but as a sign. I am convinced that you will see no image or symbol, because every symbol is a sign of something, an image of some kind of being or reality.

CATACOMB CULTURE[26]

The theory and practice of the great NOTHINGNESS. Spiritual non-being engenders ennui. Everyone is bored: the bureaucrat-boss who commissions a work of art; the bureaucrat-artist who executes it; the bureaucrat-functionary who unveils it. And, of course, the people for whom this tedium was created.

Boredom has become a distinctive form of patriotism. Soviet society is mired in boredom and apathy, but even the terror of all before all does not make existence meaningful. After all, boredom cannot replace the natural, innate human need for a spiritual life.

BOREDOM PRODUCES PROTEST.

We frequently overlook the influence of boredom on history. It is precisely stagnation and spiritual mustiness of societies and institutions that have stimulated, as protest, outbursts of spiritual energy.

The best people would go underground into the catacombs to create a new culture mightier than the official one, a culture more sincere, more substantial.

In Russian reality the artist has always assumed moral and philosophical responsibility. Even before the appearance in Russia of philosophy in the Western sense of the word, there existed the concept of philosophical speculation in Russian religious painting. This tradition has been preserved to this day.

The fathers of the Russian revolutionary avant-garde perceived form as a continuation of metaphysics, as a path to spiritual heights.

The messianic tendencies[27] of Russian intellectuals quite often arouse indignation in the West. It is obvious that messianism is not only a Russian trait. But in its pure, refined, almost caricatured form there were indeed a greater number of artists in Russia with prophetic inclinations.

When a person deprived of rights cannot get a reply to his inquiries from official institutions, when an individual craving spiritual perfection cannot trust official spiritual pastors, then THE ARTIST ASSUMES RESPONSIBILITY FOR SPEAKING THE TRUTH.

Such was the case even in more liberal Tsarist Russia. At the present time this tendency is intensified a thousand-fold.

Art has become not a profession, but the serving of higher values, a MISSION. As Dostoevsky once wrote: "Beauty will save the world."[28]

Dostoevsky, beginning to describe the "insulted and the humiliated,"[29] discovered that it was not enough to describe, that – no matter where he turned – there were lacunae: ethics, law, religious and moral problems. The framework of purely professional literature became too narrow for his sensitive, wounded soul. He created a model of the Gothic cathedral in which his own novels were elements, parts. In order to work, Dostoevsky was obliged to create his own ethics, aesthetics, sociology, microcosm.

The same thing happened to Tolstoy.[30] It was not enough for him to be a writer. He began to create a microreligion: Tolstoyanism.[31]

The same thing is happening to Solzhenitsyn,[32] for an adequate circle of knowledge of modern Russian history simply did not exist. And he had to fill this gap. His pain was the pain of millions. To a greater or lesser degree this pain concerns any serious Russian artist today.

The Soviet bureaucrat understands this tendency of living Russian culture and fears it like fire.

The terror of those who live in fear is becoming greater than that of those persecuted. More and more, catacomb culture is struggling against official culture, sometimes boldly, sometimes through Aesopian language[33] within the bounds of a literary text.

Terrible nightmares haunt the Soviet bureaucrat: the conspiracy of uncontrolled art and subtexts. The bureaucrat's nightmare has spawned a new profession: SPECIALIST IN UNCONTROLLED SUBTEXTS.[34] The irony lies in the fact that if there's a specialist in any given area, then a specialist on the specialist must arise. And then a whole section of specialists on specialists. And finally a ministry of specialists. And so on in a geometric progression.

As a result of this bureaucratic logic, the entire country ought to cease growing grain, producing metal, and working in general: everyone ought to be spying on everyone else to ferret out "uncontrolled subtexts." And although this happens to a certain extent, life all the same is not the "House that Jack Built."[35] Somewhere a critical limit is reached, not subject to the will of the bureaucrat.

CATACOMB CULTURE, THE HOPE OF THE FUTURE, IS ALIVE.

II.

Efficiency is the Western economic principle. The cultured individual is a "self-actualizing personality."[36] But a free personality clashing with a free, well-organized market system is often defeated. The free market, based on economic efficiency, supports socialist realism – not communist, but hedonistic.

SENSUAL SALON CONFORMITY

The bourgeois consumer wants artists to serve him, to adorn his life, to dispel his ennui, or to be a source of income. The questions – WHERE DO WE COME FROM? WHO ARE WE? WHERE ARE WE GOING? – cease to interest a person who has become a market personality.

For the artist to raise such questions is generally considered improper, a violation of the rules of good taste. The modern artist, like a gentleman, is expected to speak only of trifles. The existing pluralism of form and the enormous diversity of styles in contemporary art do not dispel this problem. If we were to measure contemporary art by the great questions of human life, it would approximate socialist realism in its conformity and monotony.

Post-industrial society. The society of gentlemen. A society oriented to leisure demands hedonistic art, just as the masses demand bread and circuses. The *nouveaux riches* today look upon the artist as a decorator or a clown. Picasso,[37] Dali,[38] Duchamp,[39] and other modern artists wore the tragic mask of a clown. Wisdom beneath a buffoon's mask is an ancient tradition. They were provocative, tragic clowns. But the challenging role of the tragic clown is, apparently, a thing of the past. The new generation of clowns is comic. They neither provoke nor educate; they only serve. Although they wear the masks of artistic revolutionaries, they are really poodles clipped to resemble lions.

What are the causes of conformity in art? The decline of society, accursed alienation?

Or do the same values permeate the worldview of both the market and the artist?

Man is created for happiness, as a bird for flight. Who said that? A representative of the aesthetic revolt of the 1960s?[40] A young follower of sensual Orpheus[41] rising up against diligent Prometheus?[42] No, this is one of the basic slogans of socialist realism.

"Paradise at once." Who said that? The creator of socialist realism? No, this is one of the basic tenets of the aesthetics of revolt.

By happiness is meant not spiritual elevation, but material possessions. Nor does it matter that mystical motifs of early Christianity, the Tantras,[43] and Buddhism[44] appear in the pied movement of the new counter-culture. The personages of cosmological myth are freed from ontology. Freudian anthropology,[45] Rousseau's noble savage,[46] and many other elements have mated with Marxism, that is, with the most consistent materialism. Carnival, the mass action of mysteries, and psycho-drama are nothing new: they were all known in antiquity.

And gradually the gay and varicolored costumes of individuals assembled in a crowd begin to resemble the uniforms of an army. Extravagant Narcissuses[47] no longer appear extravagant: they look like everyone else. Carnival has assumed an institutionalized character. After all, the organized revolutionaries of the French Revolution walked in Roman dress. And now appears a "new" slogan: "To find a political function for art that does not seem to be conservative." But that was the same slogan with which socialist realism began. The circle is closed: aesthetic Orpheus has been transformed into practical Prometheus. But Prometheus, as you know, knew how to count.

THE CULT OF ORGASM AND THE CULT OF MAMMON MERGE.

Modern art is the best created during the twentieth-century. It has exerted a mighty influence on the face of our time, on people's way of thinking. By means of mass culture the influence and popularity of artists has attained proportions unheard of in history.

But, as often happens, the victor was vanquished by his own weapon. The new, as the aim of art, has become the foe of new art.

Newness has acquired market meaning. Technological concepts appropriate for evaluating machines are now used to assess spiritual human activity. The new has come to mean the better. New cars, TVs. A person lying on a new sofa needs new art. And new "geniuses" are created by merchants of art. Totally fresh. A genius of the last fifteen minutes. Commissioned revolt is packaged in the cellophane wrappers of fashionable journals and sold in doses like pharmaceutical preparations for debility, potency, insomnia. But the market is sensitive and dynamic; it reacts instantly to any change of consumer taste. Here, as nowhere else, is revealed the interaction of reciprocal relations. Times change. "The radical children of liberal fathers" began to replace the "conservative children of radical parents."[48] A longing for fixed values appears. And the market itself returns to us the names of artists who had the courage to withstand the pressure of fashion.

The free market has no ideological reason to kill Mozart. In the USSR the killing of creative potential in a person proceeds from the practical foundations of socialist realism. In the West the artists themselves are imbued with a market psychology. For an artist with the courage to stand alone, the market is not frightening. It is the business of the market to sell; it is the business of the artist to develop his or her God-given talent.

Freedom frequently spawns evil. But freedom also provides the opportunity to create the good. It is up to the individuals themselves. I believe in the spiritual power of the American concept of freedom. It is possible to draw courage from the awareness of one's personal responsibility before a free choice.

The enormous expanses of this country are not simply geographical space. Spaciousness becomes an element of human psychology. Space unites all nations and peoples of the world. Step by step, in struggle and contradiction, authentic culture is formed that absorbs the past and the present from the most diverse civilizations.

Russian catacomb culture – defending freedom beneath the symbols of the Cross and the Star of David and emerging from the underground – is imparting to America its long-suffering experience, in which the concept of freedom encompasses purpose, meaning, choice, will, and idea.[49]

America is the youthful land of permanent revolution, the land of swift and perpetual change. Movement is hope. In America there is hope for the appearance of an art in which the profound vertical axis containing ontological, metaphysical, and other historically-formed values intersects with the impetuous horizontal axis assimilating contemporary values of the age of technical revolution. And, where the vertical and the horizontal meet, a new art will arise.[50]

[1] Francisco Goya (1746-1828), Spanish painter and graphic artist known for his etchings, *The Disasters of War* (1810-14).
[2] Jean-Paul Sartre (1905-80), French existentialist philosopher and writer.
[3] Mozart (See Chapter Eight, note 18).
[4] Renaissance (c1350-1650), the transition from the Middle Ages to modern times.
[5] Niccolo Machiavelli (1469-1527), Florentine statesman and writer, author of *The Prince* (1532).
[6] Francis Bacon (1561-1626), English philosopher and statesman
[7] Ontology, a branch of metaphysics that studies the nature of being and existence.
[8] Sir Isaac Newton (1542-1626), great natural philosopher and mathematician, discover of calculus and author of the theory of gravitation.
[9] Socialist realism (See Chapter Eight, note 16).
[10] Socialism, an economic philosophy and social movement which seeks to establish a just, classless society through public ownership of the means of production and distribution of goods.
[11] Humanism, Renaissance revival of classical Greek, Latin, and Hebrew literature.
[12] Utopia, an imaginary ideal state envisioned by Sir Thomas More in his *Utopia* (1516).
[13] Entropy (See Chapter Eight, note 5).
[14] Union of Soviet Artists, one of the "creative unions" established by Stalin to enforce conformity to socialist realism in the arts.
[15] KGB (See Chapter Six, note 10).
[16] Andy Warhol (1930?-80), American filmmaker and exponent of Pop Art.

[17] Khrushchev (See Chapter Six, note 8).
[18] Iosif Vissarionovich Stalin [Soso Dzhugazhvili] (1879-1953), dictatorial leader of USSR (1924-53).
[19] Reference to the dystopian novel, *1984* (1949) by George Orwell [Eric Arthur Blair] (1903-50).
[20] Salieri (See Chapter Eight, note 17).
[21] Marx (See Chapter Three, note 45).
[22] Gothic, the dominant style of European architecture from the twelfth through the fifteenth centuries, characterized by pointed arches, ribbed vaults, and flying buttresses.
[23] Impressionism, influential art movement developed by Manet, Monet, and Pissarro in late nineteenth century France and based on the use of bright colors to convey the illusion of light.
[24] Abstractionism, non-representational art.
[25] Pop Art (See Chapter Four, note 16).
[26] Catacomb culture: Neizvestny's term for unofficial, underground culture in the USSR.
[27] Messianic tendencies (See Chapter Three).
[28] See Chapter Three, note 23.
[29] See Chapter Four, note 14.
[30] Tolstoy (See Chapter One, note 22).
[31] Tolstoyanism, a system of ethics based on non-violent resistance to evil.
[32] Solzhenitsyn (See Chapter Three, notes 31 and 53).
[33] Aesopian language: the animal allegories attributed to legendary Greek author, Aesop (c6th century BC).
[34] Subtext, underlying system of allegorical allusions in a work.
[35] *The House That Jack Built*, a children's song based on the cyclical repetition of elements.
[36] A reference to the theory of self-actualization postulated by Abraham Maslow (1908-70).
[37] Picasso (See Chapter Two, note 45).
[38] Salvador Dali (1904-89), Spanish surrealist painter whose works juxtaposed images from dreams and hallucinations.
[39] Marcel Duchamp (1887-1968), French artist and pioneer of Dada, Cubism, and Futurism.
[40] A reference to the "counter-culture movement" of the 1960s in the United States.

[41] Orpheus, Thracian musician of Greek myth who tamed wild beasts with his lyre-playing.
[42] Prometheus, titan of Greek mythology who stole fire from the gods to benefit humanity.
[43] Tantras, the texts of Tantrism, a system of esoteric Hindu and Buddhist practices.
[44] Buddhism, the ascetic religious philosophy developed in India in the sixth century BC by Siddhartha Gautama, the Buddha.
[45] Freud (See Chapter Two, note 63).
[46] Jean-Jacques Rousseau (1712-78), Swiss-born French philosopher, writer, and political theorist who affirmed nature as the source of all virtue; author of *The Social Contract* (1762) and *Emile* (1762).
[47] Narcissus, a beautiful youth whom Nemesis caused to fall in love with his own reflected image in a fountain and to be transformed into the flower that bears his name.
[48] Reference to *Fathers and Children*, a novel by Ivan Turgenev.
[49] Reference to Christian and Jewish dissidents in the Soviet Union.
[50] An earlier form of this translation was published in *Proceedings of the Summer 1986 Intensive Workshop in Chinese and Russian*, edited by Albert Leong, 253-63 (Eugene: University of Oregon Press, 1988). Reprinted with permission from Oregon *Studies in Chinese and Russian Culture*, edited by Albert Leong (New York: Peter Lang Publishers, 1990)

CHAPTER TEN

Genius and the Art Market

What is art? Is there an answer? There have been many definitions given by philosophers, art critics, and sociologists. But allow me to begin with a definition of art handed down by an American court of law.

The former director of the Museum of Modern Art and father of American photography, Edward Steichen,[1] told me this story. The court case was connected with Steichen's suit against United States customs officials who would not allow him to bring in duty-free a small abstract sculpture by Brancusi.[2] In general, according to American law, art objects brought in from other countries are not subject to taxes. But, evidently, the Brancusi work Steichen brought back did not correspond to the custom officials' concept of art. And although the tax he had to pay was not much, Steichen considered the issue at stake of fundamental importance. Therefore, the case reached the court, which rendered the following judgment: "Any object can be considered an art object if its creator considers it as such and if another person also agrees that it is art."

At first glance, this appears to be a typical example of judicial casuitry devoid of any sense. Does it mean that any graphomane who smears something unimaginable on canvas to the rapturous praise of his wife or mistress can proclaim himself a creator of art? But, as often happens in a court of justice, that which first seems absurd and alogical turns out to be full of profound meaning. Yes, our graphomane will call himself a Van Gogh[3] or a Raphael[4] and he may be acknowledged as such by his partner (that is, the presence of a second person affirming the artist's genius), but he will all the same remain a nonentity until he receives the acknowledgment of society. However, the most important point is something else: namely, that anyone can take brush in hand or a sculptor's chisel and embark on the path of art. In this sense the court decision in Steichen's case was a great triumph for freedom of art. This freedom is given to all. There are no legal limits keeping one from demonstrating one's artistic genius. The rest depends on the artist's personality. Society disclaims responsibility for art: the artist himself is responsible.

In the USSR there are 14,000 artists listed. What distinguishes them from everyone else? Only one thing: their membership in the Union of Soviet Artists,[5] whether municipal, regional, or national. If Picasso[6] or Salvador Dali[7] are not members, let them remain nobodies. Raphael, if he is not invited to join the Union of Artists, means nothing and nobody needs him.

In New York alone there are 470,000 artists, that is, more than thirty times greater than in all of the Soviet Union. And this figure includes only people with American passports. How many additional émigré artists, legal or illegal, are there?

What, then, distinguishes the American artist from all other people? In New York there are no creative unions. In New York no one answers for the artists. No one instructs them in anything. Their mark of distinction is that they call themselves artists and are ready to prove this in the art market. After all, out of 470,000 artists competing for this market, less than 10% manage to support themselves by art alone. I believe that these two figures dramatize the plight of art in the United States: extraordinary tension and unbelievably sharp battles among artists to survive and to affirm themselves in the art market.

Another question arises: where did all those artists, all those people claiming to be part of art, to be intellectuals and even geniuses, come from in such a short period of time? Let's start with the fact that three technological revolutions in America have liberated an enormous number of people from physical labor. Until recently 40% of the people were farmers who fed the other 60% of the American population. Today, as we know, only 2% suffice to feed the whole country. And all these changes took place in the course of a single generation. What happened to the other 38%? Part of them, no doubt, went into business, another into the military, others into medicine, some into law. But all those people still did not make up the majority. The majority of people, hard to believe, had neither the desire, the determination, nor the money to get an education and rise to the highest intellectual levels of society. Thus, under these conditions, the easiest role to play was the "intellectual": writer, poet, artist, inscribing "self-employed writer" or "self-employed artist" under occupation in customs declarations. It took no more to become an "intellectual" in this country.

We can only guess how this "intellectual revolution" proceeded, how much narcissism, ardent hope, and wounded ambition rushed into this "breech," how a sea of dilettantes mingled with professional artists, how an armada of psychopaths proclaimed themselves unacknowledged geniuses, how many pseudo-intellectuals turned up side-by-side with people of really lofty spirit.

All this defines the context of the art market, where it is harder and harder to distinguish the dilettante from the creator, the innovator from the merely vulgar provocateur, the creators of brilliant provocative works from their pathetic imitators in this muddy, roaring flood of graphomania.

Each artist claims to have an exceptional personality and, what seems more often to those around him, believes in his own genius. The inability to prove this produces in him a wounded sensibility and boundless ambition. Sometimes he becomes depressed or hysterical and is ready to negate everything, first of all the reality that surrounds him. And quite often, when I see the crowds of leftist intellectuals, artists, and writers demanding creative freedom (which society has somehow taken away from them), when I look upon their turbulent protest demonstrations, I begin to understand that they are pouring out the bitterness brimming in their hearts at their personal lack of success. Their protest against the age that gave them the opportunity to do what was genetically against their nature is a revolt against fate, which did not make them a Michelangelo[8] or a Dante[9] at once. That's why they flipped their lids. After all, for themselves, for those around them, and for their wives or mistresses they have already declared themselves geniuses and ardently believe that this is the case. Now they hurl curses at the society that is not ready to recognize their talent. Their external radicalism essentially poses as genius, as in the game of love when demurring is actually an invitation in the form of protest. The hysterical cries of "No! No! I don't want to!" in fact serve as passionate appeals: "I'm ready! I'm here! Why don't you take me?!"

I shall cite a scene from my early notes about the New York art market. The scene is an inspired caricature written under my first, keen impressions of life in New York. Therefore, having apologized to the reader in advance, I shall not change a single detail.

> "Many art exhibits recall youthful masturbation, a cynicism born of a fear of life, the superficial wit of pimpled youth, adolescents admiring their own freedom, kids who boldly tell their mothers that they won't eat their jello for dessert. Here's one bold guy in glasses dragging stones across a parquet floor in a fine home off limits to others. And without rhythm or any kind of visual tension he simply throws the stones on the parquet floor. Ladies, smoking, champagne, collectors, movie cameras. And this 'artist,' proud, independent, and flushed with success hears comments like: 'Well, you know, it's a form of protest. The concept of protest. Anti-aesthetics. Would you like some champagne? Excuse me, but I must go now. The critic from *Art America* has just arrived.' At that very moment I visualize my peers blown up with stones, flying and falling to earth, into the ocean, into swamps, and even onto a parquet floor.[10] I have seen stones from explosions on parquet floors in Vienna and Budapest; I have seen stones falling on the parquet floors of palaces. And I myself have shattered

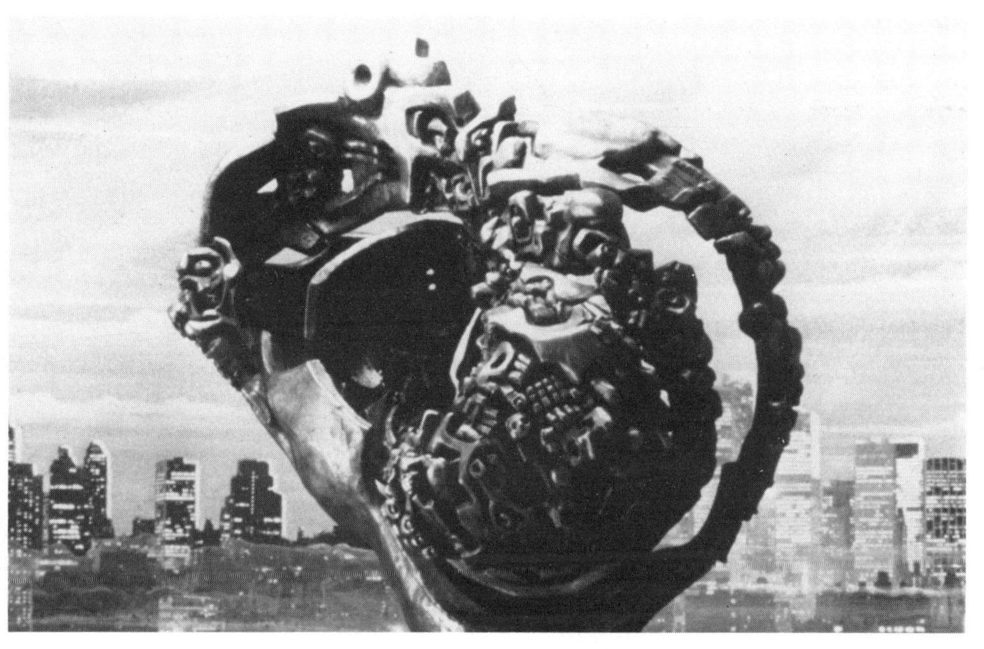

Drevo zhizni (Tree of Life), 1968-76
Bronze, 60.96 x 60.96 x 60.96 cm.
New York

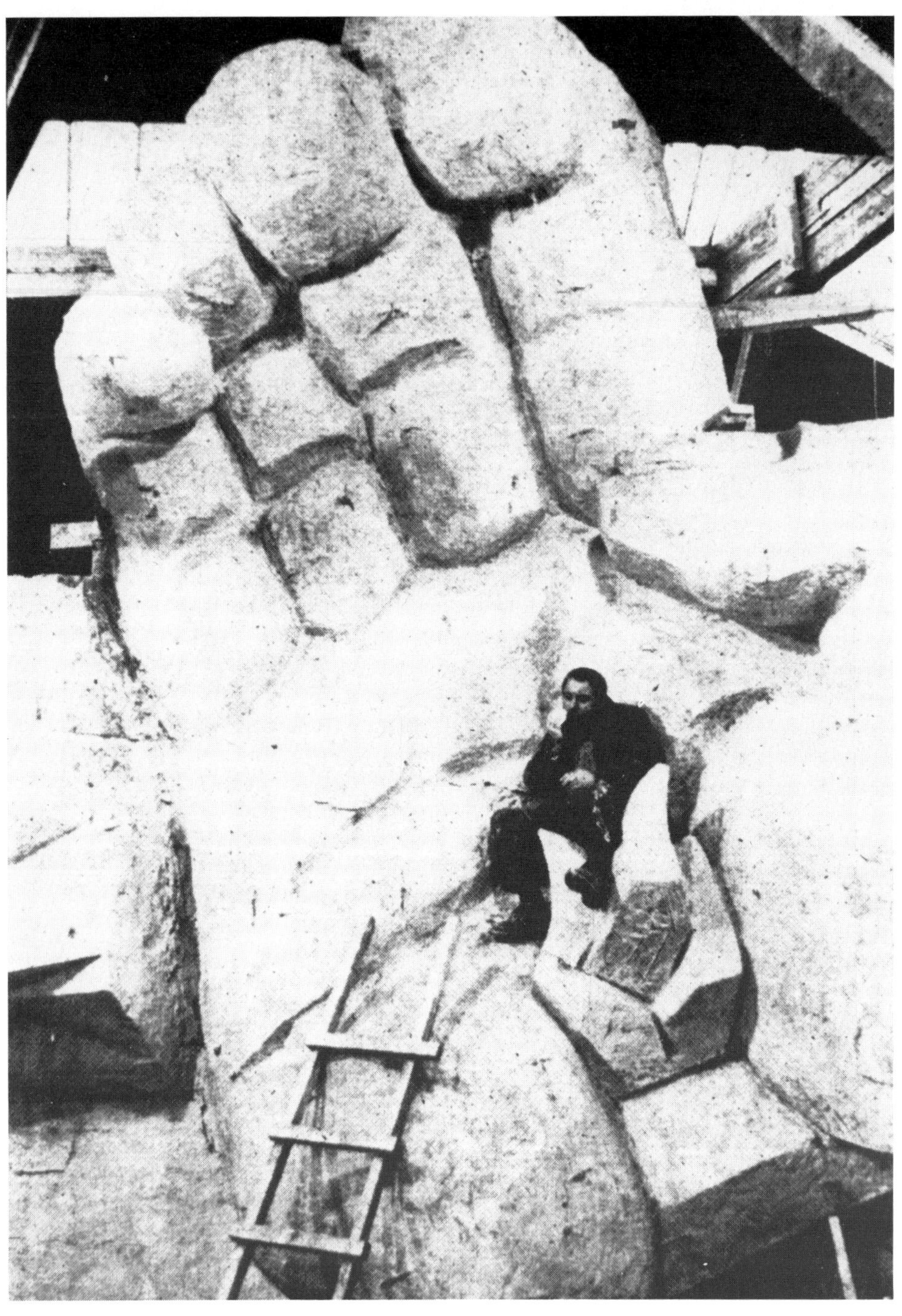

Detail, *Ruka i ia* (The Hand and I), from *Prometei* (Prometheus), 1966
Latvian tuff, 150 sq. meters
Artek Pioneer Camp, USSR

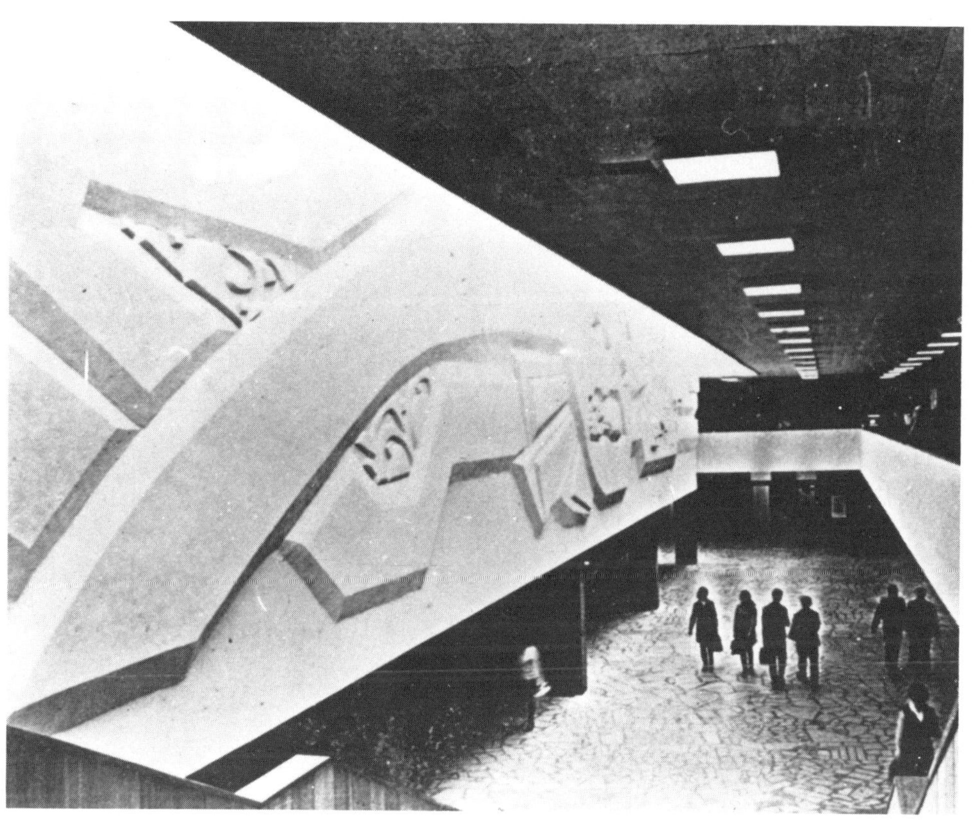

Chelovek i nauka (Man and Science), 1974
Concrete relief, 970 sq. meters.
Institute of Electronics and Technology, Moscow, USSR

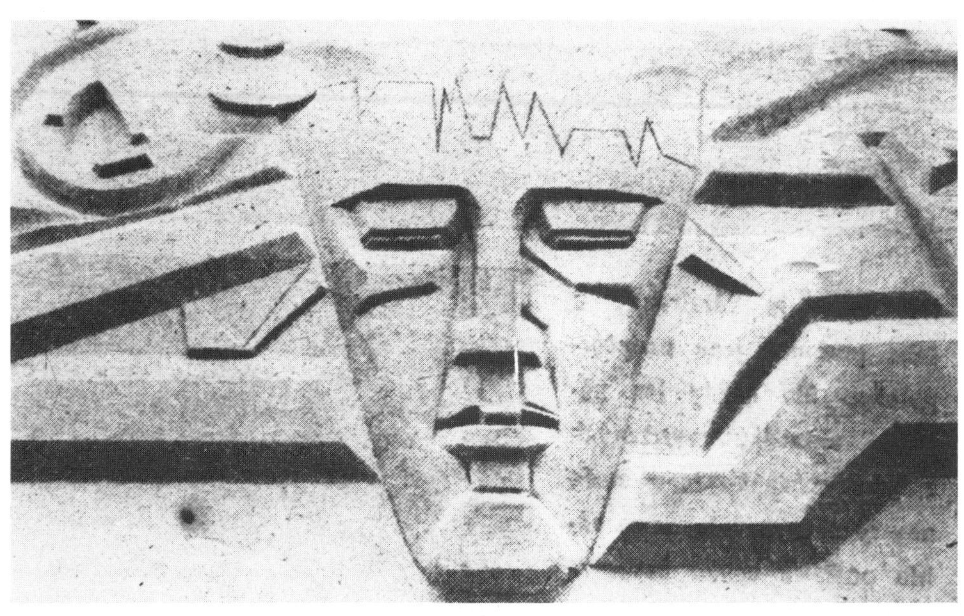

Detail, *Chelovek i nauka* (Man and Science), 1974
Concrete relief, 970 sq. meters.
Institute of Electronics and Technology, Moscow, USSR

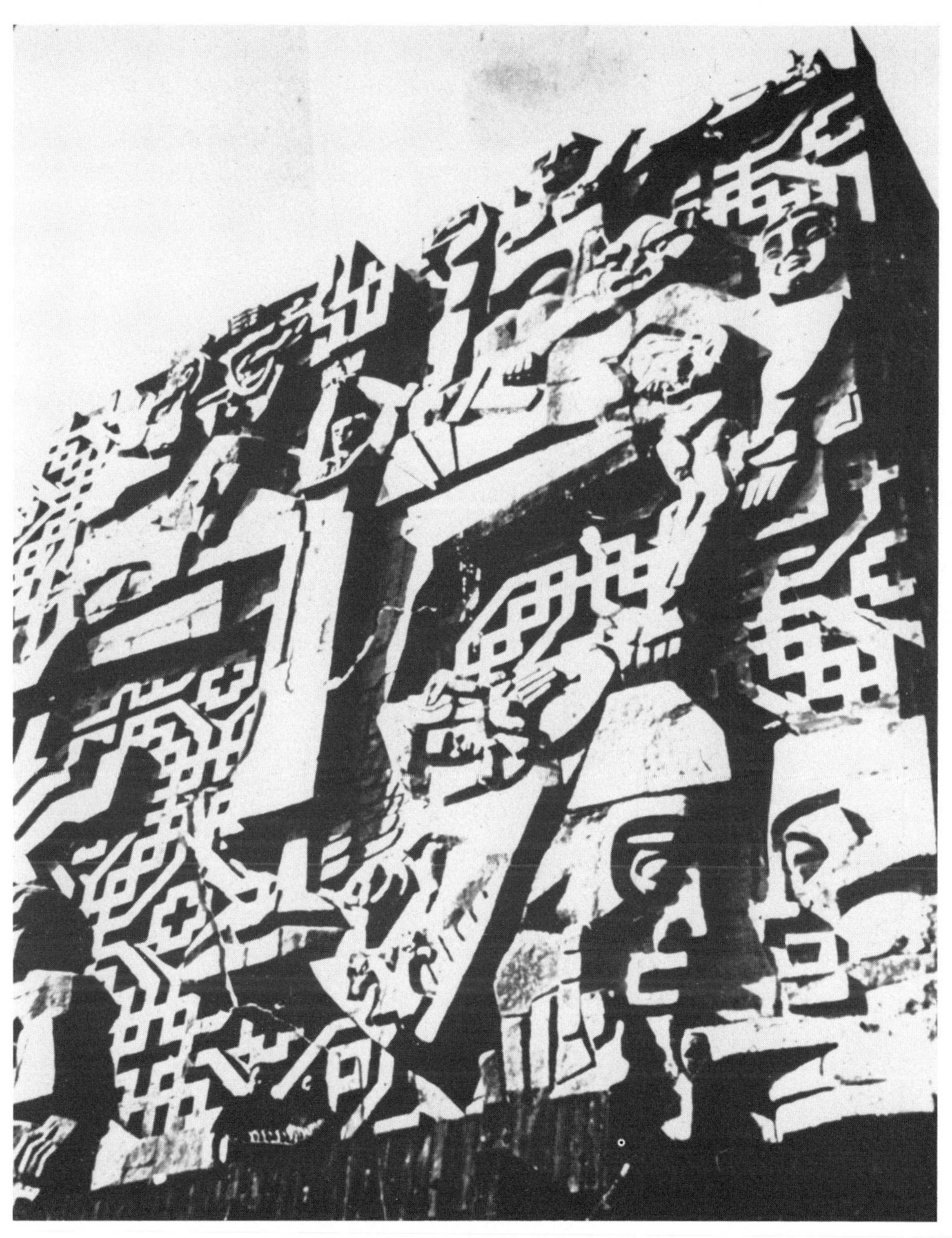

Rel'ef (Relief), 1974-75
Concrete, 400 sq. meters
Central Committee Headquarters, Ashkhabad, USSR

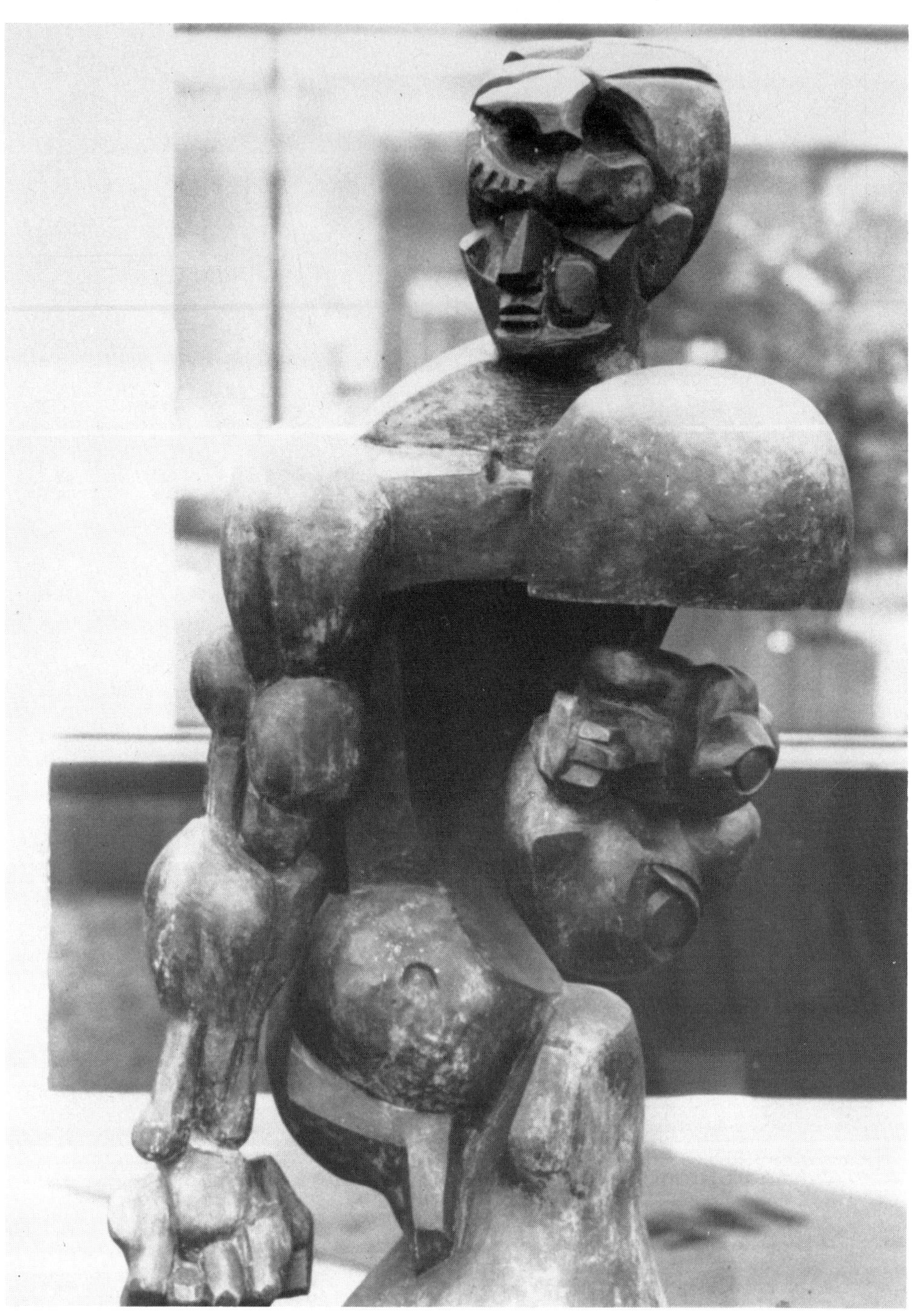

Prorok (The Prophet), 1970-80
Bronze, 157.48 cm.
New York

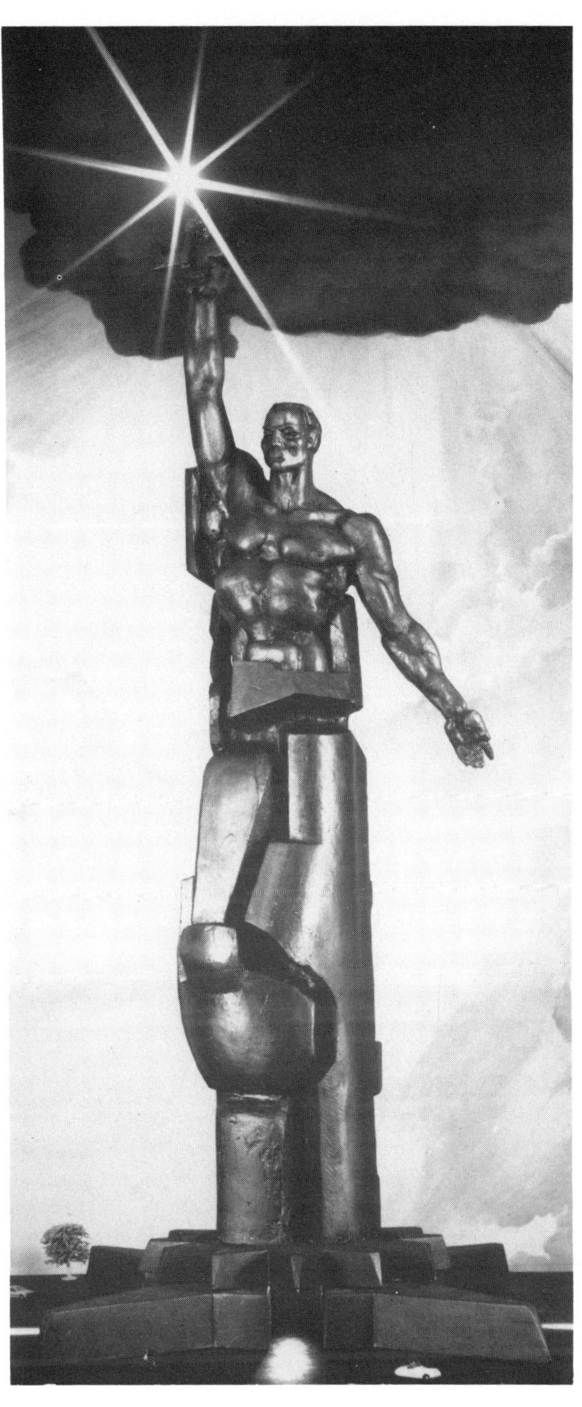

Novaia statuia svobody (New Statue of Liberty), 1988
Copper, 124.46 x 27.94 x 40.64 cm.
Kaohsiung, Republic of China; The Vatican

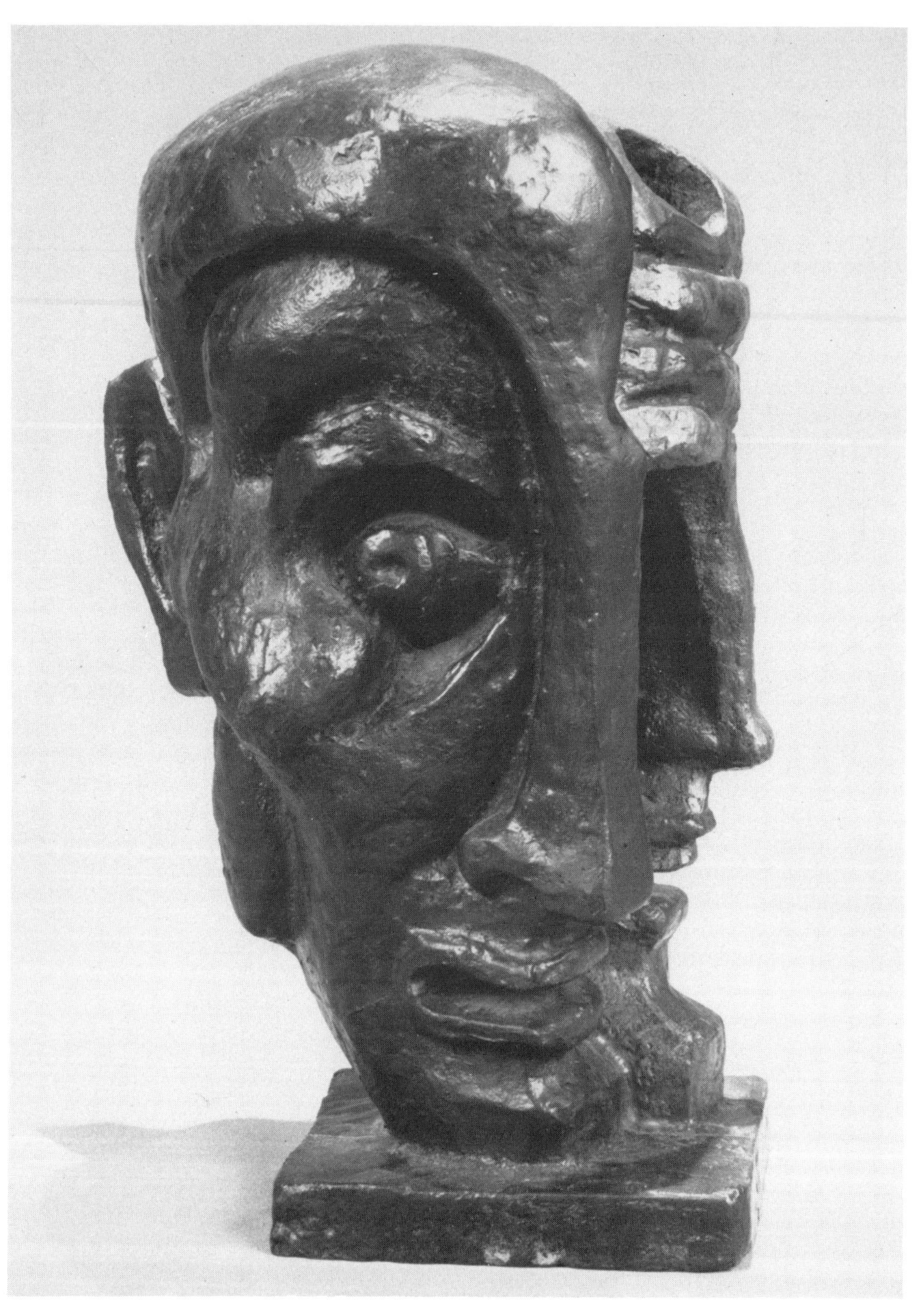

Dvulikii (Man with Double Face), 1988
Bronze, 55.88 x 22.86 cm.
Private collections

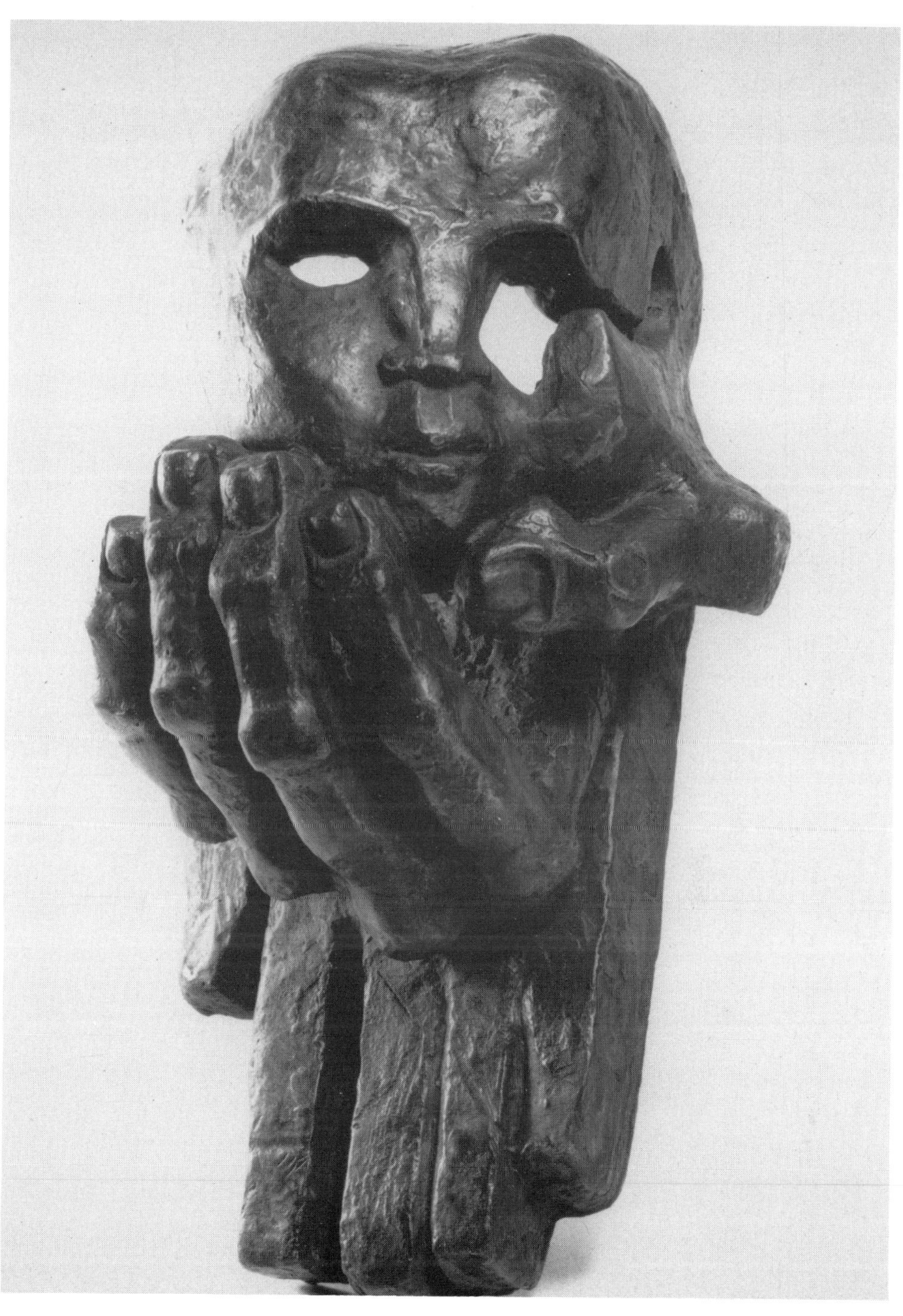

Pamiatnik v chest' mertvykh (Monument in Honor of the Dead), 1974
Bronze, 43.18 x 22.86 cm.
Tree of Life Museum, Uttersberg, Sweden
Photograph by Edward V. Gorn

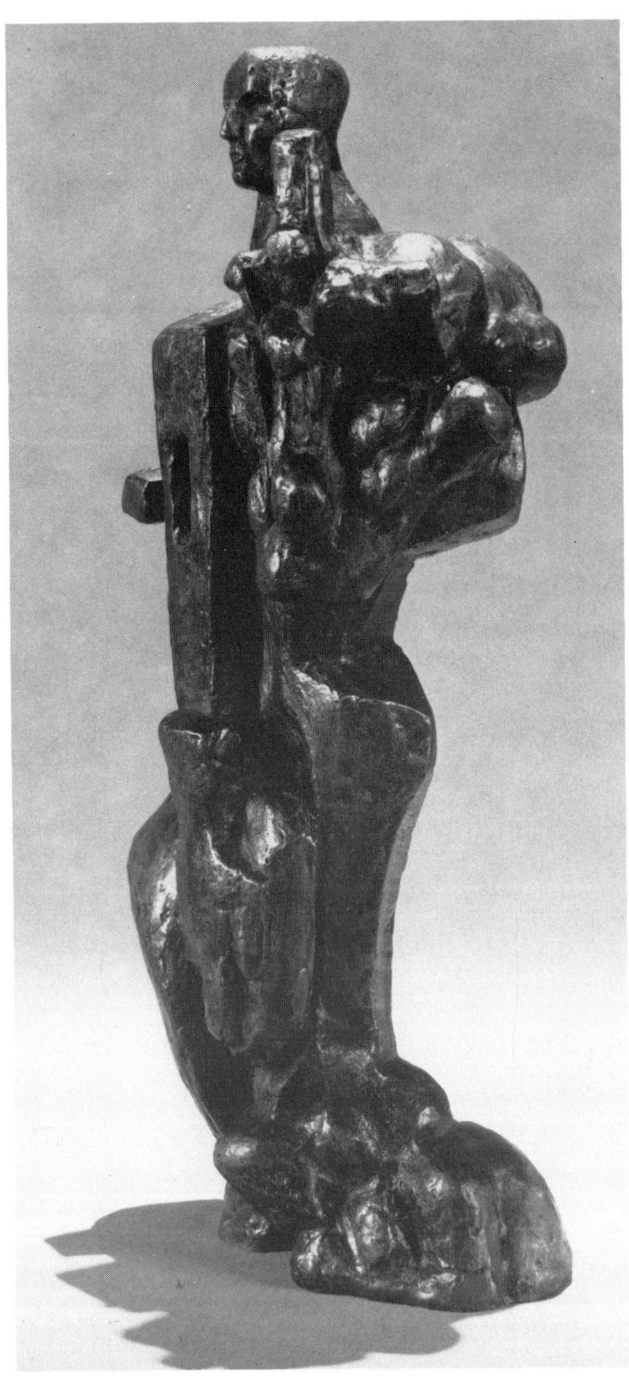

Zheleznyi prorok (Iron Prophet), 1978-88
Bronze, 35.56 x 16.51 x 10.80 cm.
Tree of Life Museum, Uttersberg, Sweden

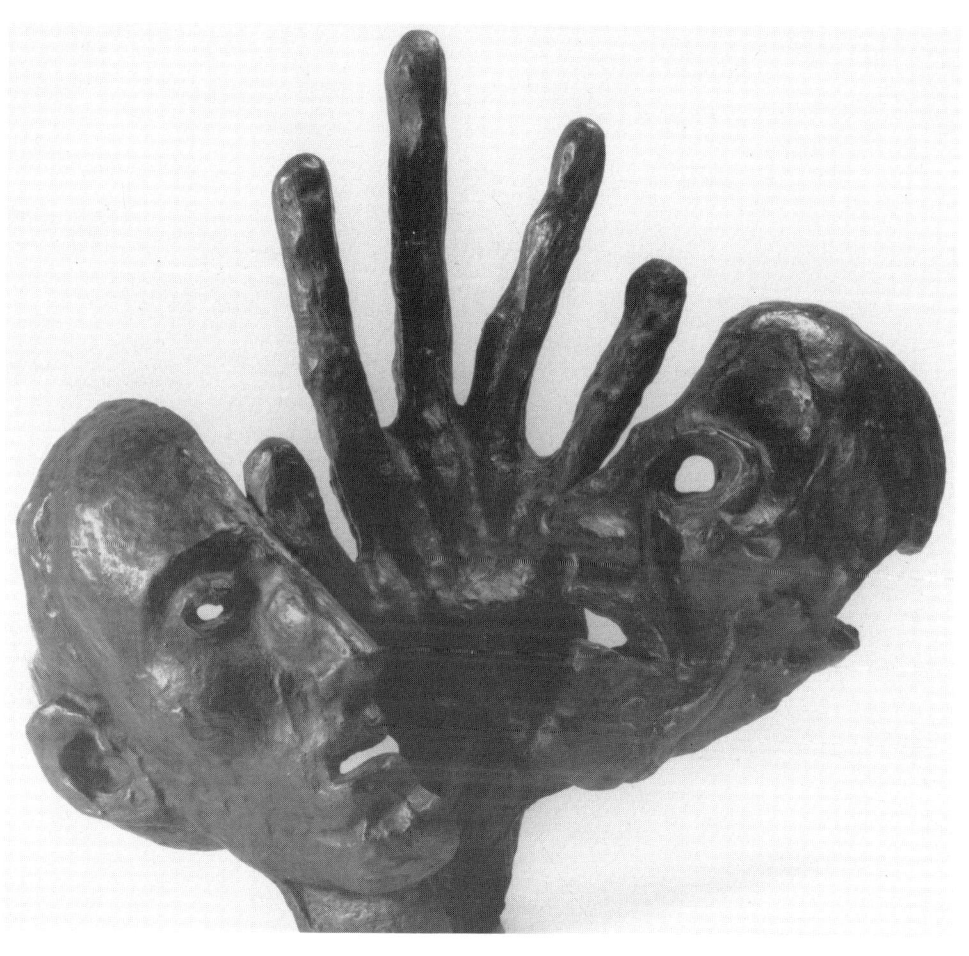

Atomnyi vzryv (Atomic Explosion), 1957
Bronze, 40.64 x 55.88 cm.
Tree of Life Museum, Uttersberg, Sweden
Photograph by Edward V. Gorn

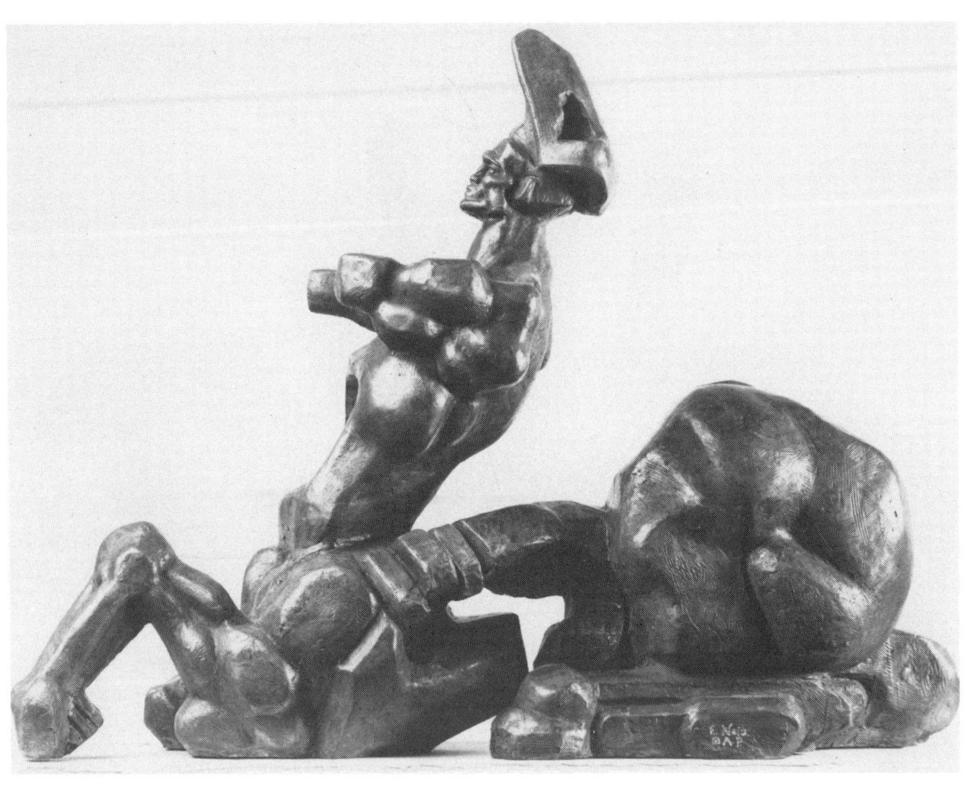

Kentavr bez ruk (Centaur without Hands), 1989
Bronze, 66 x 91.50 cm.
Tree of Life Museum, Uttersberg, Sweden

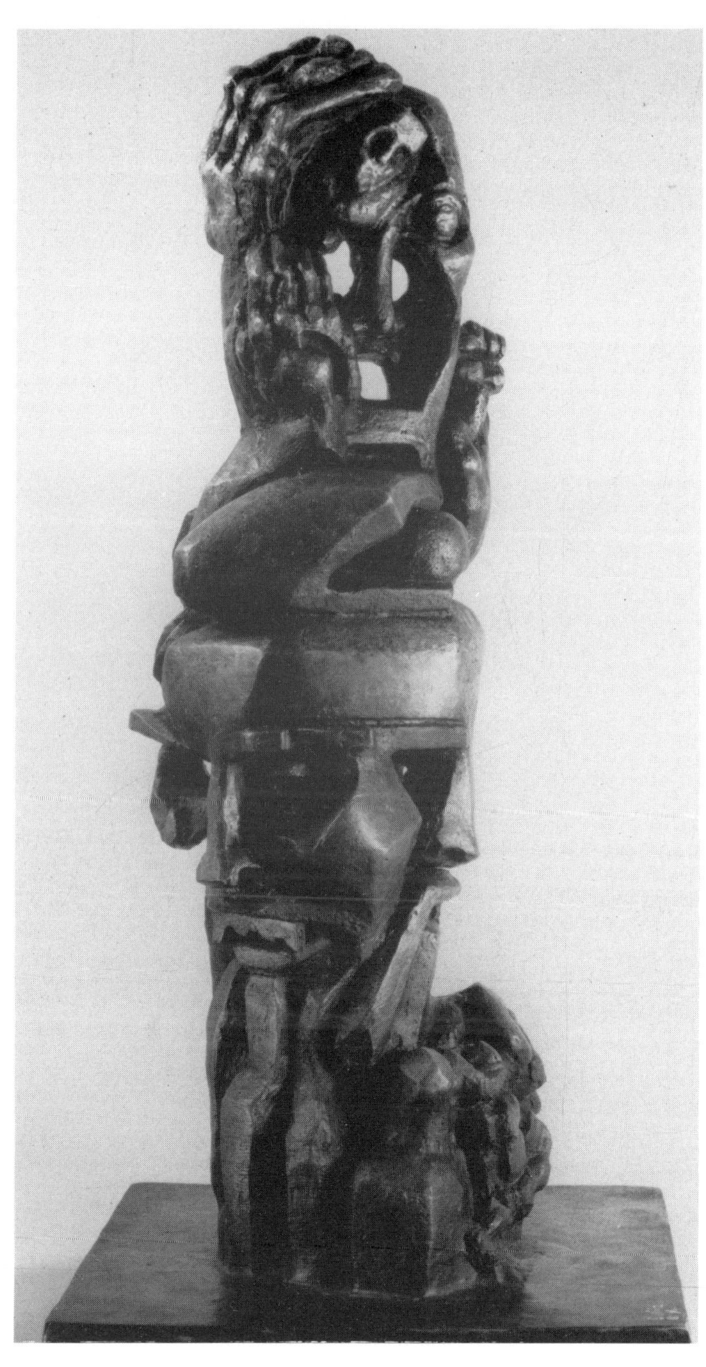

Totem (Totem), 1970s
Bronze, 68.58 x 30.48 x 33.66 cm.
Tree of Life Museum, Uttersberg, Sweden
Photograph by Edward V. Gorn

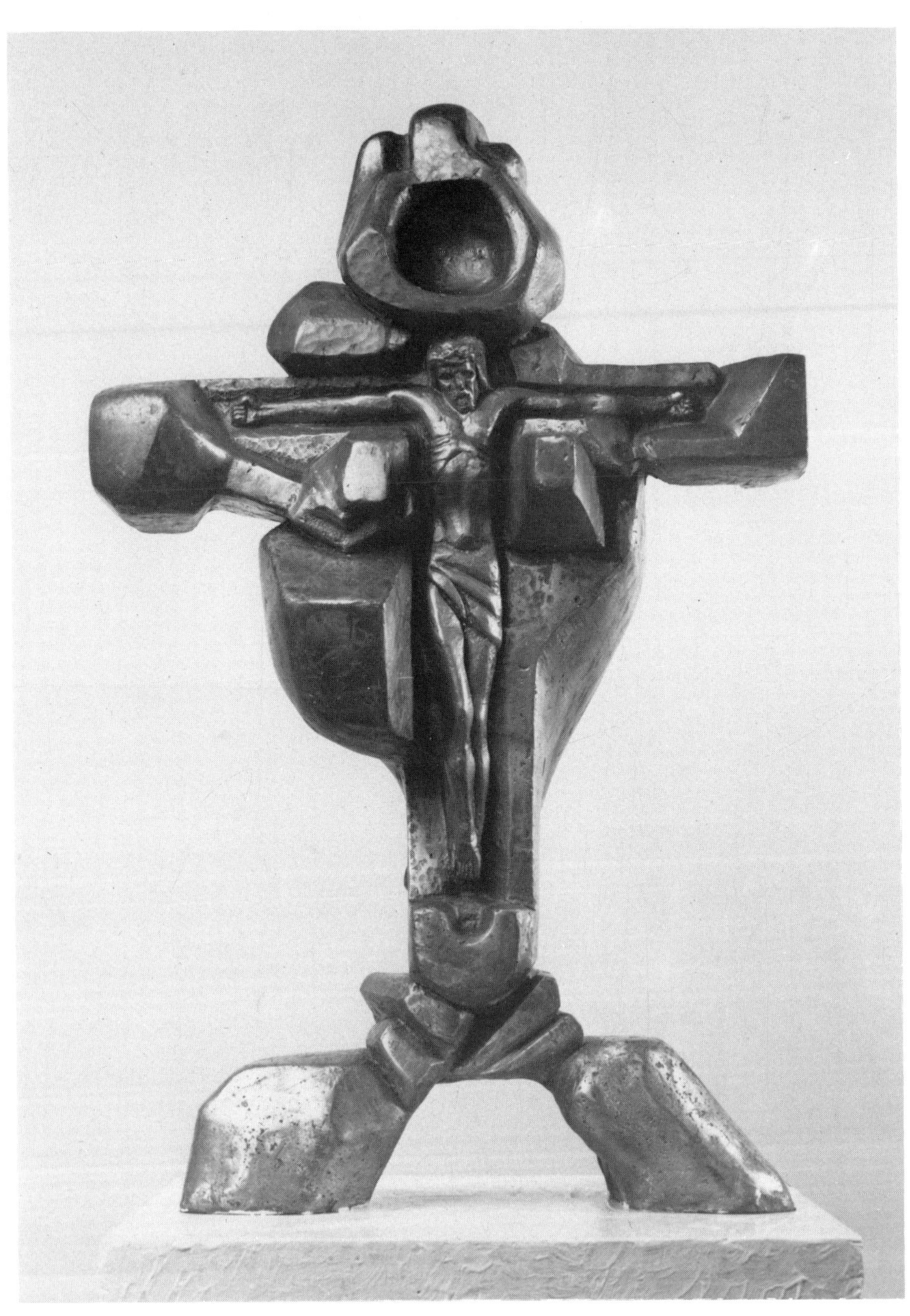

Serdtse Khristosa (Heart of Christ), 1973-75
Bronze, 62 x 41 x 25 cm.
Tree of Life Museum, Uttersberg, Sweden

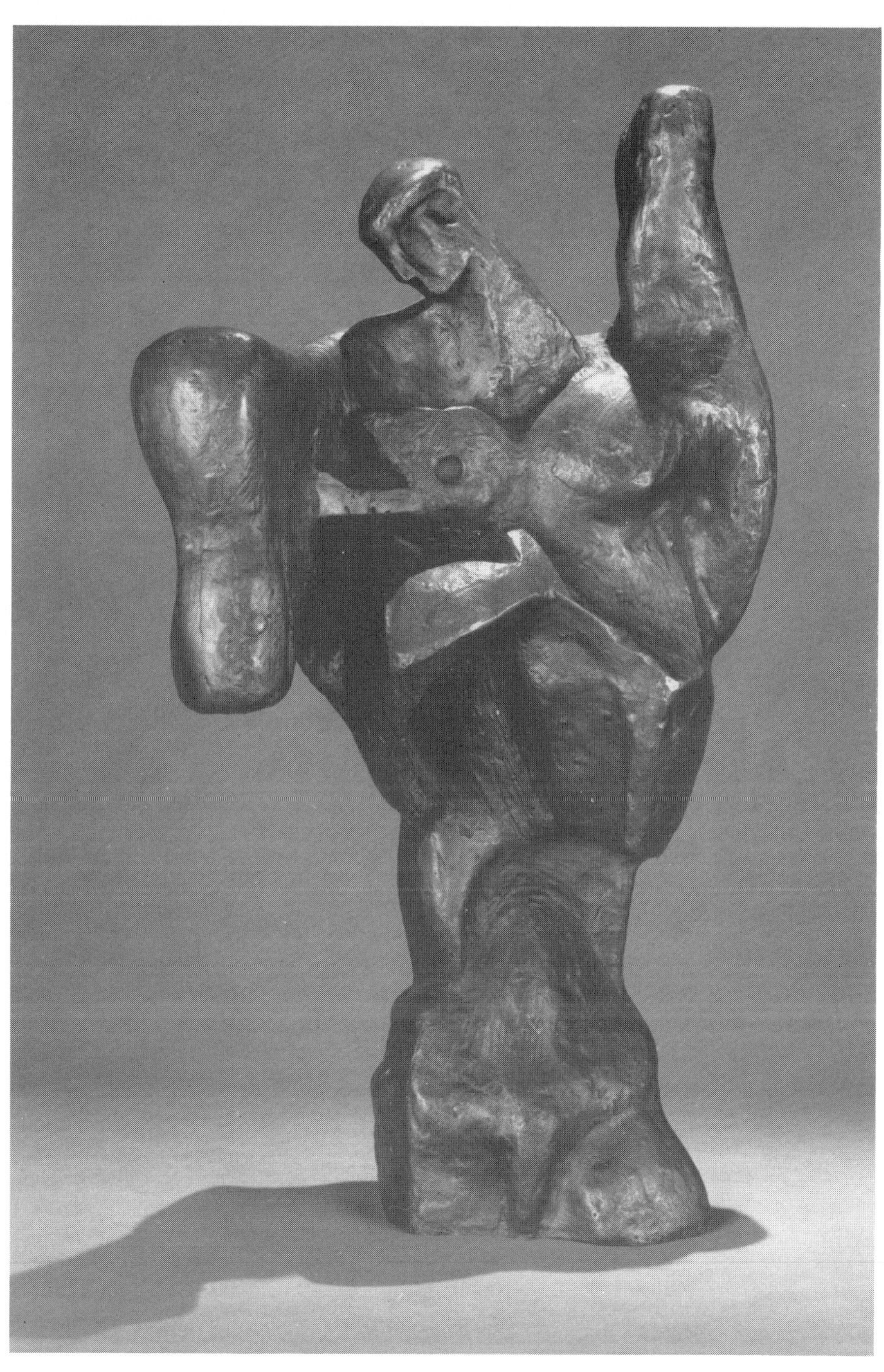

Tors kentavra (Centaur's Torso), 1961-62
Bronze, 54 x 35 x 30 cm.
Tree of Life Museum, Uttersberg, Sweden

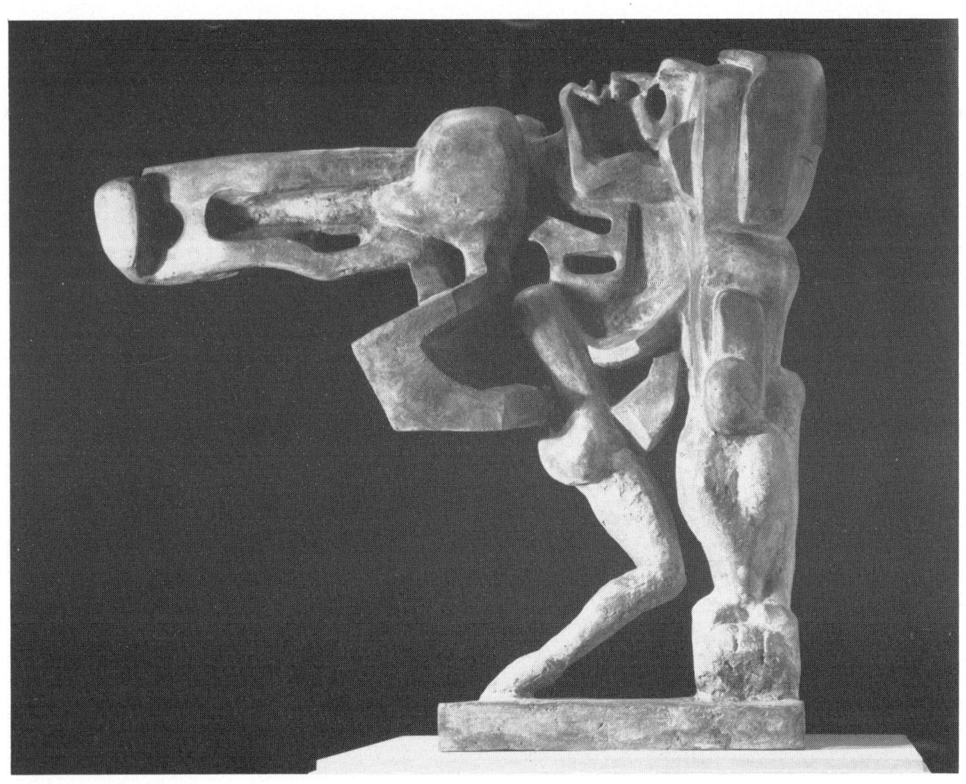

Raspiatyi gigant (Crucified Giant), 1971-89
Bronze, 78.74 x 87.63 x 25.40 cm.
Tree of Life Museum, Uttersberg, Sweden

> stone. Believe me, those stones looked more dramatic and contained more tension and art because bitter fate cast them. Social and spiritual forces shattered those stones, and not the pitiful, impotent concepts of commercial success. Look at those stones cast by the Devil today, and see if you do not hear the echo of dice games played in the past. And feel shame, and learn to throw stones. Hurl them so that the stones' screams can be heard, and not the rustle of nyloned thighs of rich old women afraid of being out-of-fashion. When hurling stones, remember that there's a time for throwing stones, as well as gathering them."

Maybe it's humane to pity these failures and protestors in art. But the social processes in the world do not take our emotions into account. And today the art market is the highest and sole judge of an artist's works. There is simply no other judge. Other criteria come from the Devil, who's a match for those who cast stones to the rustle of rich old women's nyloned thighs.

But what does it mean to be recognized by the art market? A man making an appearance in God's world and receiving the name of John or Ivan can live out his whole life without altering himself. He might try to surpass his father and grandfather, or try to have more land or cattle, or enjoy greater respect than his forebears. But he essentially remains himself, the same John or Ivan named by his family, to the end of his days. Everything has changed in our hyperdynamic age, which has transformed millions of people into robots carrying out certain functions in society. Man is lost in this world; he is nothing. The name given him at birth is only a sign that has no meaning until his second birth takes place and the world learns about him. This second birth of a person is a social christening. In reality a person is recognized as a personality only when the press, television, or radio declares to the whole world that on earth has appeared some kind of remarkable movie star, brilliant writer, or outstanding stage actor. Not parents, but the mass media have become the true godparents of people. The struggle in the world among actors, scholars, writers, politicians, prostitutes, and terrorists occurs for the sake of this social christening. To break out of social nonexistence by any means, legal or illegal, is the main task. Look at the graphomane carrying a manuscript to a publishing house. Does he not express the craving of a little person for recognition, the sublimation of his protest against social nonbeing? Or when a terrorist before the eyes of the world willingly blows himself up with explosives concealed on him? Or when I see a guy on the street with a ghetto-blaster at full volume? These are the outcries of souls lost in the labyrinth of a tumultuous age that crushes human personality.

Well, what about the artist? The artist is at the forefront of the vicious struggle for social christening or recognition. Any artist, not only the talentless ones and nihilists, needs the compliments and recognition of the public. But the public is the newspaper, the critic, and the art market mercilessly tended by the bourgeoisie. It is they who ultimately decide the fate of an artist by acquiring or rejecting his works. But can the artist comprehend this? That's the dramatic question that courses through the history of art and is paid for by the blood and sweat of many generations of artists. For the bourgeoisie, art was always a kind of diversion and clowning to satisfy their often undeveloped tastes. But, for the artist, art is a means of expressing himself, of turning his soul inside out, an outcry of the soul that the bourgeoisie always spat upon.

So it has been for ages until something comparable in significance to the French Revolution[11] took place in art at the beginning of the twentieth century. But if the French Revolution ended with the triumph of the bourgeoisie, then the revolution in art overthrew the bourgeoisie and led to the greatest triumph of art. This revolution was achieved by great artists of the avant-garde like Picasso, Dali, Duchamp.[12] They imposed their will on the bourgeoisie and taught them to buy works *they did not understand,* and thereby proclaimed the right of the artist to create the *incomprehensible* in art. This meant that henceforth the artist had the right to express himself in his art and to be free from pandering to the bad taste of the bourgeoisie. This was the challenge of artistic freedom, the meaning of which is hard to overemphasize. The artists of the avant-garde beat the bourgeoisie at their own game in the art market. With the help of those artists the bourgeoisie came to understand that they had overlooked Cézanne,[13] Modigliani,[14] and Van Gogh, and they decided not to make the same mistake again. The bourgeoisie came to the unanimous decision that they were not competent to judge what artists create. And, if art is business, then it's a special kind of business that the bourgeoisie cannot figure out easily.

This triumph of the artists of the avant-garde was a victors' feast during which they could not refrain from punishing the bourgeoisie for their stupidity. Taunting the bourgeoisie, avant-garde artists created deliberate provocations, clowning, and absurd shows to force the bourgeoisie to bow down before them. They avenged the artist, the unrecognized genius oppressed and humiliated by philistines for generations.

However, not only did the masters of the avant-garde stand up for the right of artists to create the unintelligible, they also became the innovators and shamans[15] who transformed universal archetypes and symbols into the new rhythms and music of technological progress.

This was a paradoxical and dialectically dualistic process. It created freedom and unfreedom simultaneously and complicated conditions even more for the constantly tense art market. Turbulent technical progress instilled in consumers the idea that the newer the better. And people began to talk about objects of spiritual culture in the categories of technological progress. A new painting or, say, a new poem was considered categorically better than the old ones. All that was not new was declared routine by critics and considered anathema. An artist wishing to pass for an innovator had to break records and arrange provocations as the latest word in art in order to amuse the philistines.

On the other hand the tempi of technological development began to influence art. Just as old furniture, television sets, and household goods are thrown out as garbage each year, music that changed each season made its appearance. Alongside sculpture that was created agonizingly in marble and bronze over a period of years appeared modernistic works thrown together from cardboard and bits of iron. A new facile style was spawned that was essentially a profanation of art by dilettantes. A new type of artist was born – an instant genius, a genius of the last fifteen minutes. This kind of artist preserved only one tradition of the avant-garde, the tradition of provocation. But if Picasso, Duchamp, and Dali were lions throwing a challenge to society, then today's avant-garde artists, who always pander to the public, remind me of poodles clipped to resemble lions.

From what I have said it should be obvious why it is so hard to define real values in the art market. The art field is truly open to the self-displays of failures, graphomanes, and capricious Narcissuses[16] who flaunt themselves as geniuses before television cameras for a brief moment, if only for fifteen minutes.

On the other hand, I understand the unbelievable burden of work that lies on the shoulders of a genuine artist. True, he has every opportunity to prove he's a genius. But then, according to the court ruling in Steichen's case, the same opportunities exist for everyone who wants to call himself an artist. So everyone struggles, makes orations, howls. And the art market is transformed into a jungle through which genius must make his way. This, in essence, is the price he must pay for the freedom granted him by fate.

The situation might be considered hopeless were it not for the appearance of one other person in this art market: the gallery owner, the art dealer who sells works of art. It might seem strange why, in an essay devoted to the psychology of artistic creation, I have introduced a type of person far removed from creative work, a person who perhaps earns millions of dollars dealing in art, but whose role cannot be compared to that of an authentic master of art. But the fact remains that in the jungle of the art market today, the art dealer plays as decisive a role in art as the artist himself. You might ask, how can a person make his way through the maze of this art market, in this raging ocean of human passions, in this infinite mosaic of tastes, styles, artistic manners, and traditions? In this bazaar how can diamonds be distinguished from pathetic imitations?

We live in an age of narrow specialization. People do not heal themselves, but instead go to medical specialists, just as they do not defend themselves in court, but turn to legal specialists. Thus, an art dealer is an expert and specialist in the field of art and a person to whom the buyer turns. Hence, the art dealer has a mission, a mission that is creative in many ways. While he does not create works of art, he is a creator of tastes in art. The art dealer alone has enough power in the art market to render judgment on works of art and the real value of an artist, on whether or not a person is a master whose work is suitable for sale.

But in fact all is much simpler than it appears at first glance. The art dealer does not have the goal of rendering expert opinion in the art market. He merely wants to do business (like all other businessmen in this country), to buy art works cheaply, and to sell them for maximum profit. And the artist approaches a gallery owner with no great love for him (what love could there be for someone who takes the lion's share of the money earned by the artist?). And the buyer goes to an art gallery out of necessity: where can he find an artist's works if not in a gallery? He knows that he will buy an artist's works there at three times the going rate, but he nevertheless is willing to pay the gallery owner for guaranteeing the value of the work purchased. By overpaying the gallery, the buyer is paying a percentage for its expert opinion. As we see in this triangle – artist, gallery, buyer – there are no sentimental feelings. But, lacking emotion, the mechanism of this market nonetheless selects the best works of art, at least if one looks at it in the context of time. And what's the result? The result is the growth of superstar art galleries. Alongside the artist of genius stands the art dealer of genius who becomes the creator of geniuses in the art market. The art dealer does not merely purchase an artist's works. Today such transactions come from the era of primary accumulation. The superstar-gallery owner invests money in the artist, in publicizing his work through the mass media. And, after investing hundreds of thousands of dollars in a future genius, the art dealer tries to make millions of dollars off of him. The public has boundless faith in such art dealers, regardless of what it thinks of any given artist. The important thing is that the artist is exhibited in the Castelli or Marlborough galleries in New York. The gallery itself is transformed into a kind of alchemist's workshop. A garbage bag lying at the entrance to the Castelli Gallery is only a garbage bag. But once it is brought inside the gallery, it becomes a work of art worth a fabulous price.

Thus, art is transformed into big business, a fact that perhaps might not arouse extreme rapture in us. No matter what people say, the sound of money is not the best accompaniment for immortal works of genius. But, apparently, there is no other mechanism for developing art in the free world. Perhaps it would be more pleasant if there were some kind of Areopagus[17] or higher Reason capable of selecting perfect works of art and directing them towards loftier human ideals. But we know the dire consequences of similar social utopias, in which dreams of one controlling Reason assume the form of ministries of ideology and unions of artists capable only of being mortuaries for genius.[18]

[1] Edward Steichen (1879-1973), pioneer American photographer.
[2] Brancusi (See Chapter Six, note 23).
[3] Van Gogh (See Chapter Four, note 21).
[4] Raphael (1483-1520), Italian painter and architect of the High Renaissance.
[5] Union of Soviet Artists (See Chapter Nine, note 14).
[6] Picasso (See Introduction, note 26).
[7] Dali (See Chapter Nine, note 38).
[8] Michelangelo (See Chapter One, note 27).
[9] Dante (See Introduction, note 59).
[10] A reference to Neizvestny's experiences as an airborne commando officer in World War II.
[11] French Revolution (1789).
[12] Duchamp (See Chapter Nine, note 39).
[13] Paul Cézanne (1839-1906), major French painter influenced by the Impressionists.
[14] Amedeo Modigliani (1884-1920), Italian painter and sculptor known for his portraits and use of elegant, elongated forms.
[15] Shaman (See Chapter Three, note 52).
[16] Narcissus (See Chapter Nine, note 47).
[17] A reference to the Athenian council which tried criminal cases on a rocky promontory west of the Acropolis.
[18] This essay was published in Russian under the title, "*Genii na rynke iskusstv*" (Genius on the Art Market) in *Vremia i my*, No. 100 (1988): 187-97.

CHAPTER ELEVEN

On Egyptian Art

The opportunity to visit Egypt came rather suddenly in the fall of 1968.[1] After a brief acquaintance with Cairo we traveled to Karnak, Luxor, and Alexandria, looked at ancient Islamic and Egyptian temples, and visited the Valley of the Kings. Immediately afterwards we arrived at the great Aswan Dam, where my friends and I were to erect the *Lotus Blossom* monument that represents our contemporary plastic culture in a land of perfected monuments of deep antiquity. This task, by affirming once more the linkage of epochs and continents, was deeply human and responsible.

The tradition of raising monuments to crown great events is dear to the peoples of Russia and the East.

The grandiose scale of the dam, the lake, the hydroelectric station, and the boundless surrounding landscape call for a monument of great size. In form the monument is in the shape of a lotus blossom, a traditional form in Egyptian sculpture. Its height, 85 meters, is taller than a 25-story skyscraper. Five petals form planes, which create an intense dynamic space to be covered by reliefs. The figures of the relief are distributed on the surface of the spiral created by the tongues of flames. The monument rises from the lower figures of slaves pressed together, bent, and fallen, to people now standing erect, and finally to the gigantic figure of Free Man.

Two parallel roads lead to the monument. Where these paths symbolizing two peoples intersect is a pool of life-giving water from which blossoms the 85-meter flower as a symbol of life. Of course, the problem of monumentality is not limited by the volume or size of a work in space, since we mean not only a constructively organized mass when we speak of monumentality. Monumentality, above all, is spiritual content and a special attitude towards the viewer. A monument is not rhetorical and stilted, but heroic. Gazing at Egyptian pyramids, temples, and mosques, I could not isolate myself from professional problems for even a moment.

That is how I remember Egypt, a culture about which volumes have been written. Therefore, without reiterating commonplaces, I shall relate my impressions as a sculptor. What shook me about Egyptian culture? Knowing it only by illustrations in books, I was prepared to find a certain adherence to canon, homogeneity, and constraint. All was familiar to me since childhood: the silhouettes of pyramids and sculptures, reliefs and wall inscriptions, the outlines of tombs and rectangular buildings. Consequently, the most unexpected thing for me was the passionately pulsating vitality of Egyptian art and its extraordinarily convincing verisimilitude. We were familiar with the clarity of construction, laconicism, and monumentality that glorified and immortalized the art of ancient Egypt. But, suddenly, within its homogeneous system of constructing figures and reliefs were revealed a remarkable diversity and almost a kind of mysterious vitality. And the gigantic metaphorical legacy stored up over thousands of years by the art of Egypt seemed quite close to me.

The first thing that obviously struck me was the false notion that the large scale of Egyptian structures, their plastic construction, and their magical essence were designed to crush and debase human beings. Perhaps this is so in a bookish sense. Indeed, the Pharoahs[2] exalted themselves, oppressed people, and exploited the labor of slaves to erect structures which, from the vantage point of our particularly pragmatic twentieth century, were practically useless. But, if you look with clear eyes and without preconceived notions that are often biased, you will see nobility and dignity in all of Egyptian art – from pyramids to dishes, from a colossus to a household statuette.

You will find no cruelty, even in scenes of war and hunting. Egyptian art is an art of extraordinary monumental power and impact that never turns into the crudity, obtrusiveness, and irksomeness of rhetorical monumentality, which tries to drum in a moral through sheer size. For such an art, monumentality and humanity are incompatible.

Despite the enormous scale and grandiose colossi, the ceremonies and rituals, and the mighty constructions, gravity, and static quality characteristic of Egyptian art, that art is refined, fragile, and even feminine. Power does not contradict humaneness, but brings it to light. In reality all Egyptian representations bear the imprint of a strict system of hieroglyphs. Their combination of figures and their poses are signs. But the phenomenon of art lies in the extraordinary vitality of the representation, which is expressed through, and apparently due to, and not in spite of, a system of constraints. And, illuminated by natural light, the sculptures themselves are not as stiff and canonical as we see them in reproductions.

The given scheme as if compresses the powerful flesh, which is quite alive in spite of its conventionality. And this creates tension. The constraint of Egyptian sculpture is not tranquillity, but enclosed motion within a form. Even if we simply take a hieroglyph,[3] the character and depth of the relief vary within the representation depending on the illumination to preserve the contour of a written sign. This hieroglyph resembles a single musical theme that contains a number of diverse variations. The result is external contradiction and contrast: constraint and canonical representation versus vividness and vitality of spiritual content. These qualities in general characterize folk art, such as icons and temple painting, which developed through prolonged repetition and refinement in a time of specified techniques of representation. The repetition of a single theme or plastic subject and the fixed affirmation of one and the same thing characterize not only holistic civilizations, but also great individual artists.

What seems dead and academic to me is the idea of primitiveness and inadequate rendering of reality in Egyptian art. This notion of certain Egyptologists is not only questionable, but simply false. As a sculptor, I can say that deformation[4] (if we can call it that) in circular Egyptian sculpture and relief is not primitive out of ignorance, but complex and profound.

Egyptian reliefs, indeed, do not display perspective, although the Egyptians knew how to use perspective, were familiar with geometrical proportions, and knew how to apply reduced and enlarged scales. Among the Egyptians the measurement of direct perspective was related to a mathematical formula. The representations of Egyptian structure should be understood not as the dawn of youth and ignorance, but as maturity and old age, as metaphysical thought, just as the perspective of icons, especially Russian icons, cannot be understood without penetrating into their spiritual essence. In precisely the same way the shaping of space in ancient Greek sculptures is connected with the whole system of thought elaborated by the Greeks of the early slave-owning period. Therefore, reproaching the Egyptians for being naive is not justified. It is merely that their sense of spatial unity in art differs from the space of Euclid[5] or Kant.[6] All of Egyptian civilization, from the earliest excavations to the tombs discovered by the archeaologist Petri,[7] contains an astonishingly holistic hymn to Aton,[8] life, and the sun through its classical epochs up to the Ptolemaic period.[9] What amazing human universalism it contains! And what wholeness of religious and philosophical spirit, what faith in immortality must they have possessed to transmit these feelings directly and spontaneously to me, a man of the twentieth century! I stretch out my hand, and the warm stone, which lives as a book of time, is a silent but mighty epistle that passes through the magical symbolism of a representation, through the incomprehensibility of hieroglyphs.

Yes, here, on this spot and under the same sun where thousands of years ago stood builders and stonemasons who built these stone epistles with their own hands, one begins to think: "These people had no terror before the trumpet voice of time. Many things tormented them, and life was no doubt terrifying for them. But existence, death, and terror were not meaningless. And what is an artist? A narcissus or a stonemason who objectifies a holistic world in art?"

I once again experienced an unbearable longing for holistic art, for a whole vision of the world that does not consists of pieces of existence. No, of course, it is not necessary to reject modern discoveries, experiments, the accretion of facts, or the whole flood of information. But one must find a spiritual core, a general plastic idea. And do we artists with our localized aims not resemble children who break up the alphabet into letters and forget that letters make words and that words form the book of existence?

Egyptian art once more strengthened my idea of developing a symphonic and monumental art. But the fear of monumentalism that we often observe even among serious people in the West is antithesis and fright before the rhetoric and didacticism of mass means of propaganda. Perhaps this fear is linked with a saturation of plastic culture against a narrow, compressed western European concept of space. Or maybe there is such a saturated solution or layer of culture in the West that the striving of, say, the Mexicans and developing countries towards monumental art seems somehow childish, native, and possibly barbaric. In conversations with West Europeans when I was still in the USSR, I was often obliged to listen to their indignation on the subject of how Soviet artists who can make small works to their satisfaction can strive for the "old-fashioned and primitive" art of monuments.

Yes, there are many contradictions between the falsely understood idea of monumentality and the personal idea of humankind. There exists an art that we can call liturgical in which a person, independent of others, freely confronts the small space of a canvas or the small mass of a sculpture and comes to know the beautiful.

The greatness of ancient Egyptian culture is the same as that of our temples: they both create the idea of mass activity and free individual access to it. Hence the meaning of *sobornost'* – together with everyone, but without losing one's own personality. This idea inheres in the very process of creating ancient folk art.

We know in detail how Russian icons were created. I have seen analogous forms of collective creativity in Egypt. In the Valley of the Kings there are unfinished tombs. As soon as a Pharoah comes to power, he begins to build his own resting place. When the Pharoah dies, construction ceases. We saw inner decorations on the walls of a tomb that reflect cessation of work upon the sudden death of a Pharoah. The god of death, the jackal Anubis,[10] is drawn in paint on a stone wall plastered in a particular way by the hand of an apprentice. Corrections made in the firmer hand of a master and a black line made by a substance resembling slate are placed over this drawing. And a third person has already begun to cut the stone along a contour to transform the drawing into a relief. A fourth person has begun to paint the relief in white, ochre, turquoise, and gold.

How can we reconcile a complex and refined modern metaphor with mass monumentalism? It seems to me that the Egyptian system of metaphors and fantastic juxtapositions consists in combining a single plastic image with what appears to be externally incompatible: human beings and animal elements (jackal, lion, snake, hippopotamus), people and plants, parts of human beings (eye, hand, phallus), and the cosmos are converted into a symbol, into a semantic sign. Of course, we do not know the ultimate ritual essence of these images. But what we do know makes these metaphors meaningful without taking away the sensual principle characteristic of art in general. A metaphor has an end; it is transformed into a symbol.

This is what distinguishes Egyptian art from a modern application of metaphors such as Salvador Dali's.[11] I mention Dali as the most vivid and talented example. His metaphors have no end. He takes a certain complex fantastic situation where objects, beings, and events have no ultimate connection. Thanks to this situation, these elements arouse a feeling of alarm and dissatisfaction. The craving to take away this feeling of anxiety arouses rapt attention and a desire to understand what is happening there. But there is no answer. This kind of art poses questions but does not answer them. The metaphor is not transformed into a symbol. But Egyptian art does.

Although I have not named specific temples and concrete works, my reflections and judgments have been elicited by immediate experience of everything I have seen. And strange as it might seem, my holistic impression of Egyptian culture was even intensified when we arrived in Cairo and visited the museum of ancient Egyptian culture. What an astonishing impression of a superabundance of masterpieces! From the exhibits of this museum alone one can fill dozens of first-class European museums. Moving from floor to floor, from everyday objects to cult objects, from washing vessels to the gigantic representation of a Pharoah helped my memory to unite the disparate impressions from the whole trip.

And I once again confirmed the goodness, humanity, and nobility of ancient Egyptian art.[12]

[1] A reference to the international competition Neizvestny won in 1968 with his design of a "Lotus Blossom" monument to top the Aswan Dam in Egypt.
[2] Pharoahs, the kings of ancient Egypt believed to be the personification of the gods Horus and Amen.
[3] Hieroglyphs (See Chapter Six, note 22).
[4] Deformation (See Chapter One, note 29, and Chapter Two, notes 11 and 22).
[5] Euclid (See Chapter Seven, note 3).
[6] Kant (See Chapter Two, note 26).
[7] Petri (See Chapter Two, note 27).
[8] Aton, Egyptian solar deity.
[9] Ptolemy, name used by the fifteen Egyptian kings of the Macedonian dynasty (323-30 BC).
[10] Anubis, Egyptian god of the underworld.
[11] Dali (See Chapter Nine, note 38).
[12] This essay was first published in Russian under the title, "O Egipetskom iskusstve" (On Egyptian art) in *Novoe Vremia* (New Times) [January 1969]. The present English translation is based on the slightly abridged Russian version published in *Govorit Neizvestnyi* (Neizvestny speaks) [Frankfurt: Possev-Verlag, 1984], 167-74.

CHAPTER TWELVE

Reflections of a Centaur

1. The Centaur

When my mother arrived in New York from the Soviet Union, she brought with her drawings I had made when I was eight, nine, ten, and eleven years old. Even then centaurs could be found roaming throughout my sketches. While I knew nothing about centaurs in theory, I was drawn for some reason to those fantastic creatures from the very beginning. I do not know which came initially: did I sculpt them or did I explain them first? At any rate centaurs were two beings fused into one and dialogical in nature. I have never liked monological things: my sculptures are dialogical, my life is dialogical, and all my aspirations are bound up with affirmations and negations, with theses and antitheses. There are stable and transitional periods. Ours is the age of the centaur, that is, a time of transition in which fixed forms undergo change. In reality the centaur is a pantheistic, dualistic union of two natures, the animal and the human. For me the centaur is a fusion of human nature, animal nature, and technology. We are centaurs. For instance, while I am speaking, my voice is amplified by a microphone and my face is being recorded on film. Technology extends and continues the action of our eyes, hands, voices, and hearts. We are fused with technology just as, in antiquity, a Scythian and his horse were one,[1] or the centaur's union of a human torso with the body of a horse. We ourselves do not realize how much this second nature of technology has become a part of our lives: eyeglasses and typewriters, not to speak of telescopes and computers. In general I do not believe in Freud's theory of the conscious and the unconscious, because no one yet has determined their boundaries.

2. Dostoevsky's *Notes from the Underground*

When I was living in Zurich I quite unexpectedly made the acquaintance of Ingold Wildenauer, a brilliant stage director and actor in the *Spielhaus*, one of the leading German-language theaters in Switzerland and in all of Europe. He looked me up because he had heard that there was a Russian artist living in Zurich who could serve as a consultant on his production of Dostoevsky's *Notes from the Underground*. We hit it right off, and Wildenauer asked me to be his artistic director for this production. After all, my favorite works by Dostoevsky are *The Double [Dvoinik]*, which I believe is the key to his works, and the *Notes from the Underground*, which I know by heart. Wildenauer was so struck by my interpretation of the *Notes* that he decided to stage it according to my conception.

My concept of the *Notes* is amazingly simple. First of all, time has stopped. For forty years the hero has been sitting in his cellar and repeating the same thing, namely, that time has stopped for him. I believe that Samuel Beckett's play *Krapp's Last Tape* is a variation on the same idea: Beckett's hero listens to a tape recording and believes that it is repeating the thoughts he just uttered. It is an idea based on a Dostoevskian notion in reverse form or possibly on Heraclitus' assertion that one cannot step twice into the same river.[2]

Because time has stopped for the narrator of the *Notes*, on the floor of the stage we draw a chalk circle confining the hero to a finite space. Our hero says that he is speaking and writing only for himself and totally ignores the spectators *(Mne plevat' na zritelia:*

Literally, "I spit on the spectator."). How can one stage a play and the monologues of an actor who disdains the spectators without lapsing into falsity? A false note is struck when the hero turns to the full house and asserts that "I wish to see and hear no one," and the audience immediately reacts with irony to the hero's words. It is crucial to ignore the existence of the spectator. I told Wildenauer to disregard all dramatic theories and to imagine himself masturbating in a hotel room while the spectators peep through a crack in the wall. The spectators, like peeping toms or eavesdroppers, ought to have the sensation of seeing and hearing things they shouldn't. I instructed Wildenauer as the hero to ignore the audience completely, to behave indecorously, like a person gone to seed who is used to chomping his teeth, scratching himself, and assuming the most unattractive poses.

This idea was developed in my series of paintings entitled *The Outcry (Krik)* and *The Kiss (Potselui)*, both of which depict intimate human behavior. The classical Greek representation of the kiss between Cupid and Psyche is merely the sign of a kiss, and not an actual sensual experience, just as the ancient Egyptian representation of a male figure of adult size with a finger to its lips is the traditional sign of a child, although we do not have the sense experience of a child. By contrast take Rodin's *The Kiss,*[3] in which a third person or spectator present is ignored by the lovers. This, of course, is not pornography, but the genuine, tender kiss of lovers in which the spectator is a co-participant. What I depict in my series *The Kiss* is the inner experience of a kiss, when I am doing the kissing.

I explored the same phenomenon in my series *The Outcry.* Leonardo da Vinci[4] with anatomical precision depicted the mask of an outcry. Contrast this with Edvard Munch's *The Scream,*[5] in which everything cries out: the man, the bridge, the clouds. We experience the outcry ourselves. But suppose I am screaming. In my series *The Outcry,* and occasionally in Dostoevsky's works, you will see mouths and figures contorted in an outcry. I am the one who is screaming. What do I experience during such an outcry? The sounds "a - a - a . . .!" While crying out, I sense the vibration of my larynx, lips, and ears, and I depict these sensations in my series *The Outcry.*

Thus, in my staging of the *Notes from the Underground,* I establish an atmosphere of eavesdropping, as in the case of Rodin's *The Kiss* or Munch's *The Scream,* by placing a coffin-like bunk on stage, so that the hero would seem to rise naked from the grave. When he's lying down, only his penis is covered. I let the hero, the recognizable Russian solitary drinker, make contact with the audience by means of a bottle of vodka. The towel or rag over his penis suggests that the character may or may not masturbate, but nonetheless is lonely. He stands up, the rag drops off, and a stark naked man with dangling testicles, absolutely without constraint, begins to pace the chalk circle drawn on the stage. In the center of this circle lies a large mirror. I trample this mirror to bits and paint one part of the mirror yellow and leave the rest white. That's all the stage decoration there is. Why a mirror? The extremely simple and primitive lighting barely changes throughout the play, falls on the mirror, and is reflected upwards in yellow and white rays, which is precisely the lighting of Dostoevsky's visions. And it is this lighting that creates a spiritual, Cubo-Futurist space on stage.[6] And my hero pacing this chalk circle dramatizes the fact that time is enclosed. The hero, sometimes standing on all fours, talks to the mirror, to his own reflection, and not to the audience. Since his entire monologue is structured according to the laws of memory, reverse time and perspective, as well as compression and displacement of time, exist, as in a dream. Consequently, the clothing of my hero takes place in a totally strange way. A clothes rack, a mirror, and a coffin-cot make up the stage set. On this clothes rack hang the hero's whole stage accoutrements. Nor does he dress himself by the normal rules of dressing. For instance, the hero begins to put on his long underwear and suddenly remembers his psychological "duel" with the officer who would not yield an inch when passing him on the street on a number of occasions. The fact is, the officer simply did not notice him at all, as if he were a louse. One time our hero decided to dress up, thinking that the officer ignored him because he was usually poorly dressed, but the result was the same. So our hero, while dressing up, suddenly takes off his top hat and staggers along the chalk circle half-naked, in underpants alone, like a dissolute Petersburg dandy. This creates the horror of a nightmare. In general I would dress him as Goya dressed his heroes in his *Capriccios.*[7]

The hero's monologue takes place in this enclosed, frozen space and time, in a circular space where he behaves as if the audience were eavesdropping on him. That was my idea, and Ingold acted it out so brilliantly that even I myself became terrified and ashamed. At times I felt like covering myself up, so powerful was his acting. The play lasted almost four hours, and no one coughed or even got up. Besides the hero's monologue, there were specific scenes arising from his recollections. I retained only Dostoevsky's main scenes: the hero's encounter with the prostitute Liza in the bordello and his earlier run-in with his "friends" at the restaurant. How were these scenes staged? The chalk circle and my hero were illuminated while, for example, the small table and his "friends" sitting around it stood in darkness. As my hero steps out of this circle and enters his recollections, the lighting of the circle would dim and light would illuminate the staging of his memories, where the characters would sit without stirring before coming to life, as in Meyerhold's[8] staging of the concluding scene of Gogol''s *The Inspector (Revizor)*.[9] Then they freeze again as the hero returns from his memories to the present. The principle underlying the entire spectacle seems simple only because a brilliant actor plays the lead. If the actor could not carry it off, it would get complicated. Moreover, I would have to coach the other actors according to my rules, and not those of Stanislavsky[10] or Meyerhold, that is, I would have to draw for each of them a sketch that captures the essence of his or her role. The drawing, then, becomes the archetype of the role. What is an archetype? What is a cross, for instance? It is a person with outstretched arms, that is, the cross contains a human being within itself. This is true of any hero: for the sake of clarity and simplicity, my heroes are all reduced to archetypal masks. Sometimes an archetype can be found in a character's name. Ferfichkin, for instance, is a crooked spiral.[11] After seeing a crooked spiral, an actor would portray him as fleet and furtive *(iurkii)*. Since the play was long and incomprehensible, it was first performed in a small experimental theater before moving to the main stage of the *Spielhaus*, where it remains in the repertoire to this day.

3. Marcel Marceau and Charlie Chaplin

When I watch Marcel Marceau perform, I admire his masterful control over the body. He seems to experience the plastic form of the image from within. As a professional mime, Marceau may know how he is perceived by the spectators, but not by a sculptor like myself. What do I mean by this? In a sculpture, every position of the human body in a three-dimensional space represents the most or least expressive visual outline or silhouette. And each culture exploits its own type of expressiveness. In ancient Egyptian reliefs we see people sandwiched between two panes of glass, one in back and one in front, as between the covers of a thin book. For the human body to be most expressive under such constraints, the head is presented in profile, one eye faces the viewer directly, the torso is turned slightly, and the hands and feet are placed in profile.

To heighten the comic movements of his feet, Charlie Chaplin stands in the first ballet position and accentuates the length of his feet with oversized shoes. Then he wobbles towards the viewer like a sea lion. A sea lion's gait is more expressive than a person's because his flippers turn outwards. That is why Chaplin became a cinematic sign: his exit from the screen into the depths of cinematic space is the sign of a man walking. There would be no expressiveness whatsoever in Chaplin's movements were it not for those turned-out feet.

Like Chaplin, the figures in Egyptian reliefs, and Kabuki dancers whose gestures are not only beautiful, plastic, and expressive, but are also related to the semiotic structure of the action, Marcel Marceau contorts his body in essentially the same way. In his Moscow performance Marceau would suddenly turn towards the spectators with his elbows sticking out, so that the viewer from his vantage point would lose sight of the mime's general contours. Although Marceau would change his position for the sake of expressiveness, it occurred to me that his movements would be even more expressive if he moved as if he were in a confined space. Later, when we met at the French Embassy, I outlined to him my theory of space and expressiveness: "Marcel, suppose you were to create an imaginary glass structure in which you would constantly be moving while sensing one panel of glass pressing against the back of your head and the other against your chest, and to mark the stage to suggest that you were moving not in free three-dimensional space, but between two glass panels standing on stage, as in the spatial confines of an Egyptian relief. Those glass panels should grow into a labyrinth through which you pass, but always in such as way as to maintain optimum expressiveness *vis-a-vis* the audience." Marceau got the point at once and has performed accordingly ever since.

In my essay, "Body: Man as Visual Sign," I wrote that puppets are often more expressive than a human being. Why is that so? A puppet is expressive in a particular way. If you watch a puppet and puppeteer on a television show, you will remember the puppet but not the puppeteer, unless the puppeteer is also a ventriloquist, in which case the puppet amplifies the ventriloquist's face in a grotesque way. The German scholar Heinrich von Kleist, while researching the motion of marionettes, developed the theory of bionic movement in 1810 in relation to drama and the theater. According to his theory, marionettes are more expressive than live actors because they are not bound by the law of gravitation. A marionette, manipulated by the puppet master from above, exhibits refined movements that are free from purely biological conditions such as weight. Therefore, a marionette is always psychological: its lament is always a lament, and its running is pure running. That is, a marionette exhibits pure psychology, pure psychological archetypes. Thus, in great esoteric cultures, actors quite often do not imitate live movements, but rather the motion of puppets. That is what Marcel Marceau and Charlie Chaplin do. There is the concept of puppet tragedy, Pierrot,[12] for instance, in the Romantic[13] repertoire. To a certain extent the movements of Marcel Marceau, Charlie Chaplin, and the Kabuki theater can be viewed as puppet tragedies.

4. Picasso[14]

Everything made by Pablo Picasso[15] is significant. According to my theory, works of art are created by an artist either as individual masterpieces or as an integral part of a holistic process.[16] Picasso is an artist who created works as a holistic process. No one work by Picasso can be said to represent Picasso entirely, but only a part of the artist. He is wholly a manifestation of flow *(potok)* and process. Just as one cannot extract a phrase, a plot, or a separate idea from the works of Dostoevsky,[17] it is equally impossible to pick out isolated elements from the works of Picasso. Picasso exists only as a whole.

In the Picasso exhibition at the Museum of Modern Art, the flow from work to work is always crowned by a kind of semantic accord, period, or conclusion. We can see this in his Suprematist,[18] Cubist,[19] Realistic,[20] or Expressionistic[21] compositions. One can discern how Picasso's Blue Period gradually turns into his Rose Period as he acquires greater compositional power. As a construction of his becomes dominant, it squeezes out other elements, so that it is finally bared. And then color reappears in his works. But this color, already transformed into a construction and a flat Suprematist vision, becomes decorative and so forth.

But the power of Picasso lies in his enormous academic culture, which constantly shines through his works. This cultural foundation sharply distinguishes Picasso from his plagiarizers and other light-weight modernists. Through his deformations[22] and transformations one can always discern a powerful drawing, a mighty spatial conception, and a strong classical foundation. It's the same with contemporary music: in any form of pop music – whether rock, Pink Floyd, Wings,[23] Edith Piaf,[24] or the Beatles[25] – as soon as we sense a solid foundation, we begin to experience infinity, the "depths of the iceberg." But if this foundation is cut off, we sense this at once, when the music becomes "light."

Speaking of periods, I can add the following. I have a certain hypothesis or thought-instrument that helps me personally to understand Picasso. A complex relation exists between an artist and the world. In the language of cybernetics these relations are called "direct" and "inverse." All of us can perceive the color red or the beauty of a flower. But, for some reason, not everyone can draw a flower or even simply depict the color red, although this requires no special training. Why is this?

Between the eye and the hand two kinds of relations exist. Initially there is a direct relation of eye to color. Then comes the inverse relation of hand to color, to the representation. And from time to time these relations in an artist are obscured due to stereotypes or repetitions of a device.[26] The device has become ossified, and the work no longer emanates the living breath of creativity, but merely artfully reproduces conventional views of an object, of nature herself.

It seems to me that Picasso changed his periods not according to external circumstances (as art critics often allege), and not for speculative reasons. Picasso was a real madman in the highest sense of the word. When he began to feel that a certain balance or a stereotype of his vision had been established, and that the reverse relation of hand to representation had been destroyed, he began to seek a device to restore his vision anew. An artistic period of his would last as long as he was looking for a new way of seeing. And when he tired of the quest, he would discard the style of that period.

As Picasso himself once said, "A canvas is always the sum of destruction." He annihilated precisely what I wish to put together. By analyzing art, he created masterpieces. But I would rather create a synthesis. Picasso was a typical creator of works of art in a holistic process, as a kind of objectified meditation. His creative work is a definite state of soul and body: consciously or unconsciously Picasso was striving for immortality. Power over the transient moment is the main feature of Picasso's works. These words by Boris Pasternak[27] apply to Picasso:

> No byt' zhivym, zhivym i tol'ko,
> Zhivym, i tol'ko do kontsa.
> ("But to be alive, and only alive,
> Alive, and only to the end.")

As for the relation between art and life, the French publishing house Skira, which specializes in art books, once suggested that I write an autobiographical book. As an example of what they wanted, Skira sent me a copy of Eugene Ionesco's book.[28] I was expected to describe how my life influenced my art. I sat down and began to juxtapose my life and work year by year. What did I discover? That my life and my creative work do not correspond at all. When I was happy, I produced the most dramatic works. But when I was in love, I created ascetic works. And so on.

Journalists have always written of my creative work as some kind of opposition to the Soviet regime, as if it were a struggle against collective farms,[29] rather than resistance to universal human tragedy. But my art has no direct connection to everyday life. Relatively speaking, I am an ideological artist, although the term "ideological" has become pejorative.

Picasso is a visual artist, although he is also a conceptual artist to the highest degree. The visual element is always present in his works. However, Picasso does not reflect directly or realistically what exists, but rather his own artistic vision. Changes in color, structure, or way of perceiving the world were developed, of course, in connection with Picasso's inner state of being, and not with any kind of external stimuli or irritation. But if you look carefully at where this is done, it will be clear that even color appears, shall we say, biographically: the artist has departed into nature. But what came first: did the canvases blossom after the master caught sight of colorful nature, or did the artist wish to see colorful nature and sought it out? This is a complex question.

I prefer the viewpoint that the artist constructs his own world and his own vision, and this construction becomes apparent later on. But bear in mind that this does not suit everyone. For instance, if we examine Turner[30] or the Barbizon School[31] in France, we see that real life breaks out within their artistic world. Sea mists. A Barbizon sun. And Van Gogh's[32] paintings changed after the artist moved to Arles in the south. Such an approach is justified only in the case of visual artists, and applies only partially to Picasso. Closer to me in their perception of the world are artists such as Michelangelo[33] or William Blake.[34] For these artists the state of the soul, and not visual stimuli, influenced their use of color and form.

I have described Picasso's work as objectified meditation because meditation is a way of entering a state which is close to religious Nirvana.[35] It is not a religious condition, but a psychological state of self-knowledge. It is an attempt to turn one's eyes inward in order to see oneself. This is exactly what I had in mind, and not Picasso's concrete religious experiences. But since I generally support metaphysical definitions of art, I think that there is simply no artist outside of religion, even if he were an atheist. If the person is beyond religion, then he or she is no artist.

As for his communism and portrait of Stalin,[36] Picasso was only too human. Like all major artists, Picasso was a natural and elemental anarchist and avenger. He clearly did not consider bourgeois society ideal, and found himself inwardly opposed to it. Many honorable and good people of Picasso's generation were simply drawn to communism as the sole alternative to fascism.[37] I think that Picasso's communism was more ethical opposition to fascism rather than hard-core communism itself.

The Spanish Civil War[38] and resistance to fascism left an imprint on a whole generation. There were people who joined the Communist Party for speculative reasons. But others joined to oppose fascism. Picasso could not have found a place for himself within the confines of the Party, if only by force of temperament. He, in essence, was a Spanish anarchist who approached communism as a form of opposition to fascism and the Nazis.

As for the view that Picasso boldly borrowed elements from Braque,[39] Matisse,[40] Velazquez,[41] and others, I would say first of all that Jupiter[42] is permitted what a simple ox is not. Picasso once said of himself: "People call me a questing artist. This is false. I do not seek, I find. No one is interested in a person who wanders through Paris looking for a million dollars. We are interested in the person who has found it."

In spite of the external cynicism of these remarks, they express a profound truth about people like Picasso. There exists a particular type of artist who regards art as nature produced by man and who considers this second nature his property. Dante,[43] Rabelais,[44] Swift,[45] and many others were such artists. If an artist of this type is not a great master, then he plagiarizes. But when such an artist is also a great master, as in the case of Picasso, there is no plagiarism. In spite of moments of convergence with other artists, Picasso invariably maintained his own distinctive resonance, so that ultimately a work of his is always something other than derivative. Picasso was able to assimilate African art, esoteric hieroglyphs, spatial compositions from different countries and peoples, and Eskimo art and to meld these styles together creatively.

Whether or not Picasso influenced my art is a complex question. I do not think that he influenced me directly. To speak frankly, although this may appear to be immodest, Picasso was a genius who took apart the machine which I intend to reassemble. We take different paths as artists.

The Picasso exhibition at the Museum of Modern Art confirms what I have suspected for a long time. The remarkable layout of this exposition reaffirms my idea that Picasso's art, despite its surface diversity, is actually one integrated whole. This exhibition is constructed so that we can see the evolution and transformation of Picasso, not by design, but as the natural movement and development of a single artist who, like a tree, changes and grows not in spurts, but gradually.

5. The Methodology of Creativity

I like to read a writer's notebooks more than I do the novels themselves. I prefer to read about the process of creating a work. Dostoevsky's notebooks are much more interesting for me to read than his novels. I have often wondered why. And suddenly a curious thought occurred to me. I love to watch bad movies and to look at bad sculptures because anatomy interests me much more than beautiful art. Anatomy conceals how something is made, and the consumer should be interested in how things are made. I am always suspicious of an artist with impeccable taste. He or she either wishes to appear more cultured than they really are, or at least to seem to have good taste. When you ask the greatest creative artists what they love, they invariably give terribly absurd replies. At times it seems as though they were provoking the public with their tastes, for they liked second-rate things. Take Dostoevsky, for instance. I do not wish to suggest that George Sand[46] is a bad writer, but it's rather odd that Dostoevsky preferred her writings over those by the titans of world literature. But I can understand why he did. In George Sand's writings he could see how things were done. When people ask me what I like, I must admit that I like bad sculpture. I do not like bad sculpture as such, but merely prefer it to the pinnacles of sculpture. In Greek sculpture there is Phidias,[47] the summit of Greek culture. But in earlier, more primitive Greek sculpture, or later Greek sculpture from the period of Alexander the Great or the decline of Greece, the process of creation is revealed, and I can learn something from it. But when I look upon a work by Phidias, I can only admire it. Therefore, I sometimes prefer a minor icon from the northern Russia to acknowledged masterpieces, because it intimately reveals how it was made.

6. Holistic Civilizations

The sign of a great civilization is always a sensation of wholeness. Let's take the Egyptian Pyramids as an ideal example. You can cut off the top of a pyramid and still recognize what it is. You can level a pyramid almost to its foundations and still make out its basic structure. Similarly, paleontologists can reconstruct the cultural level and rhythm of an entire civilization from fragments of a Greek or Egyptian torso. This feeling of wholeness is what distinguishes major from minor works of art. That is, the least part of a work embodies the laws governing the entire structure, and I study from ancient civilizations how this is done. I do not know whether I succeeded or not, but, in principle, when I was illustrating Dante, I continued the spiral formations and vortical movement of my *Tree of Life*. The rhythms of the circles of Hell or the circles and spirals of the *Tree of Life* ought to permeate each part and stroke of my body of works. Indeed, Apollonian stasis is preserved in the presence of Dionysian destruction and chaos.

7. Faith

I do not wish to speak about religion because it would be immodest, nor do I wish to speak about God because that would be superfluous. But I am deeply convinced that real achievement in art cannot exist without faith, because in reality art cannot be reduced to satisfying man's rational needs. Rational needs may exist within art, but that does not exhaust art. Without faith creative work is impossible. What is faith? Faith is a striving, an endeavor, a means of overcoming man's cosmic solitude, and a premonition of the ultimate answer which simultaneously resounds both within and outside oneself. Great art has the power to inspire people with hope in the meaningfulness of everyday existence.[48]

[1] The Scythians, a nomadic people from Western Siberia or Central Asia, were among the earliest peoples to master horsemanship.
[2] Heraclitus (See Chapter Two, note 9).

[3] Rodin (See Chapter One, note 1).
[4] Leonardo da Vinci (1452-1519), noted Italian painter, sculptor, scientist, architect, engineer, musician, and mathematician.
[5] Edvard Munch (1863-1944), Norwegian painter and printmaker who foreshadowed Expressionism in his anguished representations of loneliness, love, and death.
[6] Cubo-Futurism, the central movement in Russian Futurism, cultivated novelty and innovation in the arts. Cubo-Futurist stage designs made use of abstract geometric forms and unusual lighting effects.
[7] Goya (See Chapter Nine, note 1).
[8] Vsevolod Emilievich Meyerhold (1874-1942), Russian stage director and actor whose system of "bio-mechanics" revolutionized the Russian theater.
[9] Gogol''s *The Inspector* is considered to be Russia's greatest comedy.
[10] Konstantin Stanislavsky (1863-1938), Russian actor, director, and producer who founded the Moscow Art Theater in 1898 and developed the "method" theory of acting.
[11] Ferfichkin, a devious and unsavory character from the *Notes from the Underground,* whose name suggests obscenities through repetition of the sound and shape of the Cyrillic letter "f" in his name.
[12] Pierrot, male character in French pantomime.
[13] Romanticism, style of art that subordinates form to emotion, imagination, and exotic content.
[14] This discussion of Picasso was published in Russian as "O Pablo Picasso" (On Pablo Picasso) in *Novyi Amerikanets* (New American), Vol. 1, No. 27 (12-17 August 1980).
[15] Picasso (See Introduction, note 26).
[16] Neizvestny divides all artists into two categories: "artists of masterpieces" or "artists of process."
[17] Dostoevsky (See Introduction, note 60).
[18] Suprematism, non-representational art movement founded by Malevich in Russia and distinguished by its use of a limited palette and simple geometric forms.
[19] Cubism, twentieth century art movement founded by Braque and Picasso that reduced natural forms to geometrical shapes.
[20] Realism, art movement emphasizing the objective evolution of people and events in historical context.

[21] Expressionism (See Chapter One, note 2).
[22] Deformation is a technical term used by Russian Formalist critics to describe the intentional reshaping of a specific literary device to make the work's form more palpable.
[23] Pink Floyd and Wings, popular rock music groups of the 1980s.
[24] Edith Piaf (1915-63), popular French cabaret singer.
[25] Beatles, influential British pop music group of the 1960s.
[26] See Viktor Shklovsky's formalist concept of "art as device" (*"iskusstvo kak priem"*).
[27] Pasternak (See Chapter Eight, note 12).
[28] Eugene Ionesco (1912-), Romanian-born French playwright and pioneer in the theater of the absurd.
[29] Collective farm *(kolkhoz)*, Soviet form of agricultural organization in which peasants cultivate common land for the state and retain small acreage for their private needs.
[30] Joseph Mallord William Turner (1775-1851), great British Romantic landscape painter.
[31] Barbizon School (1830-70), a group of French painters who frequented the village of Barbizon and depicted natural, rural subjects.
[32] Van Gogh (See Chapter Four, note 21).
[33] Michelangelo (See Chapter One, note 27).
[34] William Blake (1757-1827), visionary English painter, poet, and prophet.
[35] Nirvana, the highest state of existence in Hinduism and Buddhism and the final escape from the cycle of rebirth.
[36] Stalin (See Chapter Nine, note 18).
[37] Fascism, the authoritarian and anti-democratic political and social system of Italy under Mussolini and Germany under Hitler which calls for absolute obedience to a deified leader.
[38] Spanish Civil War (1936-39), a conflict between liberal and conservative forces that resulted in the victory of the fascist leader, Francisco Franco (1892-1975), despite military aid from the Soviet Union to the republicans.
[39] Georges Braque (1882-1963), seminal French painter and sculptor who, together with Picasso, developed Cubism and the technique of collage.
[40] Henri Emile Benois Matisse (1869-1954), major French painter and graphic artist.
[41] Diego Rodriguez de Silva y Velazquez (1599-1660), great Span-

ish court painter.

[42] Jupiter, Roman equivalent of Greek god Zeus, the lord of heaven.

[43] Dante (See Chapter Seven).

[44] Rabelais (See Chapter Two, note 58).

[45] Swift (See Chapter Seven, note 5).

[46] George Sand (1804-76), pseudonym of French romantic novelist and feminist, Amandine Aurore Lucie Dupin.

[47] Phidias (See Chapter Eight, note 1).

[48] These reflections, with the exception of the section on Picasso, are edited from taped interviews with Neizvestny conducted in New York and Uttersberg, Sweden, by Vladimir Bondarev in 1988-89 in connection with the Soviet documentary film, *V otvete l' zrachii za sleptsa* (Will the visionary answer for the blind?) [1989].

BIBLIOGRAPHY

A. Works by Neizvestny

"Art and Freedom." *Studies in Comparative Communism,* Vol. XVII, Nos. 3 & 4 (Fall/Winter 1984-85): 235-39.

"Art and Society." In *Proceedings of the Summer 1986 Intensive Workshop in Chinese and Russian,* 2d ed., ed. Albert Leong, 253-63. Eugene: University of Oregon Books, 1988. Reprinted in *Oregon Studies in Chinese and Russian Culture,* edited Albert Leong. New York: Peter Lang Publishing, Inc., 1990), 313-26. Also in Ernst Neizvestny, *Space, Time, and Synthesis in Art: Essays on Art, Literature, and Philosophy,* ed. Albert Leong, 109-24 (Oakville: Mosaic Press, 1990).

"Beda i schast'e russkikh khudozhnikov: Beseda s Ernstom Neizvestnym" (The woe and fortune of Russian artists: a conversation with Ernst Neizvestny) *Posev* (Sowing) No. 5 (1980): 35-37. Also in *Govorit Neizvestnyi* (Neizvestny speaks), 131-38. Frankfurt: Possev-Verlag, 1984.

"Body: Man as Visual Sign." In *Proceedings of the Summer 1986 Intensive Workshop in Chinese and Russian,* 2d ed., ed. Albert Leong, 89-106. Eugene: University of Oregon Books, 1988). Reprinted in *Oregon Studies in Chinese and Russian Culture,* ed. Albert Leong. New York: Peter Lang Publishing, Inc., 1990), 106-32. Also in Ernst Neizvestny, *Space, Time, and Synthesis in Art: Essays on Art, Literature, and Philosophy,* ed. Albert Leong,19-42 (Oakville: Mosaic Press, 1990).

"Bronze." In *Ernst Neizvestny: Bronze.* New York: Eduard Nakhamkin, 1989. Also in Ernst Neizvestny, *Space, Time, and Synthesis in Art: Essays on Art, Literature, and Philosophy,* ed. Albert Leong, 81-90 (Oakville: Mosaic Press, 1990).

"Budushchee rezhima" (The future of the regime). In Ernst Neizvestny, *Govorit Neizvestnyi* (Neizvestny speaks), 110-30. Frankfurt: Possev-Verlag, 1984.

"Creativity in Disgrace." In Ernst Neizvestny, *Space, Time, and Synthesis in Art: Essays on Art, Literature, and Philosophy,* ed. Albert Leong, 101-07 (Oakville: Mosaic Press, 1990).

"Dante." In Ernst Neizvestny, *Space, Time, and Synthesis in Art: Essays on Art, Literature, and Philosophy,* ed. Albert Leong, 91-99 (Oakville: Mosaic Press, 1990).

"Dante's Hell." In *Ernst Neizvestny: Dante's "Inferno."* New York: Eduard Nakhamkin, 1987. Expanded text, "Dante," in Ernst Neizvestny, *Space, Time, and Synthesis in Art: Essays on Art, Literature, and Philosophy,* ed. Albert Leong, 91-99 (Oakville: Mosaic Press, 1990).

"Dialog s Khrushchevym" (Dialogue with Khrushchev). In Ernst Neizvestny, *Govorit Neizvestnyi* (Neizvestny speaks), 5-36. Frankfurt: Possev-Verlag, 1984.

"Discovering the New." In Ernst Neizvestny, *Space, Time, and Synthesis in Art: Essays on Art, Literature, and Philoso-*

phy, ed. Albert Leong, 71-80 (Oakville: Mosaic Press, 1990). Russian text, "Otkyrvat' novoe," in Ernst Neizvestny, *Govorit Neizvestnyi* (Neizvestny speaks), 156-66. Frankfurt: Possev-Verlag, 1984.

"Drevo zhizni" (Tree of life). In Ernst Neizvestny, *Govorit Neizvestnyi* (Neizvestny speaks), 139-55. Frankfurt: Possev-Verlag, 1984. Included in English translation, "The *Tree of Life*," in Ernst Neizvestny, *Space, Time, and Synthesis in Art: Essays on Art, Literature, and Philosophy*, ed. Albert Leong, 55-69 (Oakville: Mosaic Press, 1990).

"Fragmenty opyta" (Fragments of an experiment). In Ernst Neizvestny, *Govorit Neizvestnyi* (Neizvestny speaks), 78-109. Frankfurt: Possev-Verlag, 1984.

"Genii na rynke iskusstv" (Genius on the art market). *Vremia i my* (Time and we), No. 100 (1988): 187-97. English translation, "Genius and the Art Market," in Ernst Neizvestny, *Space, Time, and Synthesis in Art: Essays on Art, Literature, and Philosophy*, ed. Albert Leong, 125-34 (Oakville: Mosaic Press, 1990).

Govorit Neizvestnyi (Neizvestny speaks). Frankfurt: Possev-Verlag, 1984.

"Ia vsiudu odin i tot ze" (I am the same person everywhere). *Druzhba narodov* (Peoples' friendship), No. 12 (1989): 63-81.

"Interv'iu *Russkoi Mysli* s Ernstom Neizvestnym" (Interview of *Russian Thought* with Ernst Neizvestny). *Russkaia Mysl'* (18 June 1981): 12.

"Katakombnaia kul'tura i ofitsial'noe iskusstvo" (Catacomb culture and official art). *Posev* (Sowing) No. 11 (1979): 37-41. Reprinted in *Govorit Neizvestny* (Neizvestny speaks), 37-49. Frankfurt: Possev-Verlag, 1984.

"Krasnen'kie, zelenen'kie i p'ianen'kie" (The reds, the greens, and the tipsy). In *Govorit Neizvestny* (Neizvestny speaks),

50-77. Frankfurt: Possev-Verlag, 1984. Also in *Kontinent* No. 21 (1979): 7-33.

"*Lik – Litso – Lichina:* Novye glavy iz odnoimennoi knigi" (Visage – Face – Mask: new chapters from a book of the same title) *Kontinent* 27 (1981): 110-40.

"Lik – Litso – Lichina" (Visage – Face – Mask). *Kontinent* 37 (1983): 42-54.

"Lik – Litso – Lichina" (Visage – Face – Mask). *Sovetskii ekran* (Soviet screen) [October 1989]: 19-22.

"Moi dialog s Khrushchevym" (My dialogue with Khrushchev). *Vremia i my* (Time and we), 41 (1979): 170-200. Reprinted in Ernst Neizvestny, *Govorit Neizvestyi* (Neizvestny speaks), 5-36. Frankfurt: Possev-Verlag, 1984.

"On Egyptian Art." In Ernst Neizvestny, *Space, Time, and Synthesis in Art: Essays on Art, Literature, and Philosophy,* ed. Albert Leong, 135-41 (Oakville: Mosaic Press, 1990). Russian text in Ernst Neizvestny, *Govorit Neizvestyi* (Neizvestny speaks), 167-74. Frankfurt: Possev-Verlag, 1984.

"O Pablo Picasso" (On Pablo Picasso). *Novyi Amerikanets* (New American), Vol. 1, No. 27 (12-17 August 1980). Part of "Reflections of a Centaur," in Ernst Neizvestny, *Space, Time, and Synthesis in Art: Essays on Art, Literature, and Philosophy,* ed. Albert Leong, 149-54 (Oakville: Mosaic Press, 1990).

"O sinteze iskusstv" (On synthesis of the arts). *Voprosy filosofii* (Problems of philosophy), No. 7 (1989): 73-82. *Also in Ernst Neivestny, Space, Time, and Synthesis in Art: Essays on Art, Literature, Philosophy, ed. Albert Leong, 1-18 (Oakville: Mosaic Press, 1990)and O sinteze v iskusstve* (On synthesis in art). Ann Arbor: Hermitage, 1982.

"Preface to Poems by Bella DeJour." *Kontinent* 42 (1984): 60.

"Reflections of a Centaur." In Ernst Neizvestny, *Space, Time, and Synthesis in Art: Essays on Art, Literature, and Philosophy*, ed. Albert Leong, 143-58 (Oakville: Mosaic Press, 1990).

"Son: Iz knigi vospominanii *Lik, litso, lichina*" (Dream: from a book of memoirs *Visage, Face, Mask*). *Strelets* (Archer) 1 (January 1984): 31-32.

Space, Time, and Synthesis in Art: Essays on Art, Literature, and Philosophy. Edited, with introduction, translations, and notes by Albert Leong. Oakville: Mosaic Press, 1990.

"Three Fragments: Chapters from a Book." In *Kontinent 4: Contemporary Russian Writers*, edited by George Bailey. New York: Avon Books, 1982.

"Tragediia svobody" (The tragedy of freedom). *Kontinent 46* (1985): 219-32.

"The Tree of Life." In Ernst Neizvestny, *Space, Time, and Synthesis in Art: Essays on Art, Literature, and Philosophy*, ed. Albert Leong, 55-69 (Oakville: Mosaic Press, 1990).

"Tri fragmenta: glavy iz knigi" (Three fragments: chapters from a book). *Kontinent 21* (1979): 7-33

B. Works Illustrated by Neizvestny

Aksenov, Vasily. *Aristofaniana s liagushkami* (Aristophanes with frogs). Ann Arbor: Hermitage, 1981.

Beckett, Samuel and Neizvestny, Ernst. *Concepts and Representations*. London: John Calder, 1991 (In press).

Bestuzhev, Lada. *Kontury griadushchego* (Contours of the Future). Moscow: Znanie, 1963.

Dante Alighieri. *Malye proizvedeniia* (Short works). Moscow: Nauka, 1968.

De Jour, Bella. *Shadows of the Soul: The Poetry of Bella De Jour*. New York: Moyers-Bell, 1990.

Dostoevskii, F. M. *Prestuplenie i nakazanie* (Crime and punishment). Moscow: Nauka, 1970. Also Japanese and Norwegian editions.

The Foreseeable Future (in Russian). Moscow: Znanie, no date.

Japanese Poetry. No publication data.

Kontinent 2. Garden City, NY: Anchor Press/Doubleday, 1977.

Nauka i chelovechestvo (Science and humanity). Moscow: Nauka, no date.

O sinteze v iskusstve (On synthesis in art). Ann Arbor: Hermitage, 1982. Also German and Swedish editions.

C. Works about Neizvestny

Alovert, Nina. "Monument tret'emu miru" (A monument for the Third World). *Novoe Russkoe Slovo* (New Russian word) [10 July 1987].

________. "Mezhdu vostokom i zapadom" (Between East and West). *Novoe Russkoe Slovo* (New Russian word) [24 May 1985].

________. "Muzei Ernsta Neizvestnogo" (Ernst Neizvestny's museum). *Novoe Russkoe Slovo* (New Russian word) [2 November 1983].

Amlinskii, A. "600 strok o Neizvestnom: Moskovskie vstrechi znamenitogo skul'ptora" (600 lines about Neizvestny: Moscow meetings with the renowned sculptor).

Komsomol'skaia pravda (Komsomol truth) [29 June 1989]: 4.

Arkus, Liubov'. "Ernst Neizvestnyi: Khudozhnik – eto Gulliver" (Ernst Neizvestny: the artist is a Gulliver). *Sovetskii ekran* (Soviet screen) [October 1989]: 18.

"An Artist's Brush with a Leader." *Insight* (30 March 1987): 17.

Astrachan, Anthony. "Why Khrushchev's Favorite Sculptor Chose Exile." *New York Times* (11 April 1976).

Balsamo, Dean Duveen. "Ernst Neizvestny: An Artist for the 21st Century." Unpublished essay (1986).

________. "Nature Machine." *Cover* (January 1987): 5.

Batchan, Aleksandr and Sharymova, Natal'ia. "Desiat' voprosov Ernstu Neizvestnomu" (Ten questions to Ernst Neizvestny). *Novyi Amerikanets* (New American). No date.

Bazarov, Konstantin. "Ernst Neizvestny." In *Contemporary Artists*. 2d ed. New York: St. Martin's Press, 1983.

Berger, John. *Art and Revolution: Ernst Neizvestny and the Role of the Artist in the USSR*. New York: Pantheon Books, 1969.

________. "The Anguish of an Artist Forced into Solitary Confinement." *The Times* (26 July 1975).

________. "Arts in Society: A Soviet Sculptor." *New Society* (8 September 1966): 374-76.

________. "A Modern Mind at Work." *Daily Worker* (10 March 1962): 3.

________. "A Revelation from Russia." *Observer Weekend Review* (28 January 1962).

________. "The Unofficial Russians." *Sunday Times* (6 November 1966).

Bering-Jensen, Henrik. "Arts and Crafts of the State." *Insight* (30 March 1987): 16-18.

Betaki, Vasilii. "Sotvorenie universuma" (Creation of a universal). *Kontinent 46* (1985): 393-97.

Bowa, Matthew Cullerne. *Contemporary Russian Art.* New York: Phaidon Press, 1989.

Bowlt, John E. "Artists in Transit." In *Transit: Russian Artists between East & West,* 47-50. New York: Eduard Nakhamkin, 1989.

________. "A Brave Collector's Passion for 'Artists Who Dared to Fly.'" *Art News* (January 1982): 100-03.

________. Review of *Govorit Neizvestnyi* (Neizvestny speaks). *Slavic Review* (Summer 1985): 387.

________. "Moscow: The Contemporary Art Scene." In *New Art from the Soviet Union: The Known and the Unknown,* 20-25. Washington: Acropolis Books, 1977.

Brown, Tony. "Sculptor's Works Reflect Homeland." *Wichita Eagle-Beacon* (1 October 1987).

Chemiakin, Mikhail. *Chemiakin: Art and Life.* Vol. 1. Oakville: Mosaic Press, 1988, 41.

Chen, David. "An Asian Statue of Liberty." *The China News* (28 August 1988).

Cheporov, Edgar. "Bol' zhivoi pamiati" (The pain of living memory). *Moskovskie novosti* (Moscow news) [13 October 1989].

________. "Drevo zhizni" (The tree of life). *Novoe vremia* (New times) No. 13 (1989): 46-48.

________. "Monument chelovechkoi skorbi" (A monument to human grief). *Moskovskie novosti* (Moscow news) [13 November 1989].

________. "The Pain of Living Memory." *Moscow News* (13 October 1989).

Crafts, Fred. "The Tree of Life." *Eugene Register-Guard* (14 April 1983): 1,3D.

Darov, Anatolii. "Pobeditel' Khrushcheva" (Khrushchev's conqueror). *Novoe Russkoe Slovo* (New Russian word) [9 September 1976].

Davies, Margaret. "Ernst Neizvestny: A Man to Match Mountains." *Art and Artists* (April 1983): 10-11, 15.

"Defector Russian Artist Creates Liberty Statue for Kaohsiung." *China Post* (3 June 1988): 13.

Delli, Bertrun. "Ernst Neizvestny: Tradition or Avant-Garde?" Unpublished essay.

De Micheli, Mario. *Ernst Neizvestny.* Milan: Giangiacomo Feltrinelli Editore, 1978.

Dodge, Norton and Hilton, Alison. "Introduction." In *New Art from the Soviet Union: The Known and the Unknown,* 9-19. Washington: Acropolis Books, 1977.

Doria, Charles, ed. *Russian Samizdat Art.* New York: Willis Locker & Owens Publishing, 1986.

Dovlatov, Sergei. "Ernst Neizvestnyi: Teoretik iskusstva" (Ernst Neizvestny: theoretician of art). *Kul'turnyi dnevnik* (Cultural diary), No. 30. No date.

Egeland, Erik. *Ernst Neizvestny: Life and Work.* New York: Mosaic Press, 1984.

________. "Kloyn ili ubiitsa Motsarta" (A clown or Mozart's murderer). *Aftenposten* (14 August 1982).

________. "Vstrecha s Neizvestnym" (A meeting with Neizvestny). *Kontinent 17* (1978): 299-313.

"Ernst Neizvestny." In *Transit: Russian Artists between East & West,* 78-79. New York: Eduard Nakhamkin, 1989.

"Ernst Neizvestny." In *Twentieth-Century Culture: A Biographical Companion.* ed. Alan Bullock and R. B. Woodings. New York: Harper & Row, Publishers, 1983).

"Ernst Neizvestny." *London Sunday Times* (17 September 1989): 9.

Ernst Neizvestnyi (Documentary Film). Moscow, no date.

"Ernst Neizvestnyi – avtor memoriala zhertvam stalinizma" (Ernst Neizvestny – author of a memorial to the victims of Stalinism). *Novoe Russkoe Slovo* (New Russian word) [1989].

"Ernst Neizvestnyi – rezhisser" (Ernst Neizvestny – director). *Novyi amerikanets* (New American) [22-28 October 1980].

Evtushenko, Evgenii. *A Precocious Autobiography.* New York: E. P. Dutton & Company, 1964.

Ezerkaia, Bella. "Ernst Neizvestnyi sooruzhaet memorial zhertvam kommunizma" (Ernst Neizvestny builds a memorial to the victims of communism). *Novoe Russkoe Slovo* (New Russian Word) [3-4 March 1990]: 5.

________. "Khram vechnogo cheloveka: Interv'iu s Ernstom Neizvestnym" (Eternal man's temple: an interview

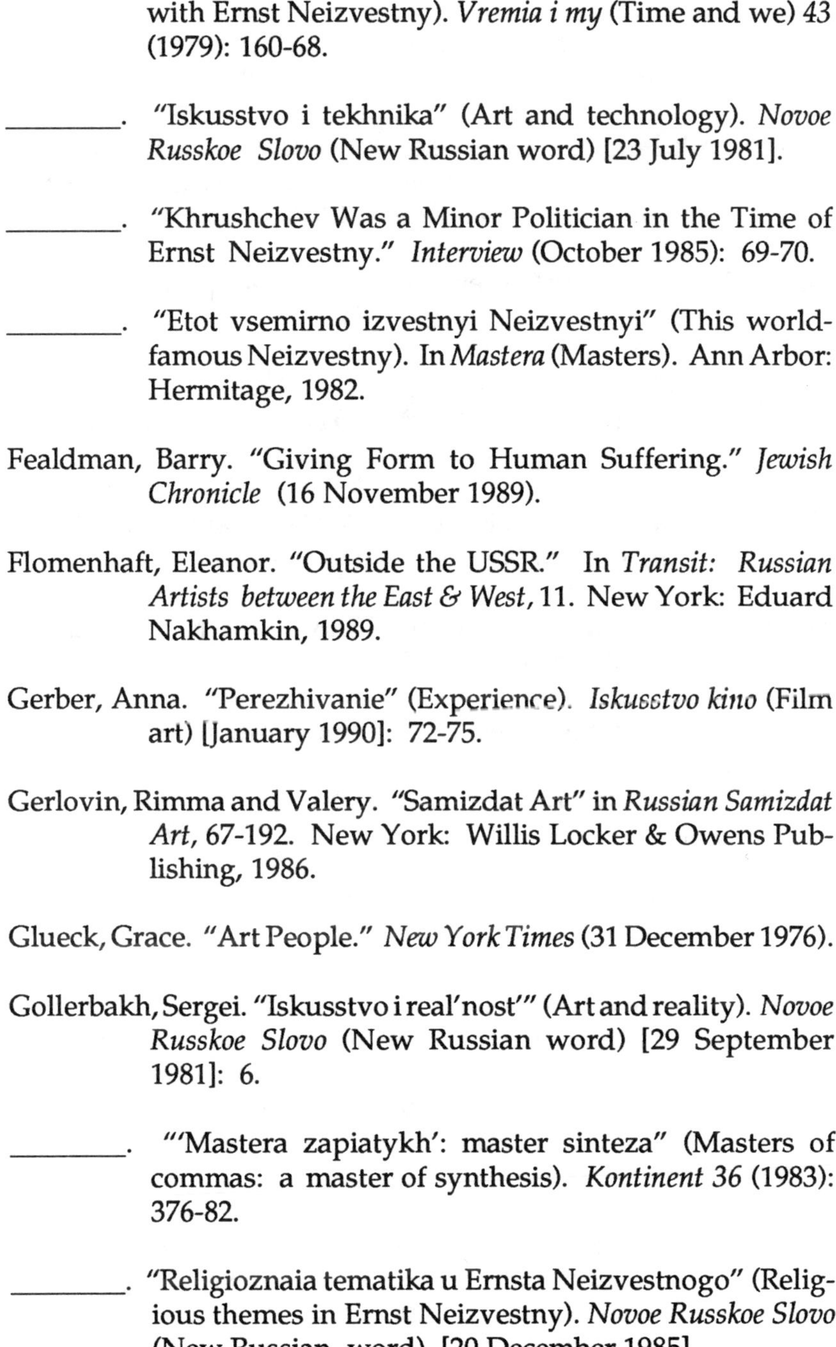

with Ernst Neizvestny). *Vremia i my* (Time and we) 43 (1979): 160-68.

________. "Iskusstvo i tekhnika" (Art and technology). *Novoe Russkoe Slovo* (New Russian word) [23 July 1981].

________. "Khrushchev Was a Minor Politician in the Time of Ernst Neizvestny." *Interview* (October 1985): 69-70.

________. "Etot vsemirno izvestnyi Neizvestnyi" (This world-famous Neizvestny). In *Mastera* (Masters). Ann Arbor: Hermitage, 1982.

Fealdman, Barry. "Giving Form to Human Suffering." *Jewish Chronicle* (16 November 1989).

Flomenhaft, Eleanor. "Outside the USSR." In *Transit: Russian Artists between the East & West*, 11. New York: Eduard Nakhamkin, 1989.

Gerber, Anna. "Perezhivanie" (Experience). *Iskusstvo kino* (Film art) [January 1990]: 72-75.

Gerlovin, Rimma and Valery. "Samizdat Art" in *Russian Samizdat Art*, 67-192. New York: Willis Locker & Owens Publishing, 1986.

Glueck, Grace. "Art People." *New York Times* (31 December 1976).

Gollerbakh, Sergei. "Iskusstvo i real'nost'" (Art and reality). *Novoe Russkoe Slovo* (New Russian word) [29 September 1981]: 6.

________. "'Mastera zapiatykh': master sinteza" (Masters of commas: a master of synthesis). *Kontinent* 36 (1983): 376-82.

________. "Religioznaia tematika u Ernsta Neizvestnogo" (Religious themes in Ernst Neizvestny). *Novoe Russkoe Slovo* (New Russian word) [20 December 1985].

________. "Skul'ptor dukhovnogo sinteza" (A sculptor of spiritual synthesis). No publication data.

Golomshtok, Igor'. "The Future of Soviet Art." In *New Art from the Soviet Union: The Known and the Unknown*, 50-54. Washington: Acropolis Books, 1977.

Golomshtok, Igor' and Glezer, Alexander. *Soviet Art in Exile.* New York: Random House, 1977.

Halloran, Richard. "Sculptor Expelled by Moscow Is in the U. S. Looking for Work." *New York Times* (26 September 1976).

Henderson, Michael. "Neizvestny: A Man 'Larger than Life.'" *Lake Oswego Review* (27 June 1985).

Hume, Paul. "Neizvestny's Bust of Shostakovich." *Washington Post* (27 September 1976).

Istratova, I. "Ernst Neizvestnyi." No publication data.

Ivanova, Ol'ga. "*Freedom of Expression:* A Film About Ernst Neizvestny." *Moscow News,* No. 36 (1989): 11.

Kaiser, Robert G. "Soviet Travel Ban Attacked." *Washington Post* (16 March 1974).

Kamin, Ira. "USSR Emigre's Art: Motion Locked Forever in Place." *Northern California Jewish Bulletin* (8 June 1984): 22.

Kenan, Naomi. "Ernst Neizvestny." *New American,* Vol. 1, No. 5/6 (May-June 1986): 12-16.

Khrushchev, Sergei. *Khrushchev on Khrushchev: An Inside Account of the Man and his Era.* Edited and translated by William Taubman. Boston: Little, Brown and Company, 1990.

Kobler, John. "Riding the Red Tide: The Power Behind the Boom in Contemporary Russian Art." *Connoiseur* (October 1989): 134-37.

Kramer, Hilton. "Art: The Social Expressionism of Ernst Neizvestny." *New York Times* (1 June 1988).

Lauridsen, Inger Thorup and Per Dalgaard. "Interv'iu s Ernstom Neizvestnom." (Interview with Ernst Neizvestny). *Russian Language Journal,* XL, Nos. 136-137 (1986): 123-31.

"Leitenant Neizvestnyi Ernst" (Lieutenant Neizvestny, Ernst). *Moskovskii komsomolets* (Moscow komsomol) [2 July 1989]: 2.

Leong, Albert. *The Art of Freedom: Ernst Neizvestny and Russian Culture* (In preparation).

________. "Centaur: The Life, Art, and Thought of Ernst Neizvestny." In *Ernst Neizvestny, Space, Time, and Synthesis in Art: Essays on Art, Literature, and Philosophy.* Ed. Albert Leong, xxv-xlix. Oakville: Mosaic Press, 1990.

________. "Ernst Neizvestnyi i russkaia kul'tura" (Ernst Neizvestny and Russian culture). *Kontinent 61* (1989): 273-83.

________. "Ernst Neizvestny and the Russian Avant-Garde." In *Proceedings of the Summer 1986 Intensive Workshop in Chinese and Russian,* ed. Albert Leong, 237-52. Eugene: University of Oregon Books, 1988). Reprinted in *Oregon Studies in Chinese and Russian Culture,* ed. Albert Leong. New York: Peter Lang Publishing, Inc., 1990.

________. "Ernst Neizvestny: Synthesis of East and West." In *Ernst Neizvestny: Exhibition Tour, 1988, Republic of China,* 7-16. Kaohsiung: 1988.

________. Review of *Govorit Neizvestnyi* (Neizvestny speaks). *Slavic and East European Journal* (Winter 1985): 487.

________. Review of *Art and Revolution: Ernst Neizvestny and the Role of the Artist in the USSR* by John Berger. *Slavic and East European Journal* (Summer 1971): 253-54.

________. Review of *O sinteze v iskusstve* (On Synthesis in Art) by Ernst Neizvestny. *Slavic and East European Journal* (Spring 1984): 130-31.

Levkova-Lamm, Innesa. "After Isolation." In *Transit: Russian Artists between East & West*, 39-43. New York: Eduard Nakhamkin, 1989.

Limonov, Eduard. "Novyi avangard" (The new avant-garde). *Novoe Russkoe Slovo* (New Russian word) [7 September 1975].

Lundegaard, Diane. "Ernst Neizvestny: Freedom Fighter, Peace Lover, Artist and Sculptor." *Sun Storm* (September 1987).

________. "Fantasticheskaia zhizn' i tvorchestvo Ernsta Neizvestnogo" (The fantastic life and work of Ernst Neizvestny). *Strelets* (Archer) [January 1985]: 20.

MacDougall, William. "How Russian Emigres Are Shaping U. S. Culture." *U. S. News and World Report* (28 March 1983): 35-36.

Martynenko, Ol'ga. "Stikhiia svobodnoi rechi" (The elements of free speech). *Moskovskie novesti* (Moscow news), No. 36 (3 September 1989): 21.

Miele, Franco. *Dinamismo Plastico in Ernst Neizvestny* (The plastic dynamism of Ernst Neizvestny). Rome: Prospettive, no date.

"Monument tragedii" (Monument to a tragedy). *Moskovskie novosti* (Moscow news), No. 27 (2 July 1989).

Morath, Inge and Arthur Miller. *In Russia.* New York: Viking Press, 1969.

Mullaly, Terence. "Russian Drawings Cut East-West Barriers." *Daily Telegraph and Morning Post* (24 May 1965): 21.

________. "Slav Labour." *Daily Telegraph* (4 May 1985).

Niezvestoe o Nievxestnom (Unkown facts about Niezvestny). Moscow: Central Studio of Technical Films, 1990.

"New Statue of Liberty." *New Yorker* (13 July 1987).

Novikov, Nikolai. *Ernst Neizvestnyi: Iskusstvo i real'nost'* (Ernst Neizvestny: art and reality). New York: Chalidze Publications, 1981.

Ogibenin, Boris. *Ernst Neizvestny. Créateur d'une archaïque nouvelle* (Ernst Neizvestny: creator of a new archaism). Lisse: The Peter De Ridder Press, 1975.

One Word of Truth (Produced by Ailsa Hamilton, Harry Howlett, and Finn Harald Wetterfors). Cambridge: Anglo-Nordic Productions Trust, 1981.

Osnos, Peter. "A Design for 'The Essence of Life.'" *Washington Post* (5 February 1976).

________. "Leading Soviet Sculptor Asks for Permission to Emigrate." *International Herald-Tribune* (5 March 1975).

"Pamiatnik zhertvam Stalina" (A monument to Stalin's victims). *Novoe Russkoe Slovo* (New Russian word) [9 December 1976].

"People: Ernst Neizvestny and Pope John Paul II." *International Herald Tribune* (21 August 1988).

Podshivalov, Ivan. "Memorial: Monument tragedii" (Memorial: a monument to a tragedy). *Moskovskie novosti* (Moscow news), No. 27 (2 July 1989).

Pomerantsev, K. Review of *Govorit Neizvestnyi* (Neizvestny speaks). *Russkaia Mysl'* (Russian thought) [30 August 1984].

"Pope Presented With Model of New Statue of Liberty To Be Erected in Kaohsiung." *The China News* (24 August 1988).

Reese, Donna. "One Branch on 'The Tree of Life'." *Willamette Valley Observer* (28 April 1982).

Robertson, Michael. "No Hammers, No Sickles, No Lenin." *San Francisco Chronicle* (10 November 1988): 44, 46.

Roditi, Edouard. "Paths of Their Own." In *Transit: Russian Artists between East & West*, 51-53. New York: Eduard Nakhamkin, 1989.

Rosenberg, Karen. "Soviet Sculptor Who Challenged Khrushchev Still Has Grand Design." *Boston Globe* (10 November 1984).

Rueschemeyer, Marilyn, Golomshtok, Igor, and Kennedy, Janet. *Soviet Emigré Artists: Life and Work in the USSR and the United States*. Armonk, NY: M.E. Sharpe, Inc., 1985.

Russell, John. "Russian Artists in Exile."*New York Times* (18 December 1981).

________. "Soviet Sculptor Thinks Big." *New York Times* (1 December 1978).

________. "Ernst Neizvestny." *New York Times* (28 November 1986).

"*Russia* Speaks With Ernst Neizvestny." *Russia 1* (1981): 29-32.

Salisbury, Harrison E. "The Monumental Dreams of Ernst Neizvestny." *Art News*, Vol. 78, No. 5 (May 1979): 102-05.

Schiefelbein, Susan. "Russian Artists in America: Is There Life After Exile." *Saturday Review* (September 1980): 12-16.

"Sculptor Who Tangled with Khrushchev Denied Visa." *Jerusalem Post* (9 July 1975).

Seddon, Richard. "Revolutionary Zeal." *Yorkshire Post* (6 November 1989).

Sedykh, Andrei. "Neizvestnoe o Neizvestnom" (The unknown about Neizvestny). *Novoe Russkoe Slovo* (New Russian word) [17 October 1976].

Seidman, Robert J. "The Politics of Art in Russia: An Interview with Ernst Neizvestny." *Partisan Review*, Vol. XLVII, No. 2 (1980): 249-63.

Shiffers, Evgenii. "Skul'pturnyi alfavit mastera E. Neizvestnogo" (The sculptural elements of E. Neizvestny, master artist). *Kontinent 8* (1976): 337-47.

Shirley, Don. "Shostakovich in Music and Bronze." *Washington Post* (25 September 1976).

Sjeklocha, Paul and Mead, Igor. *Unofficial Art in the Soviet Union*. Berkeley: University of California Press, 1967.

Sorokko, Serge. "Contemporary Russian Painters and Selected Modernists." *Wall Street Transcript* (18 February 1985).

Sokolov, N. "Razum skaly – k kartine Ernsta Neizvestnogo" (The rationality of cliffs – the paintings of Ernst Neizvestny). *Chelovek i priroda* (Man and nature), No. 7: 75-79.

Taylor, John Russell. "Lack of Inhibition Fit to Make the Earth Tremble." *The Times* (16 April 1985): 10.

Tokareva, M. "Drevo, kotoroe vzrastil Neizvestnyi" (The tree erected by Neizvestny). *Leningradskaia pravda* (Leningrad truth) [5 December 1989]: 3.

"Tribute for a Non-Person." *Time* (September 1974): 10.

V otvete l' zrachii za sleptsa (Will the visionary answer for the blind?). Directed by Aleksandr Demidov. Moscow: Moscow Film Studios, 1989.

"V otvete l' zrachii za sleptsa" (Will the visionary answer for the blind?). *Iskusstvo kino* (Film art) [January 1990].

Vasinskii, A. and Shal'nev, A. "Ernst Neizvestnyi: V iskusstve nel'zia prikazyvat' (Ernst Neizvestny: art must never be commanded). *Izvestiia* (News) [16 June 1989]: 6.

Volkov, G. "Vtoraia kniga Ernsta Neizvestnogo" (Ernst Neizvzestny's second book). *Novoe Russkoe Slovo* (New Russian word) [4 August 1989].

Voznesenskii, Andrei. "Andrei Tarkovskii: Belyi sviter" (Andrei Tarkovsky: a white sweater). *Literaturnaia gazeta* (Literary gazette) [23 September 1987].

________. "Neizvestnyi – rekviem v dvukh shagakh, s epilogom" (Neizvestny – a requiem in two steps with an epilogue). *Iunost'* (Youth) [June 1965). Included in *Akhillesovo serdtse* (Achilles' heart) (Moscow: 1966), 11-14.

Weeks, Albert L. "Ernst Neizvestny: The Artist as Philosopher." *The World & I* (January 1986): 558-65.

Whitney, Craig R. "Sculptor to Honor Siberia's Victims." *New York Times* (17 April 1990): A6.

Wren, Christopher S. "Neizvestny, Sculptor, Leaves Soviet Union." *New York Times* (11 March 1976).

Yakes, Wayne F. "Ernst Neizvestny: A Chilling View of a Darkened World." *New York City Tribune* (May 1988): 10.

________. "Neizvestny: Monumentalist of Our Time." *New York City Tribune* (28 September 1989).

Zavalishin, Viacheslav. "Ernst Neizvestnyi o sebe i o svoem tvorchestve" (Ernst Neizvestny speaks of himself and his work). *Russkaia Zhizn'* (Russian life) [21 August 1984]: 5, 8.

________. "Iskusstvo nebyvalykh katastrof" (The art of unheard of catastrophes). *Novyi Amerikanets* (New American), No. 77 (1-8 August 1981): 24-25.

________. "Krik metalla: apokalipticheskaia logika Ernsta Neizvestnogo" (The cry of metal: the apocalyptic logic of Ernst Neizvestny). *Novaia gazeta* (New newspaper) [27 November-3 December 1982]: 16-17.

________. "Press-konferentsiia Ernsta Neizvestnogo" (Ernst Neizvestny's press conference). *Novoe Russkoe Slovo* (New Russian word) [13 April 1988].

________. Risunki Ernsta Neizvestnogo" (The drawings of Ernst Neizvestny). *Novoe Russkoe Slovo* (New Russian word) [17 April 1975].

Zhavoronkov, Gennadii. "Svoboda i kul'tura" (Freedom and culture). *Moskovskoe novosti* (Moscow news), No. 26 (25 June 1989): 2.

Zinov'ev, Aleksandr. *Ziiaiushchie vysoty* (The yawning heights). Lausanne: Editions l'Age d'Homme, 1976.

________. *The Yawning Heights.* New York: Vintage Books, 1980.

EXHIBITIONS

1962	Moscow State University, USSR; Manége, Moscow, USSR
1965	Museum of Modern Art, Belgrade, Yugoslavia; Grosvenor Gallery, London, England
1966	Museum of Modern Art, Vienna, Austria; Galérie Lambert, Paris, France
1969	Astley Gallery, Köping, Sweden
1970	Musée d'Art Moderne de la Ville de Paris, France; Museo Belle Arti, Locarno, Italy
1972	Museum of Modern Art, Tel Aviv, Israel
1974	Bochum Museum, West Germany
1975	Lincoln Center, New York, USA
1976	Stedelijk Museum, Amsterdam, The Netherlands; Kunsteverein, Constance, West Germany

1977	Galérie Scheidegger, Zurich, Switzerland; Astley Gallery, Uttersberg, Sweden; Städtisches Museum, Leverkusen, West Germany
1978	Thielska Galleriet, Stockholm, Sweden; Lilla Galleriet, Umeå, Sweden; Menzoni Galleria d'Arte, Milan, Italy; Centro D'Arte Dolomite, Cortina, Italy
1979	Eduard Nakhamkin Fine Arts, New York, USA
1981	Holst Halvorens Kunsthandel, Oslo, Norway
1983	Museum of Art, University of Oregon, Eugene, USA
1984	Magna Gallery, San Francisco, USA
1985	Cathedral of St. John the Divine, New York, USA
1987	Eduard Nakhamkin Fine Arts, New York, USA; Uhlrich Museum of Fine Art, Wichita State University, U.S.A.
1988	Touring Exhibition, Taiwan, Republic of China
1989	Eduard Nakhamkin Fine Arts, New York, USA; Magna Gallery, San Francisco, USA; Connaught Brown Gallery, London, England; Clara Maia Sels Gallery, Dusseldorf, West Germany

COLLECTIONS

Dostoevsky Museum, Moscow

Erevan Gallery, USSR

L'vov Gallery, USSR

Moderna Museet, Stockholm, Sweden

Municipality of Oslo Art Collection, Norway

Musée d'Art Moderne, Paris, France

Museum of Art, University of California, Berkeley, USA

Museum of Modern Ecclesiastical Art, The Vatican

Museum of Modern Art, New York, USA

Jewish Museum, New York, USA

Kennedy Center for the Performing Arts, Washington, DC, USA

Kursk Museum, USSR

Russian Museum, Leningrad, USSR

Sculpture Park, Schulman Building, New York, USA

Sven-Olov Andersons Torg, Köping, Sweden

Tretiakov Gallery, Moscow, USSR

Värdshuset Flottaren, Vansbro, Sweden

Volgograd Gallery, USSR

Vologda Museum, USSR

INDEX

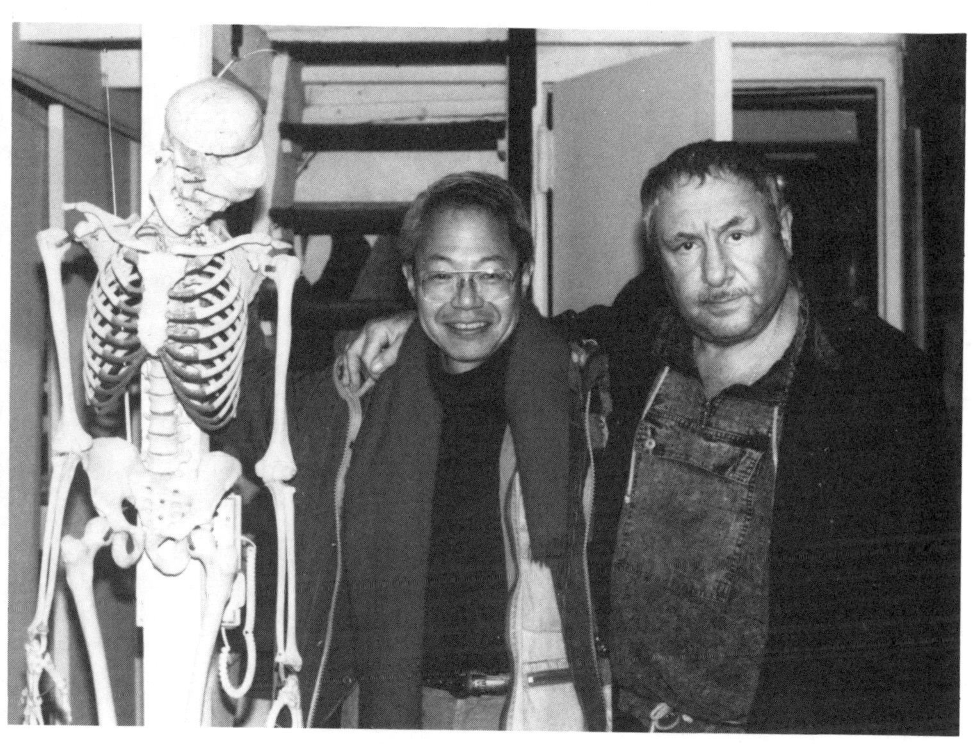

Troika: Ernst Neizvestny with Albert Leong and Skeleton. New York, 1989. Photograph by Susan Mende. Courtesy of Albert Leong.